SOUTHEASTERN UNITED STATES

showing locations of generalized physiographic provinces

Abbreviations used in the text:

I.L.P.	Interior Low Plateau
Cumb. Plat.	Cumberland Plateau
R.V.	Ridge and Valley
B.R.	Blue Ridge
Pied.	Piedmont
C.P.	Coastal Plain

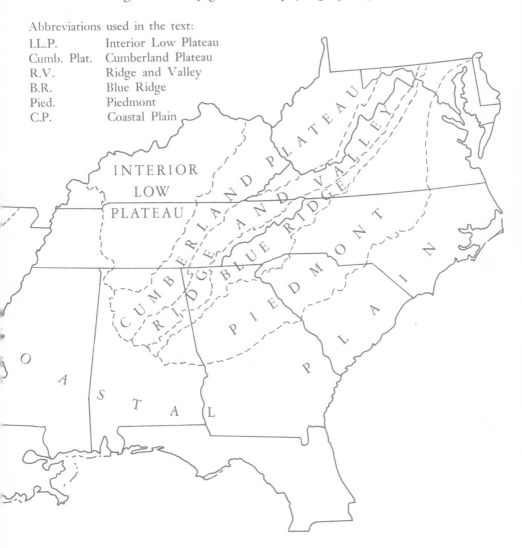

Nfld

INTERIOR LOW PLATEAU

CUMBERLAND PLATEAU

RIDGE AND VALLEY

BLUE RIDGE

PIEDMONT

COASTAL PLAIN

WILDFLOWERS OF THE
SOUTHEASTERN UNITED STATES

Wildflowers
of the Southeastern
United States

WILBUR H. DUNCAN

and

LEONARD E. FOOTE

THE UNIVERSITY OF GEORGIA PRESS

ATHENS

Library of Congress Catalog Card Number: 74–75940
International Standard Book Number: 0–8203–0347–X

The University of Georgia Press, Athens 30602

Set in Intertype Garamond
Printed in the United States of America

CONTENTS

ACKNOWLEDGMENTS

The authors are grateful to several persons who helped in the preparation and publication of this book. Dr. Daniel Ward provided information on distribution of certain species in Florida, and Dr. Donald Drapalik sent data on *Matalea*.

While the majority of the photographs in this book were made by the authors, we wish to thank the following individuals for particular photographs reproduced herein: Leo T. Barber (*Eichhornia crassipes, Zigadenus densus, Polygonatum biflorum, Clematis reticulata, Drosera leucantha, Tephrosia hispidula, Erythrina herbacea, Stillingia sylvatica, Physostegia virginiana, Pinguicula caerulea*); Jess and Anne Woodham (*Tillandsia usneoides, Cleistes divaricata, Corallorhiza wisteriana, Nymphaea odorata, Monarda punctata, Dyschoriste oblongifolia, Solidago stricta*); and George Neece (*Cypripedium reginae*).

The authors and the publisher are indebted to members of the Garden Club of Georgia for their continued support. They wish especially to thank Mrs. James T. Anderson and Governor Jimmy Carter, without whose strong support and encouragement it would not have been possible to publish this book.

FOREWORD

As a child growing up in a remote rural community of southwest Georgia, I experienced the constant and intimate fascination with the wild beauty of the woods, swamps, and fields. The changing nuances of the seasons were anticipated and savored, and our family calendar was marked by the emergence and later disappearance of certain species of plant leaves or flowers, or the ripening of particular fruits, nuts, and berries. My limited knowledge of nature was necessarily acquired by experience because my formal curriculum as a student of engineering and nuclear physics never included botany or biology.

Later, while I was governor of my state, it became more obvious to me that my own experience was quite typical. In searching for a source of information about the wildflowers of our region, I found the books and texts to be inadequate. They were either quite advanced and written for those persons already educated in the subject, or too incomplete and superficial to be reliable. Often the illustrations or photographs were not representative, and the few which were in color were of poor quality.

The superb color photography of Leonard Foote and Wilbur Duncan and the exciting and accurate descriptions of southeastern wildflowers by Professor Duncan have been combined in this volume to give us a long-awaited reference which is both comprehensive and beautiful. With its inevitably wide distribution to students, amateur botanists, outdoorsmen, and scholars, *Wildflowers of the Southeastern United States* should cause a quantum leap in knowledge and appreciation of our region's outdoor beauty. The people of Georgia are gratified to participate in the production of this fine book.

JIMMY CARTER
Governor of Georgia

Introduction

Purpose and Scope

This field guide is designed to provide a ready means of identifying most of the wildflowers found in southeastern habitats and to stimulate interest in their enjoyment, conservation, and management. The majority of the species generally considered as southeastern wildflowers consists of annual or perennial herbs. This excludes woody plants (trees, vines, shrubs) which are not usually thought of as wildflowers except for a few having scanty perennial aboveground stems, such as Pipsissewa. Ferns, and generally grasses, sedges, and rushes are similarly excluded although these great plant groups make up a substantial portion of the native southeastern vegetation. The species included here were chosen after reference to specimens in herbaria and to latest published treatments. The 485 photographs are of typical specimens and were selected to illustrate species representative of the entire wildflower population.

The text accompanying each illustration is designed to help identify that species and to show its relationships with nature and with man. Most of the texts also provide information about one or more wildflowers closely resembling those pictured, so that more than 1,000 species can be identified by using this field guide.

While emphasis is given to the more visible and widespread wildflowers, many uncommon ones are included because of the growing interest in rare and endangered species. Ordinary flowering weeds and some introduced wildflowers and garden escapes which have become naturally established are also included.

The range of this field guide includes Louisiana, Arkansas, Kentucky, West Virginia, Maryland, Delaware, and all of each state to the south and east except the southern portion of the Florida peninsula where there is a large assemblage of strikingly different species adapted to that normally freeze-free area. A majority of the species included occur outside the boundaries established, extending the usefulness of the guide well beyond the Southeast (see map inside either cover).

Nature of the Flora

The southeastern states are a mosaic of diverse environmental habitats supporting a spectrum of temperate, subalpine, subtropical, and prairie floras in addition to plants endemic to the area. The flora greatly resembles that of the northern states east of the Mississippi River, with many species either common to both areas or closely related. A similar but lesser relationship is reflected in the flora of the southwestern states. Far more surprising, however, is that many genera common to the area are also found in Asia, especially in Japan and China. Graphically illustrating relationships between these two floras are such genera as *Trillium*, *Clintonia*, *Jeffersonia*, *Lespedeza*, and *Shortia*.

The southern Blue Ridge Mountains are characterized by steep slopes, abundant rainfall, and forest canopies ranging from transitional stages of Virginia Pine to climax northern hardwoods and coniferous forests, producing a wide variety of microclimates and making this a very diverse botanical region. No less than 31 commercial forest trees occur here, resulting in a heterogeneous forest canopy which in turn influences the variety and abundance of wildflowers. Such spectacular species as Turk's-cap Lily (*Lilium superbum*), Large-flowered Trillium (*Trillium grandiflorum*), Showy Orchid (*Orchis spectabilis*), and Squirrel-corn (*Dicentra canadensis*) can be found here. Cool mountain bogs harbor Swamp-pink (*Helonias bullata*) and Pitcher-plant (*Sarracenia purpurea*).

In high mountain rhododendron thickets Small's Twayblade (*Listera smallii*), endemic to the area, grows in scattered locations. Another endemic species, perhaps more generally known but of restricted natural distribution, is Oconee Bells (*Shortia*), which was found by Andre Michaux in 1788 and lost to the botanical world for nearly a century. Other endemics such as Umbrella-leaf (*Diphylleia*) occur along moist spring-fed rivulets in high, north-facing coves.

On treeless balds and in adjacent coniferous forests of the Great Smokies are found representatives of subalpine floras which are relics of a greater range that existed during the cooler climate of the last glaciation. Mountain rains and snowfalls, sometimes exceeding 100 inches a year, produce a cool humid climate which supports northern species such as Clinton Lily (*Clintonia borealis*) and Three-toothed Cinquefoil (*Potentilla tridentata*).

At the other environmental extreme are sand dunes of the coast, arid sandhills bordering rivers of the Southeastern Coastal Plain, and the sandhills proper that are the feather edge of the Coastal Plain along the Fall Line from Virginia to Alabama. Here rainfall is much lower and temperatures are decidedly higher than in the mountains, snow seldom occurs, and soils are normally starved for water. Plants typical of this arid environment include Sandwort (*Arenaria caroliniana*), Lady Lupine (*Lupinus villosus*), and Sandhill Milkweed (*Asclepias humistrata*).

Occupying equal status with the dry sandy areas in the Coastal Plain landscape are aquatic habitats ranging from bogs to bays, ponds and lakes to streams, and swamps to tidal pools. Slow-moving, dark-colored Coastal Plain watercourses reflect the brilliant image of Golden-club (*Orontium aquaticum*), while borrow pits and shallow ponds bloom with masses of Floating Bladderwort (*Utricularia inflata*), Marsh-pink (*Sabatia dodecandra*), and Hatpins (*Eriocaulon*). Perhaps just as striking are wildflowers associated with the limy soils of the Black Belts in Alabama and Mississippi and the limesink areas of Florida, Georgia, and South Carolina.

The great alluvial valley of the Mississippi River and similar lesser valleys of the major rivers draining into the Gulf and the Atlantic shelf provide rich and productive habitats for Spider-lilies (*Hymenocallis*), Swamp Rose-mallow (*Hibiscus moscheutos*), and Butterweed (*Senecio glabellus*).

Wedged between mountains and Coastal Plain, the southern Piedmont presents two characteristic profiles. The more extensive one consists of soils derived from ancient rocks metamorphosed and eroded for eons. Here grow the Cream Wild-indigo (*Baptisia bracteata*), Southern Ragwort (*Senecio smallii*), and

Beard-tongue (*Pentstemon australis*). The other familiar landscape of the Piedmont is one of granitic outcroppings supporting such species as Elf-orpine (*Diamorpha smallii*), Rock-portulacas (*Talinum*), and Amphianthus (*Amphianthus
pusillus*).

Aquatic habitats of the Piedmont harbor Water-willow (*Justicia*), which
crowds gravel banks and bars, and Climbing Hempweed (*Mikania scandens*), a
vine familiar to most wet spots affording it an opportunity to climb.

Peculiarly, there are some species essentially absent from the Piedmont which
occur in both mountains and Coastal Plain. Examples of such broken distribution
are the Yellow-fringed Orchid (*Habenaria ciliaris*) and the Rose Orchid
(*Cleistes divaricata*). On the other hand some species are common to Piedmont
and Coastal Plain alike, as evidenced by Lizard's-tail (*Saururus cernuus*), which
frequents swamps and beaver ponds of both regions.

The Ridge and Valley Province of the Appalachian Mountains is an area with
mountaintops of acidic sandstone underlain by thousands of feet of limestone.
Among the numerous wildflowers distinctively associated with the limy soils are
Trillium (*Trillium lancifolium*), Twinleaf (*Jeffersonia diphylla*), and Leafcup
(*Polymnia canadensis*). Quite a few wildflowers peculiarly occur in this Province.
Some, such as Giant Ladies'-tresses (*Spiranthes . praecox*), Bachelor's-button
(*Polygala nana*), and Lance-leaved Violet (*Viola lanceolata* spp. *vittata*), occurring in and around natural ponds, are much more commonly found near the
coast. Perhaps more unexpected is the presence of species abundant in the western
prairies. The Coneflowers, *Echinacea pallida* and *Ratibida pinnata*, are good
examples of these.

Limy soils and outcroppings of limestone are also common to the Cumberland
Plateau, Interior Low Plateau, and Ozark-Ouachita Provinces and have wildflowers distinctively associated with them. Level outcroppings of limestone
known as "cedar glades" or "cedar barrens" occur locally in the first two provinces and in the Ridge and Valley. They are especially abundant in central Ten-
nessee. These outcroppings host a number of species with limited distribution,
Purple-tassels (*Petalostemon gattingeri*), Cedar-barren violet (*Viola eggle-
stonii*), and Leavenworthia species for example.

In various localities in the four provinces are numerous species of limited
distribution which have found places in the many special habitats occurring there.
Among these species are the Bluet (*Hedyotis canadensis*) in rocky woods on
slopes, Evening-primrose (*Oenothera triloba*) in dry often calcareous soils,
Barbara's-buttons (*Marshallia morhii*) in wet places, and Goldenrod (*Solidago
albopilosa*) under cliffs.

A newcomer to the plant scene that is fast claiming the attention of botanists
and horticulturists is the foreign or introduced species. Arriving in increasing
numbers as the result of advanced and accelerated transportation, usually from
Europe, these new arrivals adapt to local conditions, become naturalized, and
establish themselves. Unfortunately, they generally classify as weeds and distrib-
ute themselves with total impartiality. Prominent among such newcomers are
Yellow-rocket (*Barbarea vulgaris*), Wild Carrot (*Daucus carota*), Henbit
(*Lamium amplexicaule*), and Dandelion (*Taraxicum officinale*).

Tips on Identification

Pay particular attention to numbers and shapes of plant parts, especially of the flower. Be sure you recognize what constitutes a single flower. Check for heads of flowers such as in the ASTERACEAE (pages 192–230) and some of the FABACEAE (pages 64–88).

Check the list of plants with unusual characteristics (below).

Refer to the "Guide to Species Groups" (page 6) in order to find in which section of the book your particular species is illustrated and/or described.

Check your plant with the photographs for similarities, especially in the flowers. When you think these match sufficiently, check the descriptions and distributions. If either of these disagrees, then it is unlikely that the correct species for the plant in question has been found.

Should you have difficulty in determining the name of a plant and you want a check on the choice of names, you may request information from the botany department of a college or university in the state in which the plant is growing. Inquiries are welcome at the University of Georgia whether the plant is from Georgia or not.

Plants with Unusual Characteristics

Some groups of plants are set apart from others by distinctive characteristics, providing an advantage for purposes of identification. Some of these unusual characteristics and the families and/or genera exhibiting them are given below. These features are not necessarily confined to the plant groups mentioned, nor do all species in each group necessarily conform to all the characteristics listed, but in general the list below assists the user in identifying wildflowers rapidly.

1. Flowers usually small and packed tightly in heads: FABACEAE, ASTERACEAE, ERIOCAULACEAE, *Eryngium, Xyris.*
2. Flowers in simple umbels: LILIACEAE, PRIMULACEAE, ASCLEPIADACEAE.
3. Flowers in compound umbels: APIACEAE.
4. Sepals and petals 3 each and all similar: LILIACEAE, AMARYLLIDACEAE, JUNCACEAE, IRIDACEAE.
5. Stamens numerous: RANUNCULACEAE, ROSACEAE, HYPERICACEAE, MALVACEAE, ALISMATACEAE.
6. Plants lacking green color: ERICACEAE, OROBANCHACEAE, ORCHIDACEAE.
7. Plants with milky juice: ASCLEPIADACEAE, APOCYNACEAE, EUPHORBIACEAE, ASTERACEAE.
8. Petals united into a tube and with a distinct upper and lower lip: LAMIACEAE, SCROPHULARIACEAE.
9. Flowers with 4 separate sepals, 4 separate petals, and 6 stamens (2 short, 4 longer): BRASSICACEAE.
10. Leaves thick, succulent, smooth: PORTULACACEAE, CRASSULACEAE.
11. Inflorescences narrow and coiled backward at tips: BORAGINACEAE, HYDROPHYLLACEAE.
12. Inflorescences apparently fastened between nodes: SOLANACEAE, *Phytolacca.*

Guide to Species Groups

Although there are a few species which will be out of place in the scheme given below, you can save time and make identification much easier by using it. After checking the section "Tips on Identification," read below both items headed by the letter *A*.

A. DICOTS. If the sepals and petals are 4 or 5 each, the leaves netted-veined, and the vascular strands in the stem arranged in one circular line, then check *B* below. (A few Dicots are often interpreted as having parallel veins. Species of *Plantago* are the most likely to be encountered.)

> *B*. If the petals are separate, look on pages 24–117.
>
> *B*. If the petals are united, perhaps only at their bases, then check *C* below.
>
>> *C*. If the petals are of equal size and shape, look on pages 116–49, 164–67, 186–216.
>>
>> *C*. If the petals are of unequal size and/or shape, look on pages 150–64, 166–87, 190–91.

A. MONOCOTS. If the sepals and petals, which may be similar, are 3 each, the leaves parallel veined, and the vascular strands scattered (sometimes scattered in a ring such as in a bamboo stem), then check *D* below. (Some species of Monocots do not appear to have parallel veined leaves. The most common species are in *Trillium, Sagittaria, Peltandra,* and *Arisaema*.)

> *D*. If the ovulary is superior, look on pages 230–61.
>
> *D*. If the ovulary is inferior, look on pages 260–79.

Structure of Flowering Plants

The ability to identify flowering plants is basically dependent upon talent in seeing differences in structure between one species and another. As the individual develops this ability, the effort needed to find names for plants diminishes rapidly and enjoyment increases. Important plant structures are described below to help the amateur learn how to identify wildflowers. Most of these structures are easily understood, and the more advanced plant enthusiast can understand and profit from the remainder.

The structures will be considered in three categories: vegetative, floral, and fruiting.

Vegetative Structures. All vegetative parts of a plant are root, stem, or leaf, or combinations of these. One important combination is in buds, which consist of small to minute leaves on a diminutive stem. They are probably best studied in nature by dissecting a large bud from some tree, for buds on herbaceous plants are usually growing or very small and hard to see. Onion bulbs are a special type of bud.

Stems are usually above ground and bear leaves. When leaves fall off, scars are left on the stem. Each circular section of the stem which bears a leaf or leaves is a *node* and the space between any two adjacent nodes is an *internode*.

Roots are usually under ground, bear no leaves, and of course have no nodes or internodes. Stems sometimes sprout from roots and because they bear leaves of some kind can be distinguished from roots. When such stems are very short the leaves may appear to come from the root. Since roots have no leaves, they can have no leaf scars.

Leaves almost always have an expanded part (the *blade* or *blades*), usually have a stalk (the *petiole*), and often have two *stipules*. If the petiole is missing, the leaf is sessile. The term *sessile* is also applied to any other stalkless structure; sessile flowers, sessile fruits, sessile glands are examples. Stipules are always two or none. They are most often fastened to the sides of the petiole but may be attached to both petiole and stem or to the stem only. Stipules vary from conspicuous blades to very small projections. They may be thorny. Blades of a leaf may be one to many. A compound leaf with sets of opposite blades is superficially similar to a stem with opposite leaves of one blade each. Alternate blades on one compound leaf also often simulate a stem with alternate leaves of one blade each. Perhaps the single most important item in determining "what is the leaf" is to consider the position of leaves in respect to the buds (or stems that develop from them) that occur on the stem in the leaf axils.

The diagrams below illustrate various vegetative characteristics. Most vegetative structures can be recognized by referring to these. When in doubt refer also to the glossary.

VEGETATIVE STRUCTURES

SHAPE OF BLADES (LEAF, PETAL, SEPAL, BRACT)

Filiform   Linear   Lanceolate   Oblanceolate   Ovate   Obovate   Oblong

Elliptical   Cuneate   Spatulate   Orbicular   Deltoid   Reniform

VEGETATIVE STRUCTURES

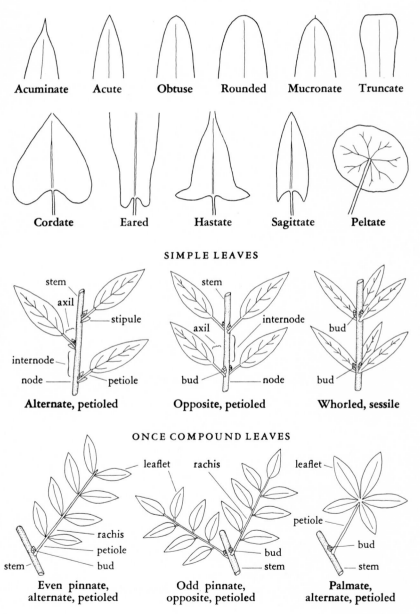

BLADE TIPS

Acuminate   Acute   Obtuse   Rounded   Mucronate   Truncate

Cordate   Eared   Hastate   Sagittate   Peltate

SIMPLE LEAVES

Alternate, petioled   Opposite, petioled   Whorled, sessile

ONCE COMPOUND LEAVES

Even pinnate,
alternate, petioled

Odd pinnate,
opposite, petioled

Palmate,
alternate, petioled

VEGETATIVE STRUCTURES

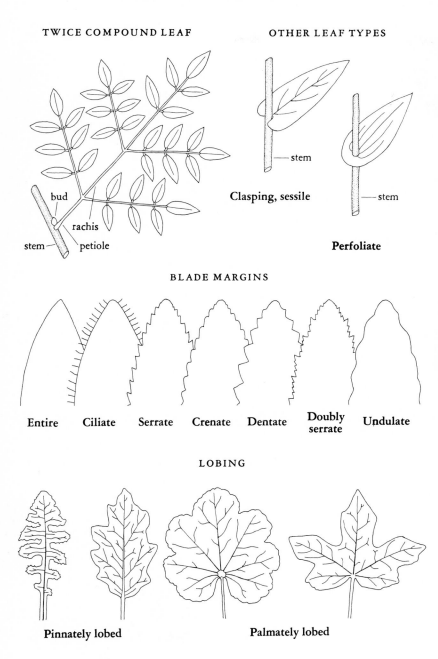

TWICE COMPOUND LEAF

OTHER LEAF TYPES

bud

rachis

stem —— petiole

—— stem

Clasping, sessile

—— stem

Perfoliate

BLADE MARGINS

Entire Ciliate Serrate Crenate Dentate **Doubly serrate** Undulate

LOBING

Pinnately lobed

Palmately lobed

Floral Structures. A complete flower is made up of four sets of parts attached to a special stem called a *pedicel.* The part of the pedicel to which the four sets are attached is called the *receptacle.* Each of the four sets is either in one or more whorls or one or more spirals. Members of each set may be completely separate, or partly or completely fused. The outermost of the sets is the *calyx,* consisting of *sepals,* which are usually green. Above these are the petals, which collectively are called the *corolla.* The corolla is usually the most colorful part of the flower. The third set of parts is the *stamens,* which bear the pollen. The final set is the *pistils.* They may be one to many, and contain *ovules.* The pistils grow into fruits and the ovules into the seeds in them.

The presence or absence of another flower part, the *hypanthium,* and variations in it are especially helpful in recognizing many species. The hypanthium is a cup-, saucer-, or disc-shaped structure found in some flowers. It supports the sepals, petals, and stamens, being between these parts and the receptacle. The diagrams below show positions and relationships of various flower parts and kinds of flower clusters.

FLORAL STRUCTURES

COMPLETE FLOWERS
WITH SUPERIOR OVULARIES AND NO HYPANTHIUM

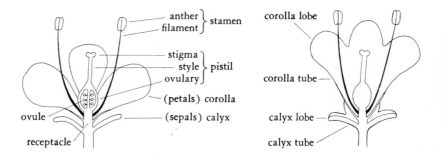

COMPLETE FLOWERS WITH A HYPANTHIUM (H)

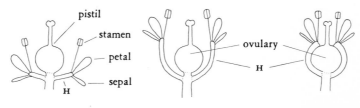

Ovulary superior   Ovulary superior   Ovulary inferior

FLORAL STRUCTURES

FLOWER FORM

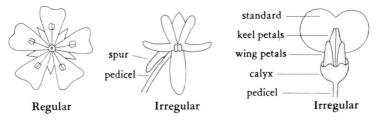

Regular   Irregular   Irregular

INFLORESCENCES (FLOWER OR FRUIT CLUSTERS)

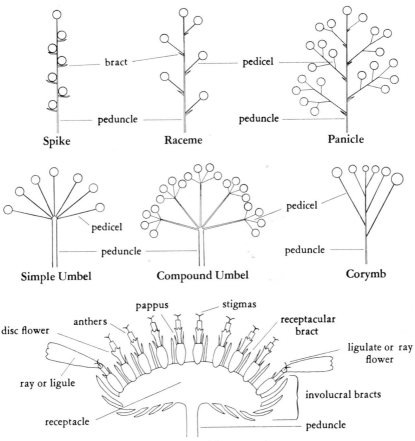

Head of Flowers (Asteraceae)

Fruiting Structures. Fruits develop from pistils, together with any other structures that may sometimes adhere to the matured pistil. A common added part is the hypanthium. For example, in the apple this structure forms the outer fleshy part that is eaten. In the banana the peels are developed from the hypanthium. In members of the sunflower family (ASTERACEAE) the hypanthium forms part of the husk covering the kernel inside. In a strawberry the receptacle is enlarged and is a major part of the fruit. A tomato, an English pea pod, and a milkweed pod, for example, develop from the pistil only. Diagrams of all these fruits except the banana follow:

FRUITING STRUCTURES

FRUIT TYPES (INTERIOR OR SURFACE VIEWS)

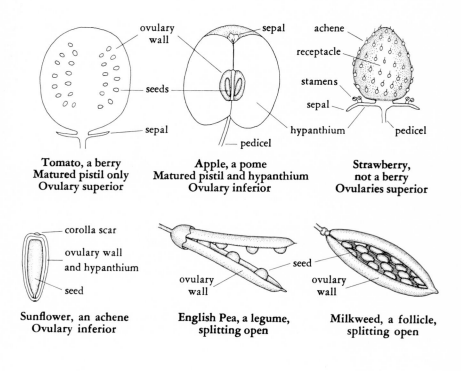

Tomato, a berry
Matured pistil only
Ovulary superior

Apple, a pome
Matured pistil and hypanthium
Ovulary inferior

Strawberry,
not a berry
Ovularies superior

Sunflower, an achene
Ovulary inferior

English Pea, a legume,
splitting open

Milkweed, a follicle,
splitting open

Photographing Wildflowers

Many wildflower hobbyists now prefer to make their plant collections through the camera lens, and most wildflowers can be identified readily from one or more good color photographs. The rise in popularity of the 35 mm single lens reflex camera has been rapid, particularly during the last decade, and even the inexpensive brands become efficient tools for wildflower photography in talented hands.

Many of the photographs included in this volume have been taken by using simple techniques which give the same control over the kind of subject lighting that is used widely by the studio portrait specialist. Aluminum reflectors covering letter-sized cardboard can be used to direct the patchy sunlight on a forest floor so that a *Hepatica* is both backlighted by the sun to expose the fine hairs on the plant stem and frontlighted to model the plant and a portion of its habitat.

A cardinal rule in wildflower photography is to get close to the flower. On a single lens reflex camera, extension tubes or a bellows attachment may be inserted between lens and camera or a portrait lens may be used in front of the standard lens. If the flower is less easily accessible, a short telephoto lens such as the common 135 mm may be used, again with or without extension tubes, bellows, or portrait lenses.

Flashguns, either bulb or electronic, will furnish adequate light when natural light is insufficient. This artificial light may be reflected by aluminum reflectors or mirrors so that the subject is more evenly lighted. With the camera on a tripod, or clamped to an available support, a long exposure combined with flash can be used to balance the lighting when natural light is low. The long exposure fills in the background and the flash highlights the wildflower.

Conservation

Any particular plant can grow and perhaps flourish where optimal conditions of climate and soil occur and where specific plant and animal associates, including microorganisms, are present. Plant colonies are formed where many individuals of a single species or a number of different species adapt to a common site and to each other and become established. These communities may remain stable for extended periods of time, or changes may occur gradually as more dominant species intrude, or they may be obliterated entirely by some catastrophic event such as fire or bulldozing. In the last circumstance succession must begin all over again with mosses, grasses, and weeds preceding shrubs, trees, and understory. Wildflowers contribute to this transition and perform an integral role in natural succession.

The southeastern states encompass an extensive range of common and specialized plant communities. Man is in the process of altering or eliminating many of these sites and the destruction appears destined to continue, at least for the time being, with the resultant decimation of some species. Highways, airports, lakes and their dams, mines, pipelines, building developments, lumbering operations, and countless other human activities are taking their toll in modifying or demolishing habitats. Some plants are eradicated immediately; others become weakened and eventually disappear. The latter process is accelerated by competition from robust plant immigrants that thrive in the converted site conditions and rapidly assume dominance. Man's activities have left few remnants of virgin environment, and the loss in genetic resources alone is incalculable.

Recent public awareness of the environmental crises confronting mankind throughout the world is producing encouraging results. Agencies and organizations at all levels of public and private enterprise are concentrating on means of preserving what is left and restoring what is destroyed. A few of the remaining natural areas are being acquired, protected, and normal plant and animal succession permitted to resume or continue undisturbed. Efforts are being made to have governmental or commercial projects redesigned so that mines, dams, highway routes, lumbering enterprises, and similar massive undertakings produce a minimum of ecological disturbance or damage.

Although encouraging progress is being made in conservation, public participation must improve or many of our much-needed natural areas will be forever destroyed. Individuals can help by supporting one or more of the numerous agencies dedicated to the protection and wise use of our environmental resources.

Comments on Photographs

Representative plants or parts of them were photographed for each species illustrated in this book. Samples of most of these plants were collected, preserved, and checked against herbarium specimens and in manuals and other literature for positive identity. The samples and field notes made it possible to relate the size of the wildflower in each photograph to its actual size. The relative size is indicated by a number placed after the scientific name. For example, $\times$ 2 means that the picture is twice that of the actual size, $\times$ 1 means the sizes are the same or natural size, and $\times$ $\frac{1}{3}$ means the picture is one-third the size of the actual subject. These values can be very helpful in getting from the picture a realistic conception of the plant's natural size.

Some photographs have been included of plants whose flowers are inconspicuous in the wild but which when magnified prove interesting. These closeups indicate what may be seen with an inexpensive hand lens and demonstrate another possibility for individual enjoyment.

Comments on Texts

The text gives for each species its common and scientific names, recognition characteristics, abundance, ecological and geographical distribution, flowering period, and often scientific names previously used. Special information is sometimes inserted to denote significant economic value (e.g., food, dye) or danger (e.g., poison).

Plant Names. Each species illustrated is identified by a scientific name and one or more common names. The name of the family to which the species belongs is listed on each page.

Both common and scientific names are useful but the latter are more exact and reliable; they are internationally constant regardless of national language, they make possible the recognizing and relating of species belonging to the same genus, and their usage is recommended. Common names are not dependable for they often vary between localities or even within a single community, leading to confusion and misunderstanding.

Scientific names, on the other hand, are controlled by international rules of nomenclature, and no two kinds of plants may have the same name. Their orderly arrangement according to genera and their frequent use of descriptive or diagnostic terms—e.g., *alba* for white, *hirsuta* for hairy—make learning them within the scope of anyone who seriously applies himself. The beginner may be surprised to find that names in common use are often the scientific names themselves, although he may be unaware of this when he speaks of Geranium, Hibiscus, Shortia, Phlox, Verbena, Lobelia, Aster, or even Chrysanthemum.

The scientific name of a species consists of two Latin or latinized words, a generic or "genus" name followed by a "species" name, the *specific epithet*. A specific epithet may be used in more than one genus—for example *Peltandra virginica* and *Silene virginica*—yet it is obvious that two different species are involved.

The scientific name of a species is followed by the name, sometimes abbreviated, of the botanist(s) who first described that species. This person's name is sometimes placed in parentheses and followed by a second name, or even two, which indicates that the second person, or persons, changed the scientific name from a previous combination to the one shown. It is often useful to know these persons' names, for with them the publication in which the species was described may be more easily located, and the names are sometimes necessary to find the proper species in a manual or other publication.

Occasionally a species is given one scientific name by one botanist and a different name by another. This difference may be due to one's ignorance of the other's work, although two names for the same species could also arise through differences in botanical opinion. For example, new studies may provide additional information which shows that two previously named and accepted species are only one. Whenever there are two scientific names for the same species, *The International Code of Botanical Nomenclature* provides that the older one is the legitimate name.

Common names are included despite the difficulties associated with their use. They do have interest and value and are frequently the only means of communication for those people unfamiliar with scientific names.

Recognition Characteristics. The names for each plant are followed by a description which provides recognition characteristics of the illustrated species. When a feature is either obvious in the illustration or requires magnification for detection it is generally omitted. Any amateur can be reasonably sure of a correct identification by comparing his plant specimen with photographs in the book and by checking the simpler characteristics in the descriptions. Less familiar descriptive terms are defined in "Characteristics of Flowering Plants" or in the "Glossary." Characteristics necessary for a positive determination are always included, although it may take the more advanced student, one who understands the entire description, to make a sure identification.

If more than one species of a genus is illustrated, characteristics common to all species of the genus may be given in the description of the first species presented. It should become a matter of routine to check the appropriate descriptions for these generic characteristics. Similarly, the description of the first species included for a family should be checked for characteristics of species in that family.

Measurement. The metric system is used in this book because of its utility. By no other practical method can comparative sizes of the small parts of flowers be demonstrated. For your convenience a metric scale 20 centimeters (cm) long has been placed inside each cover. Twenty cm equals 200 millimeters (mm). A meter is 5 times that long, i.e., 100 cm, 1000 mm, or about 39.4 inches. Ten mm equals 1 cm. These are the only metric units used in this book.

Special Items. Naturalists, botanists, ecologists, and others with similar backgrounds know that every species of flowering plant has value even though it may be negative. Plants are important in their relationships to other life and contribute balance to the environment they inhabit. Some have esthetic value and are included in this book because of their beauty. Other species may be disliked because they are weedy, noxious, or poisonous. Special aspects such as these are included in the texts.

Historically, the prime uses for herbaceous plants have been associated with food or medicine. Since many wild plants are diminishing in abundance, justification of their use for these purposes exists only in an emergency. Pokeweed, Dandelion, and other edible weeds which flourish in fields and waste places are obvious exceptions and may be used freely. Any plants from areas destined to be inundated by water, cleared for roads or homesites, or destroyed for any other reasons may also be used with impunity.

Abundance. The local abundance of many species has been established, often by numerical tabulations. Such studies are of considerable interest to ecologists and others, but these data very rarely involve the abundance of a species over its entire range. Nevertheless, a general subjective evaluation of the abundance for each species can be made on the basis of field experience, comments of other specialists, and analyses of scientific studies and specimens preserved in herbaria.

Conclusions concerning abundance for each species in this book are reported as common, occasional, or rare. Because most methods are of necessity subjective, only common and rare should be considered as significantly different ratings. Any species listed as occasional, however, is neither quite rare nor very common. Species that have limited distribution, although they may be abundant where found, are listed as rare, as are those that have wide distribution but are represented by few plants numerically. Species listed as common may also be occasional, rare or even absent in a given locale.

Distribution. The natural occurrence of a species may be conveniently considered in two categories: (1) the kind of habitat(s) in which it grows; and (2) its geographical distribution, also called range. Different habitats typically result from variations in light, moisture, soils, and kinds of associated species. Knowing that a species usually occurs in a certain habitat can be helpful in identifying a specimen or in finding plants of a given species. Geographical distributions are similarly useful, and for these reasons, as well as for general interest, the kinds of habitats and ranges are given for each species in this book.

We denote ranges mostly by states, or provinces in Canada, with standard abbreviations employed. Physiographic provinces of the Southeast are sometimes used, and abbreviations for these provinces are given with the map showing their locations inside the covers. We also refer to the Appalachian Mountains (Appalachian Mts.), which include the Blue Ridge, Ridge and Valley, and Cumberland Plateau provinces.

Distributions for each species were determined from manuals and especially from published studies of families and genera and by examining specimens in herbaria. Specific geographical sections of states have been indicated when helpful. The distributional limits of a species may be constructed simply by drawing an imaginary line from the outer margin(s) of one area to that of the next, and so on, returning finally to the first area listed. Sections of states or provinces are indicated by uncapitalized abbreviations. The basic positions of the sections and their abbreviations are shown in the following diagram:

nw	cn	ne
cw	c	ce
sw	cs	se

Flowering Period. The period of flowering is given for each species over its entire distribution in the Southeast by months. "Apr-June" means that flowering occurs during part or all of April, the entire month of May, and part or all of June in all or some portion of its range. For some species, flowering during the earliest month of spring and the last month in the fall may occur only in Florida or the southern parts of Georgia, Alabama, Mississippi, and Louisiana.

Other Scientific Names. Some scientific names which may be found in other books are not used in this one. This change in nomenclature may be due to an earlier name being found, the species being better placed in another genus, or for other professional reasons. Many of these earlier used names (synonyms) are listed after the flowering period, especially when the names will help the reader find the species in other books.

Other Similar Species. Many plants cannot be reliably identified as to species from photographs in wildflower books, and this book is no exception. A special effort has been made, however, to include in the text characteristics necessary for identification. Providing these characteristics also makes it reasonably easy to identify similar species when at least one appropriate contrasting characteristic is given. For many species this extra information has been provided in the final paragraph of the texts. Common names are generally omitted for these species because they are usually the same as for the one illustrated. Abundance, distribution, and flowering period are ordinarily given. If omitted, they are essentially the same as that in the previous paragraph. More than 560 unillustrated species are presented in the second paragraphs.

Glossary

Achene. A small dry one-seeded indehiscent fruit smaller than a nut and thinner walled than a nutlet.

Acuminate. Tapering to a point. Compare with acute.

Acute. Applied to tips and bases of structures ending in a point less than a right angle. Compare with acuminate and obtuse.

Alternate leaves. A single leaf per node.

Alternate stems. One per node.

Annual. Plant growing from seed to fruit in one year, then dying.

Anther. The pollen-bearing part of stamen.

Appressed. Lying flat against.

Aristate. Provided with a bristle-shaped tip.

Ascending. Rising obliquely or curved upward.

Awn. A bristle-shaped structure.

Axil. The space between any two organs, such as stem and leaf.

Axillary. In an axil.

Beaked. Ending in a firm prolonged slender tip.

Berry. Any fruit with fleshy walls and with several to many seeds inside, such as a grape, tomato, or pepper.

Biennial. A plant growing for two years then dying naturally.

Blade. The flattened and expanded part of a leaf, or parts of a compound leaf.

Bract. Reduced leaf, particularly at bases of flower stalks and on the outer part of the heads of flowers in the Composite Family.

Bulb. A swollen structure composed of circular layers as in an onion, usually subterranean.

Calyx. The outer set of parts of a flower, composed of sepals.

Capillary. Hairlike in shape.

Capsule. A dry fruit with two or more rows of seeds and splitting open at maturity.

Carpel. Each separate simple pistil, or section of a compound pistil.

Cauline. Belonging to the stem.

Central Placentation. Ovules and seeds on a central axis in a one-celled pistil or fruit. The axis is usually not attached at its top.

Ciliate. Marginally fringed with spreading hairs. Margin may be entire or toothed.

Circumboreal. Around northern regions.

Claw. The narrowed parallel-sided base of some petals.

Cleft. Deeply cut.

Column. The united part of the stamens in the Mallow Family; in Orchids, the fused style and stamens.

Compound. Composed of two or more separate parts united into one whole.

Compound leaf. Leaf with two or more blades (leaflets).

Compound pistil. With two or more united carpels.

Connective. The extension of the filament between and sometimes beyond the two pollen sacs of the stamen.

Cordate. As the outline of a heart with the point at the terminal end.

Coriaceous. Resembling stiff leather in texture.

Corm. A short solid thickened portion of the underground base of a vertical stem, with poorly developed scale-leaves or more commonly leafless. Compare with bulb. A swollen base of a stem, bulblike but solid.

Corolla. All petals of a flower, either separate or united, i.e., the inner series of the perianth.

Corymb. A flat-topped or rounded inflorescence with the outer flowers on the longest stalks and opening first.

Crenate. An edge with rounded teeth.

Cuneate. Wedge shaped.

Cyathia(um). The ultimate inflorescence of *Euphorbia.* Consists of cup-like involucre bearing flowers from its base.

Decumbent. Prostrate at or near base, the upper parts erect or ascending.

Deflexed. Bent or turned abruptly downward.

Dehiscent. Opening by natural splitting, as an anther in discharging pollen, or a fruit its seeds.

Deltoid. Triangular in shape.

Dentate. Toothed, the apex of each tooth sharp and outwardly directed (compare with serrate).

Disc flower. Any rayless flower in many members of the ASTERACEAE. See illustrations.

Divergent. Inclined away from each other.

Divided. Any blade cut into divisions reaching three-fourths or more of the distance from the margin to the midvein or to the base.

Elliptical. Oblong with the ends about equally rounded.

Entire. A margin without teeth. Margins may be lobed and the lobes entire.

Evergreen. Holding live leaves over winter until new ones appear, or longer.

Female flower. With pistils but no pollen-bearing stamens.

Fibrous. Composed of or resembling fibers, as many thin elongated roots.

Filament. The part of the stamen below the anther, usually slender.

Filiform. Threadlike; long and very slender.

Fruit. A mature ovulary, together with such parts that are regularly attached to it, i.e., the seed bearing part of a plant and any attached parts.

Fusiform. Cylindrical except thick near the middle and tapering to both ends.

Glabrous. Lacking hairs or other protuberances.

Glandular. Bearing swollen structures. These may be sessile, on short stalks, or on tips of hairs.

Glaucous. Surface with a very fine white substance that will rub off, as on many grapes and blueberries.

Hastate. Like an arrowhead but diverging at the base.

Herb. Any plant, either annual, biennial, or perennial with stems dying back to the ground at the end of the growing season. Any plant that has seasoning or medicinal use.

Hypanthium. A saucer-shaped, cup-shaped, or tubular organ below, around, or adhering to the sides of the ovulary. The sepals, petals, and stamens are attached at or near the outer or upper margin of the hypanthium.

Indehiscent. Not opening naturally at maturity.

Inferior. Descriptive of an ovulary surrounded by and sides fused to the hypanthium, the ovulary therefore appearing to be located below the sepals and petals.

Inflorescence. Any complete flower cluster, including any axis or bracts. Clusters separated by vegetative leaves are separate inflorescences.

Internode. A portion of the stem between one node and the next, i.e., between places where leaves are or were attached.

Involucre. A set of bracts below or around a head of flowers or a single flower.

Irregular. Flowers in which the members of one or more sets of parts are not the same size or shape.

Lanceolate. With the outline of a lance-head, much longer than wide and widest below the middle.

Leaflet. Any one of the blades of a compound leaf.

Ligule. A flattened petal-like terminal part of some corollas. Common in the AS-TERACEAE, most often on the marginal flowers of each head as in the Sunflower, but can be on all the flowers as in the Dandelion.

Linear. Narrow and elongate with essentially parallel sides.

Lip. Either the upper or lower projecting parts of the corolla or calyx of mints, snapdragons, and other plants; the odd petal (usually the lowest) in the Orchids.

Loments. A legume which is composed of one-seeded sections which separate transversely into joints, e.g., Desmodium.

Male flower. With stamens and no functional pistil.

Membranaceous. Thin, soft, and flexible.

Mesic. Moderately moist.

Mucronate. Having a short, sharp point at the apex (lip).

Node. That section of a stem from which leaves or branches arise.

Nutlet. A hard one-seeded fruit, smaller than a nut, and thicker walled than an achene.

Oblanceolate. Reverse of lanceolate, the terminal half the broader.

Oblong. Elongate and with parallel, or nearly so, sides.

Obovate. Reverse of ovate, the terminal half the broader.

Obtuse. Blunt or rounded at end, the angle at end over 90°. Compare with acute.

Ocrea. A tubular stipule surrounding the stem above the node.

Opposite. That arrangement of two leaves at a node with one attached opposing, or 180° from, the other. Also true of branches and buds.

Ovate. Having the outline of an egg with the broader half being basal.

Ovulary. That part of the pistil containing the ovules, the future seeds. Also called ovary.

Palmate. Radiately lobed or arranged.

Panicle. A rebranching flower cluster of the raceme type.

Papillate. Bearing minute nipple-shaped projections.

Papilionaceous. Having a standard, wings, and keel petals as in the corolla of many legumes.

Pappus. The outgrowth of hairs, scales, or bristles from the summit of achenes of many species of the ASTERACEAE. Generally considered to represent the calyx.

Pedicel. The stalk of each single flower.

Peduncle. The main flowerstalk, supporting either a cluster of flowers or the only flower.

Peltate. Shield-shaped and attached to the support by the lower surface.

Perfect. Flowers having both functional stamens and pistils.

Perfoliate. A leaf blade completely surrounding the stem, which appears to pass through the leaf, or two opposite leaves with bases fused to each other.

Perianth. The calyx and corolla collectively, or the calyx alone if the corolla is absent.

Petal. One of the sections, separate or united, of the corolla.

Petiole. The basal stalk of a leaf. Sometimes absent.

Pinnate. Blades of a leaf arranged along the sides of a common axis.

Pistil. The central organ of a flower, sometimes several separate ones. Contains the ovules.

Pistillate. Having pistils and no pollen-bearing stamens.

Plumose. Structured like a feather, the lateral divisions being like fine fibers.

Pod. A dry dehiscent fruit.

Prostrate. Lying parallel with the ground.

Raceme. A type of flower cluster in which one-flowered stalks are attached along the sides of a common axis.

Rachis. The main axis of a pinnately compound leaf, excluding the petiole.

Ray. See *Ligule.* Also a branch of an umbel or umbel-like inflorescence.

Receptacle. The part of the pedicel to which the other flower parts are attached. Also the enlarged summit of the peduncle of a head to which the flowers are attached.

Reflexed. Abruptly turned or bent toward the base. See *Retrorse.*

Regular. Flowers in which the members of each set of parts are the same size and shape.

Reniform. Outline of a kidney; rounded but with a wide basal notch.

Reticulate. Veins in the form of a network.

Retrorse. Directed backward or downward. See *Reflexed.*

Rhizome. A horizontal underground stem; distinguished from a root by presence of nodes, buds, or scalelike leaves which are sometimes quite small.

Rootstock. The somewhat enlarged part of a plant at or under the ground surface and from which the roots and stem(s) grow.

Sagittate. Shaped like an arrowhead. Also see *Hastate.*

Scale. Applied to many kinds of small, thin, flat, usually dry, appressed leaves or bracts, often vestigial. Sometimes epidermal outgrowths, if disc-like or flattened.

Scape. A leafless stem bearing flowers and rising from the ground or near it.

Scurfy. Surface with small scale or branlike particles.

Sepal. One of the parts of the calyx or outer set of parts of a flower, either separate or united.

Serrate. Having sharp teeth pointed terminally.

Sessile. Without any kind of stalk.

Sheath. A tubular structure surrounding an organ or part, such as the lower part of the leaf of grasses or an ocrea.

Spatulate. Somewhat broadened toward a rounded end.

Spike. A type of flower cluster in which stalkless flowers are attached along the sides of a common axis.

Spur. A sac-like or tubular extension of some part of the flower.

Stamen. A pollen-producing organ of a flower, usually consisting of anther and filament.

Staminate. Having stamens and no functional pistil.

Staminode (Staminodia). A sterile stamen or any structure corresponding to a stamen and without an anther.

Standard. The upper dilated petal of a papilionaceous corolla.

Stellate. Star-shaped. Where several similar parts spread out from a common center. Usually applied to branched hairs.

Stigma. The pollen-receptive part of a pistil, usually terminal and often enlarged.

Stipe. Basal stalk-like support of an ovulary or fruit; not the pedicel.

Stipules. A pair of structures, usually small, on the base of the petiole of a leaf or on the stem near the petiole; sometimes fused together.

Stolon. A horizontal branch arising at or near the base of a plant, taking root and developing new plants.

Style. That portion of the pistil between the stigma and the ovulary, often elongate, sometimes apparently absent.

Sub-. As a prefix, usually signifying about or nearly.

Subulate. Narrow and tapering evenly from base to tip.

Succulent. Juicy and fleshy. Either thin as in lettuce leaves, or thick as in cactus.

Superior. Said of an ovulary that is free of other floral organs.

Tendril. A thread-shaped clasping or twining structure serving as a holdfast organ.

Tepal. Used for any sepal and petal of similar form.

Terete. Circular in cross-section.

Tomentose. With matted soft wool-like hairiness.

Truncate. An apex or base nearly or quite straight across, as if cut off.

Tuberculate. Bearing small raised places.

Umbel. A flower cluster in which the flower stalks arise from the same point, as do the ribs of an umbrella. In a compound umbel this arrangement is repeated.

Undulate. With a wavy surface or margin.

Unisexual. One sex, bearing stamens or pistils only.

Whorl. Three or more structures (leaves, stems, etc.) in a circle, not spiralled.

Zygomorphic. See *Irregular.*

Plates and Texts

Lizard's-tail   *Saururus cernuus* L.

These perennials may become almost a meter tall and often form extensive colonies, spreading by rhizomes. Although the spike of flowers is drooping at the tip, the spike becomes erect as the seeds mature. Reestablishment of the beaver after near extinction in the South has increased the Lizard's-tail habitat. Common. Swamps, margins of streams and lakes, and low woodlands; Fla into e Tex, se Kan, s Minn, sw Que, and RI. Apr-July.

ARISTOLOCHIACEAE: Birthwort Family

Wild-ginger   *Asarum canadense* L.

A creeping, hairy perennial. Leaves deciduous, cordate, and mostly in pairs. Flowers single between the petioles of two leaves. Calyx with a cup and three pointed lobes. Corolla absent. The 12 stamens are closely associated with the style. In var. *canadense* the calyx lobes have long slender tips 5–15 mm long, in var. *acuminatum* Ashe they are tipped with a gradually tapering end, and in var. *reflexum* (Bickn.) Robins. the lobes are triangular, abruptly reflexed, and lack an elongate tip. The rootstock has an odor and taste suggestive of ginger and has been used as a seasoning. Residents of the southern Appalachians have told us that this species has been used in treatment of pregnant women, but we have no other information supporting such a use. Occasional. Rich woods; c SC into e Okla, e ND, and n NB. Apr-June.

Heart-leaf   *Hexastylis arifolia* (Michx.) Small

Members of this genus are aromatic perennials with thick evergreen leaves, no above-ground stems, and no petals. The 12 stamens are fastened to the style. The species are sometimes included in the genus *Asarum*.

This species has mostly triangular to ovate leaves with eared bases, sometimes in clusters to 40 cm across. Calyx flask-shaped and strongly constricted to a neck below the spreading lobes which are 3–6 mm long, the tube 15–30 mm long. Common. Moist to dry woods; w Fla into se La, e Tenn, and se Va. Mar-May.

H. naniflora Blomquist has circular-cordate leaves, the calyx tube is cylindrical and less than 10 cm long, and the calyx lobes 5–6 mm long. Rare. Deciduous woods; n SC and adj NC; s Va. Apr-May.

Heart-leaf   *Hexastylis heterophylla* (Ashe) Small

Leaves usually not variegated. Calyx tube 8–15 mm long, bulging out near the lobes but contracted between the bulge and the lobes, the lobes 5–9 mm long ascending to weakly spreading. Occasional. Rich woods; n Ga into e Tenn, w Va, c WVa, and c Va. Apr-June.

Similar species include: *H. shuttleworthii* (Britt. & Baker) Small in which the calyx is large, 3–5 cm long. Occasional. Rich woods; c Ga into c and n Ala, e Tenn, n WVa, and c Va. May-July. *H. virginiana* (L.) Small in which the calyx tube is 10–15 mm long, and the lobes 3–4 mm long. Occasional. Moist to dry and often rocky woods; n Ga into nw SC, NC, Va, WVa, and ne Tenn. Apr-May. *H. minor* (Ashe) Blomquist in which the calyx is bulged at or near the middle and the lobes are strongly spreading. Rare. Deciduous woods; nw and cn SC into cn and ce NC. Feb-Apr.

Saururus cernuus × 2/5

Asarum canadense × 1/4

Hexastylis arifolia × 1/4

Hexastylis heterophylla × 1/3

Dog-tongue; Wild-buckwheat   *Eriogonum tomentosum* Michx.

Perennial to 1 m tall, erect or often leaning. Stems hairy. Leaves densely light gray to tan, hairy beneath. Basal leaves prominent, longer than the whorled upper ones, sometimes dying with age or because of drought. Flowers in clusters of 10–20, surrounded at their bases by tan-colored bracts. Fruits about 6 mm long, 3-ribbed, surrounded by enlarged sepals. Common. Dry sandy pinelands and sandhills; Fla into upper C.P. of SC. July-Sept.

The genus consists of about 225 species most of which are in the western United States. Seeds and other parts of many species are important as food for various kinds of wildlife.

Wild Sorrel   *Rumex hastatulus* Baldw. ex Ell.

Annual or short-lived perennial to 1.2 m tall. Stems single or in large clumps, often forming extensive and colorful masses in open areas. Leaves usually with 2–4 widely divergent lobes. Male and female flowers on separate plants. Sepals at fruiting stage expanded into broad wings much wider than the achene. Various species are used as a nibble for the acid taste and to quench thirst. When eaten in large amounts poisoning may result from the oxalates present. Common. Roadsides, fields, and thin woods; Fla into e and cn Tex, se Kan, s Ill, Pied. of Ga, se Va, and locally along coast into Mass. Mar-June.

R. acetosella L., Sheep-sorrel, is similar but smaller, a perennial from slender running rootstocks, and sepals at fruiting stage just equaling the achene and enclosing it. Common. Fields, pastures, and roadsides; in most of the United States and Canada. Apr-July.

Arrow-vine; Tear-thumb   *Polygonum sagittatum* L.

Members of this genus have stipules which form cylindrical sheaths (ocreae) around the stem, the leaves are alternate and entire, the flowers are in spike-like racemes, and the fruits lenticular or triangular achenes.

This species is a sprawling freely branched annual, inconspicuous except when seen as a mass of growth. Physical contact with the plant, however, readily brings attention because of the sharp backwardly turned prickles on the stems and midveins of the undersides of the leaves. Leaves saggitate. Flowers in small tight rounded clusters. Common. Wet places, usually in the open; Fla into e Tex, s Sask, and Nfld. May-frost.

P. arifolium L. is also prominently prickly but the leaves are wider and hastate, and the flowers in loose elongate racemes. Occasional. Wet open places, often in tidal marshes; se Ga into s and e WVa, ne O, Ind, Minn, and NB. July-frost.

Dock-leaved Smartweed   *Polygonum lapathifolium* L.

An annual to 2 m tall. Ocreae thin and hairless or with a few small hairs on the veins. The peduncles bear sessile glands or are glandless. The racemes are usually arching or somewhat drooping. Various species of *Polygonum* have been used in seasoning. The leaves and seeds of many species are peppery and should be utilized with caution. They are mild in other species and are reported good in salads. *Polygonum* seeds are important food for wildlife, being eaten by many ground-feeding song and game birds, as well as by seed-eating small mammals. Occasional. Low open places, especially in disturbed areas; n Pied. Ga into Tex, Mex, BC, and Nfld. May-frost.

P. densiflorum Meisn. is similar but is a perennial and the racemes are mostly erect to slightly arching. Occasional. Swampy woods, shallow water; Fla into C.P. of Tex, se Mo, Ga, c NC, and s NS.

Eriogonum tomentosum × 1/9

Rumex hastatulus × 1/9

Polygonum sagittatum × 2/5

Polygonum lapathifolium × 1/4

Lady's-thumb   *Polygonum pensylvanicum* L.

Erect to sprawling annual with stalked glands and/or hairs on the peduncles just below
the flower clusters. The ocreae are thin and have no cilia. The fruits are flat or nearly
so on both surfaces. Common. Disturbed and often moist places; Fla into e Tex, Minn,
and w NS; scattered localities westward. Apr-frost.

Other annual species with dense racemes include *P. persicaria* L. which is glabrous
throughout and has cilia about 2 mm long on the ocreae. The calyx is not glandular-
punctate. Common. Disturbed, mostly damp places; throughout temperate N.A. Apr-
frost. *P. bicorne* Raf. is similar to *P. pensylvanicum*, but at least one side of the fruit
is convex or ridged. Occasional. Damp to wet disturbed areas; Fla into NM, Colo,
s Ill, and Pied. of Ga. *P. longistylum* Small. May-frost.

Water-pepper   *Polygonum hydropiperoides* Michx.

Perennial to 1 m tall. Leaves usually less than 15 mm wide, 3.5 or more times longer
than wide. Ocreae with cilia under 10 mm long and their sides with spreading or
appressed hairs. The calyx lacks glands. Flowers are frequently infected with smut.
Common. Swamps, water edges, in open or in woods; Fla into Tex, Minn, and NB;
scattered to west. May-frost. *Persicaria hydropiperoides* (Michx.) Small.

P. setaceum Baldw. is similar but the leaves are mostly wider and the hairs on the
side of the ocreae are spreading. Common. Similar places; Fla into e Tex, cw Mo, SC,
and s NJ. *P. cespitosum* Bl. is also similar but is an annual and the leaves are mostly
under 3.5 times as long as wide. Occasional. Damp to wet, usually disturbed places;
NC into n Pied. of Ga, s La, ce Mo, and Mass.

October-flower   *Polygonella polygama* (Vent.) Engelm. & Gray

Erect to decumbent perennial, sometimes shrubby at the base. Leaves narrowly club-
shaped to widely spatulate, under 5 mm wide, attached to cylindrical sheaths (ocreae)
which surround the stem. The ocreae are pointed on one side. The outer sepals vary
from red and pink to white. Petals absent. The stigma and style together are less than
0.2 mm long. Fruits triangular, one-seeded. Common. Sandy places, especially sandhills and pine barrens; Fla into e Tex, C.P. of Ga, and se NC; se Va. Aug-Oct. *P.
croomii* Chapm.

P. gracilis (Nutt.) Meisn. is taller, slimmer, more thinly branched, and is an annual.
Common. Sandy places in open and thin woods and scrub; Fla into s Miss, C.P. of
Ga, and se SC. Sept-Oct.

Fringed Polygonella   *Polygonella fimbriata* (Ell.) Horton

Erect annual, occasionally a perennial, 15–100 cm tall, branching well above the
ground. Leaves about 1.5 mm wide and 20–35 mm long. The flowers vary from pink
to white. The inner sepals are fringed. Common locally. Sandy soils. In open or thin
woods, especially sandhills; Fla into se Ala and C.P. of Ga. Aug-frost.

P. americana (Fisch. & Mey.) Small has similar but more abundant flower clusters
and the inner sepals are not fringed. It is a perennial, or rarely an annual, branching
near the ground and appearing as a depressed matted shrub early in the growing
season. Leaves about as thick as wide, 5–15 mm long and usually under 1 mm wide.
Common. Sandy or occasionally compact soils in open or thin scrub woods; c SC into
cs Tex, c NM, se Mo, and Pied. of Ga. Aug-frost.

Polygonum pensylvanicum × 1/4

Polygonum hydropiperoides × 1/2

Polygonella polygama × 1/8

Polygonella fimbriata × 3/5

Cottonweed *Froelichia floridana* (Nutt.) Moq.

Loosely hairy annual to 180 cm tall, usually with a few well-developed erect branches, mostly from the upper nodes. Leaves few and opposite. Upper internodes progressively longer. Spikes 10–12 mm in diameter. Mature fruit including beak, 5 mm long. Occasional. Sandy soil, pinelands, sandhills, fields; Fla into s Miss, c Ala, C.P. of SC, and se Del; La into Tex, NM, SD, nw Ind, and Ark. June-Oct.

F. gracilis (Hook) Moq. is similar but smaller, to 70 cm tall, mostly branched at the base, spikes 7–8 mm in diameter and with fruits 3–4 mm long. Occasional. Sandy soil and along railroads and highways; ce Ga into cn SC, s Va, and se NY; Ark into Tex, Mex, Ariz, Colo, and e Ind.

PHYTOLACCACEAE: Pokeweed Family

Pokeweed *Phytolacca rigida* Small

Glabrous perennial to 3 m tall. Leaves pliable, with the feel of thin kid leather. Flowering and fruiting racemes erect and appearing to be attached laterally on the stems but fundamentally terminally attached. Fruits a dark purple 5–12–carpeled berry. The flesh of the ripe berries is edible. Tender young leaves and shoots when *properly* prepared make a safe and tasty cooked vegetable and are eaten by many. Older parts and the roots are poisonous. Most persons discard the first water in which the greens are cooked to be sure to rid them of any poison. Sufficiently abundant and weedy to be considered for food by all. Common. Usually in open disturbed habitats; Fla into se Tex, s Ga, and sw SC. May-Oct.

Phytolacca americana L. is very similar but has divergent to declined racemes. Common. Fla into Tex, s Wisc, s Que, and s Me.

AIZOACEAE: Carpet-weed Family

Sea-purslane *Sesuvium portulacastrum* L.

Perennial with decumbent stems, rooting at the nodes. Leaves opposite, fleshy. Flowers solitary in leaf axils, on pedicels 3 mm or more long. Sepals 5, green outside and pink within, 7–10 mm long. Petals absent. Stamens numerous. Capsule 8–10 mm long, opening along a line circling its base. Occasional. Coastal dunes and beaches, upper parts of saltmarshes; Fla into Tex and se NC. May-Nov, or all year.

S. maritimum (Walt.) B.S.P. is similar but is an annual, is more erect, has sessile flowers, with only 5 stamens. The sepals are only 3–5 mm long. This species has been used as a potherb. Young shoots are the best. We have no record of *S. portulacastrum* being used thusly but it might be tried. Occasional. Wet coastal sands and salt flats; se Tex into Fla and NY. May-Nov, or all year.

Froelichia floridana × 1/3

Phytolacca rigida × 1/6

Sesuvium portulacastrum × 2

Talinum; Rock-portulaca *Talinum teretifolium* Pursh

Succulent perennial to 35 cm tall, the leaves terete. Flowers in long-peduncled inflorescences, opening only in the afternoon, or not at all on heavily overcast days. Petals 5–8 mm long. Stamens 15–20. Ovulary superior. Seeds shiny black. Common. Thin soil on dry rocks, dry sand; c C.P. of Ga, nw Ala, c Tenn, Va, e WVa, se Pa, and Pied. of NC. May-Oct.

In *T. mengesii* Wolf there are 50–90 stamens and the petals are 9–12 mm long. Rare. Thin soil on dry sandstone or granitic rocks; ce and nw Ala into c Pied. of Ga; c C.P. of Ga. *T. appalachianum* Wolf has only 5 stamens. Rare. Thin soil pockets on granitic rocks; c Ala only. In *T. calcaricum* Ware there are 25–45 stamens, the petals are 8–10 mm long, and the seeds are dull gray. Rare. Thin soil on calcareous rocks in cedar glades; nw Ala and c Tenn. May-Sept.

Spring-beauty *Claytonia virginica* L.

Perennial from a small globose corm. Stems 1 to several from each corm. Leaf blades linear to linear oblanceolate, more than 8 times as long as broad, the basal ones none to many, stem leaves 2 and opposite. Flowers up to 15. The species is unusual in having instability of chromosome numbers, having about 50 different chromosomal combinations. Occasional. Rich woods or open areas; sw Ga into e Tex, Minn, s Que, and NB. Feb-Apr.

C. caroliniana Michx., which is similar, has leaf blades lanceolate, elliptic, to spatulate, and less than 8 times as long as broad. Mts of n Ga into nw Ark, e Minn, s Que, sw Nfld.

Hairy Portulaca *Portulaca pilosa* L.

Annual to 20 cm tall, much-branched. Hairs in the leaf axils. Leaf blades linear to spatulate or oblanceolate. Petals to 6 mm long. Stamens 15 or more. Fruit with a lid, opening near middle at an even circular line. Seeds many, reddish-black. Occasional. Dry sandy soils in thin scrub or open; Fla into se La, C.P. of Ga and of NC. June-Oct.

P. smallii P. Wilson is quite similar but has silvery black seeds. Rare. Granitic outcrops; Pied. of Ga; Pied. of NC. June-Oct. *P. grandiflora* Hook also has hairs in the leaf axils but the petals are 15–25 mm long. Rare. Escaped from cultivation in scattered localities.

Common Purslane *Portulaca oleracea* L.

A prostrate much branched annual. Leaves alternate and opposite, fleshy, spatulate to obovate. Fruit with a lid opening just below the middle at an even circular line. Seeds dark red or black. When cooked and seasoned like spinach the tender young branches and leaves make a tasty potherb. Used as food in India for over 2000 years and in Europe for hundreds of years. It is frequently offered for sale in Mexican markets. It may be eaten raw, being a tasty addition to salad dishes. Large amounts may cause oxalate poisoning. Occasional. Cultivated areas, waste places. Throughout most of the United States. May-frost.

P. coronata Small is similar but the leaves are generally smaller, the seeds are silvery gray, and the cap of the fruit with a rim around its base. Rare. In open, granitic rocks, sandy soil; cn SC; c Ga; s Miss. June-Sept.

Talinum teretifolium × 2/5

Claytonia virginica × 1

Talinum teretifolium × 2/5

Portulaca pilosa × 1¼

Portulaca oleracea × 1

Giant Chickweed *Stellaria pubera* Michx.

All members of this family have 4–5 persistent sepals, the same number of petals, and one-celled capsular fruits with central placentation.

This species is a perennial with erect to spreading very finely hairy stems and opposite elliptic to ovate-lanceolate leaves. Flowers in loose terminal clusters. Petals white, apparently 10 but actually 5 which are deeply split. Sepals obtuse to acute, less than 6 mm long. Common. Rich woods, sometimes among rocks; nw Fla into Ala, Mo, Ind, ne Ill, and NJ. Mar-June.

S. corei Shinners is a similar species, but the sepals are acuminate and over 8 mm long. Rare. Rich woods; mts of NC and Tenn into Ind and NY. Apr-June.

Common Chickweed *Stellaria media* (L.) Cyrillo

A highly variable opposite-leaved annual with weak stems. The petals are white and appear to be 10 but actually are only 5 and deeply cleft. Stigmas 3. The sepals and some other parts are from glandular hairy to glabrous. Plants usually compact at first but later loosely branched and often forming dense masses. The young growing tips have been used as a cooked green vegetable although the plant has little taste. A complete list of birds that use chickweed for food would be a very long one. Common. Widely distributed, being especially noticeable in yards and gardens. Dec-May in South, usually dying completely by June. Flowering later northward, sometimes until frost under favorable conditions.

Some species of *Cerastium* and *Arenaria* are somewhat similar. *Cerastium* can be recognized by its having 5 stigmas, and *Arenaria* by its entire or notched petals.

Sandwort *Arenaria caroliniana* Walt.

Perennial to 30 cm tall with a dense basal cushion of decumbent to prostrate stems from a single stout taproot. Leaves opposite, linear-subulate, rigid, overlapping the ones above. Flowering stems erect, with many small glands. Sepals and petals 5 and separate. Stamens 10, five of them short and between the petals. Styles 3. Occasional. Well drained sands; Fla into C.P. of Ga, s C.P. of NC, and scattered into RI. Apr-June. *Sabulina caroliniana* (Walt.) Small.

A. uniflora (Walt.) Muhl. is another conspicuous species of this genus. It is an erect glabrous annual to 9 cm tall, often occurring in dense masses. Leaves herbaceous, oblong to linear, 2–7 mm long, acute, and entire. Sepals 2–3 mm long. Petals white, 3–4 mm long. Occasional. Shallow soil of granite rocks of Pied. of ce Ala into cs NC and of other rocks in the Upper C.P. of Ga. Apr-May. *Sabulina brevifolia* (Nutt.) Small.

Corn-cockle; Purple-cockle *Agrostemma githago* L.

Hairy annual to 1 m tall from a strong tap root. Leaves opposite and linear. Calyx partly united, with 10 strong ribs, the lobes longer than the tube, enlarging and encircling the fruit. Petals separate. Stamens 10. Styles 4 or 5. Fruit many seeded, the seeds very poisonous, 0.1–0.25 percent of an animal's body weight of ground seed being lethal. Occasional. Grain fields, fencerows, waste places; nearly throughout the United States. Apr-July.

Stellaria pubera × 1/3

Stellaria media × 2

Arenaria caroliniana × 3/5

Agrostemma githago × 1/3

Soapwort; Bouncing-bet   *Saponaria officinalis* L.

Glabrous perennial, spreading from seed and rhizomes. Stems to 150 cm long, decumbent to erect. Leaves opposite. Sepals united into a cylindrical, or nearly so, tube and obscurely five nerved, the lobes about 2 mm long. Petals separate, white to light pink. Styles 2. The scientific name comes from *sapo*, soap. The mucilagenous juice forms a lather with water and has been used as a soaplike material since ancient Greek times. When eaten the plant is poisonous. Occasional. Waste places, roadsides, fencerows, fields; nearly throughout the United States. May-Oct.

Fringed Campion   *Silene polypetala* (Walt.) Fern. & Schub.

Members of this genus have 3, or rarely 4, styles, and the sepals are partly united into a tube which has 10 main veins.

This species is a perennial to 25 cm tall. Some stems erect but most are decumbent and rooting. Leaves mostly spatulate, occasionally to elliptic or oblong. Calyx finely hairy. Petals separate. Stamens 10. Rare. Rich deciduous woods, usually on hillsides; n Fla into cw Ga. Mar-May. *S. baldwinii* Nutt.

S. ovata Pursh is another species with fringed petals. The stems are erect, to 1.5 m tall, the petals white and with only 8 linear lobes. Leaves about 6 pairs. Rare. Rich deciduous woods; ce Miss into se Ky, and cs NC.

Fire Pink   *Silene virginica* L.

Perennial to 60 cm tall, with several basal leaves and 2–4 pairs of cauline leaves, about 5 times as long as wide or longer. The basal stalk of the pistil 2–4 mm long. Sepals glandular hairy. Common. Thin woods and slopes; Ala into se Okla, se Minn, se NY, and se SC. Apr-July.

Two other pinks have similar deep red to scarlet flowers. *S. rotundifolia* Nutt., which has 5–8 pairs of cauline leaves, nearly as broad as long. Rare. Cliff ledges and slopes beneath; cn Ala into s O, e WVa, and nw Ga. June-July. *S. regia* Sims, which grows to 1.6 m tall and has 10–20 pairs of broader cauline leaves, mostly 2–3 times as long as wide. Rare. Thin woods and prairies; se Mo into sw O, e Ky. June-Aug.

Wild Pink   *Silene caroliniana* Walt.

Tufted perennial to 25 cm tall, from a thin deep taproot. In var. *caroliniana*, which is shown in the photograph, the basal leaf blades are obtuse, broadly oblanceolate, and finely hairy. Occasional. Sandy soils, usually open woods, often on slopes; se Ga into ; e Tenn, se O, s NH, and e NC. Mar-June. *S. pensylvanica* Michx.

In var. *wherryi* (Small) Clausen the basal leaf blades are acute, mostly narrowly oblanceolate, and glabrous. Occasional. Rocky upland woods, usually calcareous areas; c Ala into c Mo and cs O. Apr-May.

Saponaria officinalis × 1/3

Silene polypetala × 2/3

Silene virginica × 1

Silene caroliniana × 4/5

Yellow Pond-lily   *Nuphar luteum* (L.) Sibth. & Sm.

Perennial from a large rhizome. Leaves submersed, floating, or emersed. Leaf blades deeply cut at base. Stamens many, fastened under the ovulary. The photograph is of subsp. *macrophyllum* (Small) Beal. It is identified by having ovoid or nearly so blades and yellow inner parts of the sepals. Seeds have been used as food in the same manner as those of *Nymphaea*. Common. In fresh water; Fla into cs Tex, se Kan, se Wisc, and s Me. Apr-Oct.

Subspecies *sagittifolium* (Walt.) Beal is similar but the leaf blades are more than twice as long as wide. Rare. e SC into ce Va. In subsp. *orbiculatum* (Small) Beal the leaf blades are orbicular. Rare. n Fla into sw Ga; ne Ga. In subsp. *ozarkanum* (Mill. & Standl.) Beal the fruits and inner parts of the sepals are red-tinged. Rare. cw Ark into c and se Mo.

Yellow Nelumbo; Lotus-lily   *Nelumbo lutea* (Willd.) Pers.

Perennial from large tuber-bearing rhizomes. Leaf blades peltate, usually raised above the water, orbicular, to 70 cm wide. Flowers erect, above the water. Perianth parts numerous, the sepals grading into petals, stamens numerous. Pistils several, embedded in the top of an otherwise continuous and inverted fleshy cone. The tubers, which are starch bearing, are a tasty food when baked or boiled and seasoned. The interior of immature fruits is reported to be good either raw or cooked. In ripe fruits the shell is quite thick but can be removed by parching or cracking and the kernel inside eaten dry, baked, or boiled. Rare but common locally. In ponds, lakes, quiet streams, pools; Fla into e Tex, e Neb, Minn, and Mass. June-Sept.

N. nucifera Gaertn. is quite similar but the petals are pink. In scattered localities, Fla into La, Mo, and NC.

Water-lily; Water-nymph   *Nymphaea odorata* Ait.

Perennial from a large rhizome. Leaf blades floating or lying on mud, purple beneath, nearly orbicular, notched at the base. Sepals 4, nearly separate. Stamens fastened all over the ovulary. Seeds maturing under water. Flowers fragrant. Petals white or rarely pinkish. Flower buds have been boiled, seasoned, and then eaten. Seeds of foreign species are known to be edible. Those of our species are probably edible also. Common. In or at edge of fresh water; Fla into se Tex, s Man, and Nfld. Mar-Sept. *Castalia odorata* (Ait.) Woodv. & Wood.

N. mexicana Zucc. is similar but the petals are yellow. Rare. Fla into C.P. of NC and Ga, and e and s Tex. *Castalia flava* (Leitner) Greene.

Nuphar luteum × 1/5

Nelumbo lutea × 1/3

Nymphaea odorata × 1/5

White Baneberry   *Actaea pachypoda* Ell.

Perennial to 80 cm tall with 2 large compound leaves. The flowers are white in a single short compact raceme. Sepals 4–5, falling quite early. Petals 3–7, equal-sized, 3–5 mm long, soon dropping. Stamens numerous, the filaments thicker upward. Ovules and seeds several to many. Fruit a white berry. The plants, and especially the berries, may be poisonous. The red berries of *A. rubra* (Ait.) Willd., which occurs only north of our area, have caused poisoning. Occasional. Rich woods; n Fla into se La, e Okla, Mo, e Minn, and NS. Apr-May. *A. alba* (L.) Mill.

Golden-seal   *Hydrastis canadensis* L.

Localities recorded for this species are very few in the Southeast. It may have been overlooked and possibly has been exterminated from many areas by digging of the rootstocks for medicinal purposes. Root and rhizome preparations have reportedly been used as a hemostatic, to treat mouth ulcers, as a diuretic, and for other ailments. We know of no proof for these. Golden-seal is a perennial to 50 cm tall from a yellowish rhizome. From this develops one leaf and/or stem with 2 leaves near the top. The leaves enlarge after flowering to as much as 30 cm wide. The three sepals fall early. There are no petals, the flower being conspicuous because of the many stamens. Ovularies becoming a head of 1–2 seeded berries in fruit. Very rare. Rich woods; n Ga into Ark, e Neb, se Minn, cw Vt, and sw NC.

Black Snakeroot   *Cimicifuga racemosa* (L.) Nutt.

Perennial to 2.5 m tall, erect or the top bending, as in the picture. Leaves large with three pinnately compound divisions. Flowers in a large terminal raceme with a few to several smaller lateral ones. Sepals inconspicuous and falling as the flower opens. Petals absent. Stamens many. Pistil one and sessile. Fruit a several-seeded follicle. Common. Rich woods; ne C.P. of Ga into n Ark, s Mo, and nw NC. May-July.

   C. americana Michx. is quite similar except there are 3–8 stipitate pistils, and later fruits, for each flower. Occasional. Rich woods; mts of n Ga into Blue Ridge of NC and Tenn, se Ky, c Pa, and mts of Md. July-Sept.

Actaea pachypoda × 1/2

Actaea pachypoda × 1/3

Cimicifuga racemosa × 1/3

Hydrastis canadensis × 4/5

Wild Columbine
Aquilegia canandensis Pursh

The red and yellow flowers hang from slender nodding stems, causing the 5 long hollow spurs, one from the base of each petal, to point upward. The sepals are petal-like. The leaves are unusual in that they are divided 2 or 3 times, each time into 3 parts. Plants usually have leaves at the base and on the erect stems. The upper part of the plant is branched but not densely so. Occasional to common, especially in calcareous soils. In the open or in rocky woods, usually on slopes, and rarely in bogs; w Fla into Tex, Man, NS, and n SC. Mar-Aug.

Dwarf Larkspur
Delphinium tricorne Michx.

Not always small but averaging smaller than our other species. A perennial rarely over 60 cm tall from tuberous roots. Stems with fine hairs. Flowers white to blue or violet, each with a single spur. Seed pods usually 3 and spreading, hence the name tricorne (three-horned). All species of Larkspur are poisonous when eaten, but not equally so. In the western United States livestock losses have been heavy. Occasional. In rich woods and in open rocky areas, especially calcareous; nw Ga into e Okla, e Neb, w Pa, n Va, and cs NC. Mar-May.

D. carolinianum Walt. is similar but is usually taller, has more flowers, and the seed pods are erect and not spreading. Occasional. Dry places in thin woods and in open, often in rocky or sandy soils; ne Tex, sw Mo, cw and c Ill, La, nw and Pied. of Ga, and cw SC. Apr-July.

Rue-anemone
Anemonella thalictroides (L.) Spach

Perennial to 25 cm tall from small tuberous roots. Somewhat similar to *Anemone lancifolia* but the leaflet tips are rounded. Leaves at top of stem, with several stalked leaflets. Sepals 5–10, white to pinkish, 5–18 mm long. The fruits prominently 8–10 ribbed, one-seeded, and indehiscent. In some localities the tuberous starchy roots have been cooked and eaten. Common. Rich woods, nw Fla into e Okla, se Minn, and s NH. Mar-May. *Syndesmon thalictroides* (L.) Hoffmg. *Thalictrum thalictroides* (L.) Boivin.

Isopyrum biternatum (Raf.) T. & G. is similar but leaves usually arise from more than one level on the stem and the fruits are 2–3–seeded and split open at maturity. Occasional. Rich woods; Fla into ne Tex, se Minn, s Ont, and c NC.

Windflower
Anemone lancifolia Pursh

Perennial to about 30 cm tall, from an elongate rhizome about 2 mm in diam., with basal and cauline leaves, the latter whorled and with 3 leaflets, the lateral ones not deeply cut. Flowers single on erect pedicels. Sepals usually 5–7, white. Petals absent. Fruits are achenes and numerous. Occasional. Rich woods; c SC into ne Ala, sw Pa, and c NC. Mar-May.

A. quinquefolia L. is similar but the leaves have 5 leaflets, or with 3 leaflets and the lateral ones deeply cut. Common. Rich woods; Pied. of Ga into n Miss, s Que, and NJ.

Aquilegia canadensis × 1

Delphinium tricorne × 1/6

Anemonella thalictroides × 2/5

Anemone lancifolia × 1/2

Leather-flower; Vase-vine   *Clematis reticulata* Walt.

Perennial vine climbing by bending or clasping leaf-stalks. Leaf veins prominently netted and raised. Petals absent. Sepals petal-like, 15–25 mm long. Stamens and pistils many and separate. Fruit an achene tipped with the persistent elongated plume-like style. Occasional. Dry sandy or rocky usually open woods; Fla into e Tex, s Ark, c Tenn, Pied. of Ga, and C.P. of SC. May-Aug. *Viorna reticulata* (Walt.) Small.

In *C. crispa* L. leaf veins are not raised, sepals are 30–45 mm long with broad showy margins on the usually reflexed tips. Common. Low places, in woods or open; Fla into e Tex, s Ill, C.P. of Ga, and se Va. Apr-Aug. In *C. viorna* L. the sepals are 15–25 mm long, the tips less wide and less spreading. Leaves are green beneath. Common. Rich woods, sometimes in open and rocky places; cs Ga into La, s Mo, ce Ind, sw Pa, and ce NC. May-Sept.

Liverleaf; Hepatica   *Hepatica americana* (DC.) Ker

Perennial from a short rhizome. Aboveground stems absent. Leaves evergreen, the blades with blunt lobes, purplish beneath. Flowers appear before the leaves of the year. Sepals petal-like, bluish or less often pink or nearly white. The sepal-like structures beneath these are bracts which are persistent. Occasional. Rich woods, usually on slopes; nw Fla into e and n Ark, s Man, NS, and Va. Feb-Apr.

H. acutiloba DC. is very similar, being generally larger and the leaf blades with acute lobes. Occasional. Similar habitats, nw SC into n Ga, n Ark, c Minn, s Que, and s Me. Mar-Apr.

Bulbous Buttercup   *Ranunculus bulbosus* L.

Members of this genus have 3–5 green sepals, 5 yellow petals, many yellow stamens attached directly beneath the several to many greenish pistils. The fruits are achenes.

This species is a perennial from a firm swollen base which is not a true bulb, as the name might imply. Plants may get 60 cm tall and are conspicuous because of the many bright yellow flowers. This species and others have been reported occasionally to cause severe irritation when eaten. Common locally. Generally in low open areas; La into Ill, Ont, Nfld, NC, and c Ga. Apr-June.

There are over 20 species of *Ranunculus* in the Southeast. Flowers vary in size from 3 to 25 mm wide. Leaves are entire to lobed or palmately or pinnately divided. Identification to species is mostly dependent on the fruit characters and is often difficult.

Early Buttercup   *Ranunculus fascicularis* Muhl.

Hairy perennial usually with short tuberous roots. The achenes are smooth, flattened, and with a distinct margin. Beak of achene straight, more than half as long as the body. Common. Open areas or woods, wet to dry; Fla into e Tex, Minn, and NH. Mar-Apr.

R. carolinianus DC. is similar but is glabrous or nearly so and the roots thick and fibrous but not tuberous. Occasional. Wet habitats, in open or woods; Ga into e Tex, e Neb, s Man, and Me. Apr-July.

Clematis reticulata × 1½

Hepatica americana × 4/5

Ranunculus fascicularis × 1/5

Ranunculus bulbosus × 1½

Kidney-leaf Buttercup   *Ranunculus abortivus* L.

An erect glabrous annual, conspicuous vegetatively. Plants often with several stems originating from the base. Flowers many, inconspicuous. Achenes plump, with a beak less than 3 mm long. This is the most abundant of the species having crenate and unlobed blades on the basal leaves. Common. Usually in moist places, fields, gardens, borders of yards, low woods; Fla into e Tex, Colo, Wash, Alas, and Nfld. Mar-June.

   R. allegheniensis Britt. is similar but the achene beak is 0.6–1 mm long and curved. Rare. Rich woods; w NC into e Tenn, se O, s Vt, and Mass. *R. micranthes* Nutt. ex T. & G. is also similar but the stem and leaves are hairy. Rare. Rich woods; n Ala into ne Okla, c Ind, c Md, and cn NC.

Tall Meadow-rue   *Thalictrum polygamum* Muhl.

Perennial to 2.5 m tall. Leaves compound, the upper ones sessile. Leaflets glabrous, usually over 15 mm long. Male flowers are conspicuous and on one plant, as seen in picture, and the less conspicuous female flowers are on another. Fruits sessile. Occasional. Wet places in thin woods or open; NC into n Miss, s Ont, and NS. May-Aug.

   There are several similar species. In *T. dioicum* L. the upper leaves have petioles. Occasional; c Ga into n Ark, s Man, and c Me. Mar-May. In *T. revolutum* DC. the leaflets and fruits have very small stalked glands. Occasional. Drier places in woods or open; nw Fla into n Ark, s Ont, and Mass. In *T. macrostylum* Small & Heller the leaves and fruits are glabrous and the leaflets less than 15 mm long. Rare. Rich woods and moist meadows; SC into ne Ala and se Va.

Lady-rue   *Thalictrum clavatum* DC.

Inconspicuous but easily recognized by its stalked, curved (scimitar-shaped) fruits. Plants are perennial, to 60 cm tall. The leaves are twice divided into 3 divisions. The flowers have both stamens and pistils but lack petals. Occasional. Moist places, often in deep shade but occasionally in the open; n SC into n Ala, c WVa, and mts of NC. May-July.

   One other species, *T. coriaceum* (Britt.) Small, has stalked fruits but they are obliquely ovoid and not scimitar-shaped. Plants may grow over 1 m tall. Occasional. Rich woods; n Ga into sw Pa, and n Va.

BERBERIDACEAE: Barberry Family

Mayapple; Mandrake   *Podophyllum peltatum* L.

Glabrous perennial to 50 cm tall from long rhizomes. Flowering plants with a single flower from the junction of the petioles of the two similar leaves. Nonflowering plants have a single leaf. Leaves peltate and deeply lobed; the sepals fall early. Petals 6–9. Stamens twice as many as the petals. Ripe fruit a yellow to reddish 1-celled berry with a peculiarly-flavored pulp which is sparingly eaten raw and used to make marmalade. Seeds and vegetative parts poisonous. Long considered a medicinal plant. Indians and early settlers used it for a variety of ailments. Research has been conducted on at least 16 physiologically active compounds. Because of the poisonous nature of the plant, extracts should be used only when obtained under a doctor's prescription. Common. Rich woods or moist meadows; Fla into e Tex, Minn, w Que, and Va; escaped eastward. Mar-May.

Ranunculus abortivus × 1/2

Thalictrum polygamum × 1/2

Thalictrum clavatum × 2/3

Podophyllum peltatum × 1/4

Blue Cohosh   *Caulophyllum thalictroides* (L.) Michx.

Glabrous perennial to 80 cm tall from a knotty rootstock. A leaf with three long stalks and many leaflets is on the upper part of the stem. Above this is another (rarely two) similar but smaller leaf. At or near the stem tip are 1–3 clusters of inconspicuous flowers. Sepals 6, petal-like, yellowish-green to greenish-purple, with 3 or 4 sepal-like bracts beneath them. The 6 petals are merely small gland-like bodies. The seeds are blue when mature and are exposed, growing faster than the ovulary and splitting out of it. The plants, especially the seeds, are considered to be poisonous. Occasional. Rich deciduous woods; n Ga into n Ala, Mo, se Man, NB, and cn SC. Apr-May.

Umbrella-leaf   *Diphylleia cymosa* Michx.

Flowering plants have a single cluster of white flowers and 2, rarely 3, leaves which are at different levels and are dentate, peltate, and 2-cleft. Nonflowering plants have a single large leaf. The sepals fall early. Unlike most other dicots the sepals, petals, and stamens number 6 each. The flowers are similar to those of mayapple but smaller. The blue fleshy fruits are conspicuous late in the growing season. The genus is represented by this species and one in e Asia. Occasional. Cool moist woods in mts; Ga into Va. May-June.

Twinleaf   *Jeffersonia diphylla* (L.) Pers.

Stemless glabrous perennial from a short rootstock. Petioles at first shorter than the flower stalk, later elongating to as much as 50 cm tall. The two leaf blades are entire or toothed. They enlarge after the plant flowers, sometimes to 15 cm long. Sepals usually 4, petal-like, and dropping early. Petals usually 8, to 2 cm long. Stamens 8. Fruit erect, to 3 cm long, opening by a halfway around horizontal cleft, the upper part making a lid which is hinged at the back. Named in honor of the third president of the United States, Thomas Jefferson, for his knowledge of natural history. The only other species of this genus occurs in eastern Asia. Occasional. Rich woods, usually calcareous soils; nw Ga into n Ala, se Minn, s Ont, n NY, and n Va; sw NC. Mar-May.

PAPAVERACEAE: Poppy Family

Bloodroot   *Sanguinaria canadensis* L.

Perennial from a thick rhizome with abundant red juice. Flower single on a leafless stem. The two sepals drop early. The petals are usually 8 but vary to 16. The single leaf continues to enlarge after the petals drop and may become 25 cm wide. Stamens about 24. Fruit an ellipsoid 1-celled capsule with two rows of seeds on the inside surface of the wall. The juice has been used as a dye. Baskets and cloth colored with the juice are still occasionally available locally. The plants are likely poisonous when eaten. Common. Rich woods; Fla into e Tex, Man, and NS. Feb-Apr.

Caulophyllum thalictroides × 1/3   Diphylleia cymosa × 1/15

Jeffersonia diphylla × 2/5   Sanguinaria canadensis × 3/5

Dutchman's-breeches   *Dicentra cucullaria* (L.) Bernh.

Flowers not fragrant. Stems and leaves from a fleshy, loosely scaly, pink to light-colored bulb, the scales pointed. The two diverging spurs of the corolla base provide the legs of the "breeches," which are turned up because the flowers are nodding. There is some evidence indicating the members of this genus are poisonous when eaten. Occasional. Rich woods; n Ga, into Ark, ne Okla, ND, Que, NS, and c NC; e Ore and e Wash. Mar-Apr.

Squirrel-corn   *Dicentra canadensis* (Goldie) Walp.

Flowers fragrant. Stems and leaves arising from a rhizome bearing yellow rounded pea- or corn-like structures from which this species gets its common name. The corolla base is merely cordate. Occasional. Rich woods; n Ga into Tenn, Mo, se Minn, se Que, NS, and e NC. Apr-May.

 D. eximia (Ker.) Torr., commonly called Bleeding-heart, has similarly shaped flowers. Plants are more robust. The flowers are flesh-colored to dark pink and in panicles instead of a simple raceme. Rare. Rich, rocky woods; w NC and e Tenn into e Va, WVa, w NY, and NJ.

BRASSICACEAE: Mustard Family

Warea   *Warea cuneifolia* (Muhl.) Nutt.

Members of this family have 4 separate sepals, 4 separate petals, 6 stamens (2 long and 4 short) or rarely 2 or 4 of the same length, and a 2-carpelled fruit that splits open at maturity and retains the central partition. Indentification to genus and species often is not easy, being based chiefly on fruit characteristics.

 Erect annual to 1.2 m tall, branching in upper part. Leaves all simple, the blades cuneate. Flowers clustered in tight terminal racemes. Petals 4, clawed. Stamens 6, 4 long and 2 shorter. This is the only genus in this family in which the pistil has a stipe which elongates into a prominent stalk as the fruit matures. Occasional. Sandhills; cn Fla into se Ala, C.P. of Ga and cw C.P. of NC. July-Nov.

 W. amplexifolia (Nutt.) Nutt. (*W. sessilifolia* Nash) has rounded leaf bases. Rare. Sandy soils, pinelands or in open; cn and nw Fla. *Cleome boutteana* Raf. (CAPPARIDACEAE) has similar but larger flowers, fruits, and upper leaves. The lower leaves are palmately compound, leaflets 5–7, and the 6 stamens are the same size. Rare. Wasteplaces, cultivated areas; Fla into e Tex, ce Mo, and Conn. June-frost. *C. spinosa* L.

Winter-cress; Yellow-rocket   *Barbarea vulgaris* R. Br.

This species is a biennial to 80 cm tall, usually glabrous. Basal leaves with 1–4 pairs of lateral lobes. Cauline leaves auricled. Fruit slender, 2–3 cm long, the beak 1.8–3 mm long. Seeds in 1 row in each carpel of the fruit. Sometimes used as a salad or potherb but is somewhat bitter. The bitterness can be reduced or eliminated by changing the cooking water 2 or 3 times. Common. Damp places, meadows, fields, thin woods; NC into e Okla, Minn, s Que, and Nfld. Mar-June. *Campe barbarea* (L.) Wight.

Dicentra cucullaria × 1

Warea cuneifolia × 1/4

Dicentra canadensis × 2/3

Barbarea vulgaris × 1/4

Bitter Cress   *Cardamine parviflora* L.

Annual or biennial to 20 cm tall, glabrous or nearly so. Leaves pinnately compound and with 5–8 pairs of distinct entire leaflets. Fruits slender, erect. Seeds wingless. Common. In a variety of open and wooded habitats; Fla into Tex, Minn, and NS; Cal into BC. Mar-May.

In the similar *C. hirsuta* L. the lower petioles are ciliate. Common. Fields, lawns, waste places; Fla into ne Tex, Ill, and se NY. In *Sibaria virginica* (L.) Rollins the seeds are winged and the leaves are only deeply divided and not compound. Common. In a variety of habitats, often a weed; Fla into Tex, se Kan, s Ohio, and e Va. *Arabis virginica* (L.) Poir. The top parts of plants of *Arabidopsis thaliana* (L.) Heynh. are also similar to those of the above species, but the leaves are mostly basal, entire to indistinctly serrate, and not compound. Common. Throughout most of the United States.

Spring Cress   *Cardamine bulbosa* (Schreb.) B.S.P.

Glabrous perennial to 50 cm tall from a bulbous rootstock. Basal leaves long petioled, the blades oblong to cordate-ovate; the cauline leaves 4–12, a few of the lower ones petioled, the upper ones sessile; all entire to undulate or widely dentate. Tender young plants, including the bulbous rootstock, have been used in salads, having the flavor of horseradish. Other species of the genus have been used similarly. Occasional. Wet places, in thin woods or in open; n Fla into e Tex, e SD, s Que, and s NH. Mar-May.

C. douglassii (Torr.) Britt. also has a bulbous base. The petals are pink to lavender and the cauline leaves 2–5 and all sessile. Occasional. Wet places in thin woods or in open; n SC into c NC, e Mo, s Wisc, s Ont, and Conn. Mar-May.

Toothwort; Pepper-root   *Dentaria multifida* Muhl.

Perennial to 40 cm tall from a segmented rhizome, the segments 1–2 cm long, joined by fragile connections. Great care needs to be taken not to break the segments apart. Cauline leaves usually 2, opposite. Basal leaves 0–2 from the rhizome. Leaf segments 3–7, linear, 1–3 mm broad. Rachis of raceme glabrous. Occasional. Rich moist woods along streams and on adjacent slopes; nw Ala into se Ind, w WVa, ne Tenn, and nw Ga; c and cs NC. Mar-May.

D. laciniata Muhl. is similar but the raceme rachis is finely hairy. The upper leaves are 3, whorled, and their segments wider and toothed. Basal leaves usually absent at flowering. Common. Rich woods, calcareous outcrops; se La into se Okla, ne Minn, s Mich, s Ont, Conn, cn SC, and nw Ala. Mar-May.

Toothwort; Pepper-root   *Dentaria diphylla* Michx.

Perennial to 40 cm tall from an elongated rhizome of nearly uniform diameter. These should be uncovered only with care. Segments of basal leaves broad, similar to the cauline leaves. The rhizomes of this and other species of the genus have been used for food. With salt they taste somewhat like radishes. Makes an interesting condiment when grated and mixed with vinegar. Occasional. Rich woods; upper Pied. of Ga into nw Ala, upper Mich, NB, NS, WVa, and nw SC; c NC. Apr-May.

D. heterophylla Nutt. has similar leaves but the rhizome is segmented, the segments 2–4 cm long. Occasional. Rich woods; cn SC into nw Miss, cn O, and NJ. Mar-Apr.

Cardamine parviflora × 1/5

Cardamine bulbosa × 1/4

Dentaria multifida × 3/4

Dentaria diphylla × 1/2

Watercress   *Rorippa nasturtium-aquaticum* (L.) Hayek

Glabrous succulent perennial to 75 cm tall. Stem submersed or partly floating, creeping to decumbent, the ends erect. Leaves with 3–9 leaflets, the tip one the largest. Flowers in racemes. Fruit 1.5–2.5 mm thick and 1.5–2 cm long. In the genus *Rorippa* the fruits are curved, pedicelled and not stalked; the leaves are pinnately compound. Watercress is the only species of the genus in our area having white flowers. Frequently used as a green salad, but now often found in contaminated water. Is an important food for wildlife. Occasional, yet abundant locally. In clear running water or rooted in wet soil; nearly throughout the United States. Apr-Aug. *Nasturtium officinale* R. Br.

   Cardamine pensylvanica Muhl. is often similar in general appearance but the fruits are straight. Also good as a green salad. Common. Aquatic and drier habitats. Fla into La, Minn, BC, and Nfld.

Leavenworthia   *Leavenworthia exigua* Roll.

Annual with basal leaves only, early leaves unlobed, later ones with as many as 11 well separated lobes, the terminal one with small angular lobes. Petals 6–9 mm long, each with a broad notch. Fruits not knobby. Rare but locally common. Shallow soils of thinly bedded dolomitic limestone of cedar glades; nw Ga; c Ala; c Tenn; cn Ky. Mar.

   L. uniflora (Michx.) Britt. is similar but the petals are entire; ne Ga into n Ala, cs Ky, nw Ark, and ce Mo; cs Ind and adj Ky; cs O. The fruit is knobby in *L. torulosa* Gray. se into sc Tenn and cs Ky. All other species have petals 10 mm or more long. Of these *L. stylosa* Gray has thick fleshy fruits 12–25 mm long. c Tenn. *L. crassa* Roll. has thick fleshy fruits 6–12 mm long. cn Ala. In *L. alabamica* Roll. the fruits are thin and flat. ne Ala.

SARRACENIACEAE: Pitcher-plant Family

White-trumpet; Pitcher-plant   *Sarracenia leucophylla* Raf.

Perennial to 120 cm tall. As in all members of the genus the leaves are hollow and liquid-containing to varying degrees. Insects are caught in the hollow leaves and are digested, thus providing some of the plant's food and mineral needs. The flowers are also strange in that they all are nodding and the end of the style is expanded into a large, persistent, 5-lobed umbrella-like structure. In this species the leaves are erect, and their upper parts white and veined with reddish-purple. Occasional. Bogs, low savannahs; s Miss into sw Ga and nw Fla. Mar-Apr. *S. drummondii* Croom.

   In *S. rubra* L. the petals are also red and the leaves erect, but the leaves are green, narrow, and shorter, to 50 cm tall, and have a small opening. The hoods are only 1–3 cm wide. Rare. Similar places; nw Fla into se Miss, c Ala, C.P. of Ga, and se NC; nw SC and adj NC. Apr-May.

Rorippa nasturtium-aquaticum × 1⅓   Leavenworthia exigua × 1

Sarracenia leucophylla × 1/2

Parrot Pitcher-plant   *Sarracenia psittacina* Michx.

Perennial with decumbent leaves in a basal rosette usually mostly hidden by other vegetation. The plant in the photograph was on the edge of a depression and easily seen.
The hood almost covers the opening in the leaves. Occasional. Sphagnum bogs, wet
savannahs, open pinelands; se La into nw Fla, s Ala, and C.P. of Ga; ne Fla. Mar-July.

S. *purpurea* L. also has decumbent leaves but the hood is turned away from the
opening. The inner surface of the hood bears many stiff hairs which point toward the
open part of the leaf. These hairs may help trap insects in the hollow leaves. The flowers are red and up to 40 cm above the ground. Rare. Scattered distribution; nw Fla into
se La and sw Ga; se Ga; ne Ga into sw NC; se and c SC into e Va, e Md, Pa, ne Ill,
cw Minn, s Ont, s Lab, and Nfld.

Hooded Pitcher-plant   *Sarracenia minor* Walt.

Perennial, with erect leaves to 40 cm tall, rarely to 60 cm. Opening near top of leaves
covered by a hood. Base of hood and upper part of leaf spotted with large white or
translucent areas. Sepals yellowish, petals yellow. Common. Bogs, wet savannahs, and
open pinelands; c Fla into se Ga and se NC. Mar-May.

Trumpet Pitcher-plant   *Sarracenia alata* Wood

Perennial, the leaves erect, to 85 cm tall, yellow to greenish yellow, the veins reddish,
the margins on the base of the hood only slightly turned backward. Petals yellow. Occasional, but abundant locally. Bogs, wet savannahs, low open pinelands; sw Ala into se
La; cw La into e Tex. Mar-Apr. *S. sledgei* MacFarlane.

In *S. flava* L. the leaves may reach 125 cm but usually are a little over half that tall.
They are yellowish, sometimes veined with maroon, or occasionally entirely maroon.
The lower margins of the hood are strongly turned backward. Occasional, once common but now rapidly disappearing. nw Fla into s Ala, C.P. of Ga, and se Va; cw NC.
Mar-Apr. *S. oreophila* (Kearn.) Wherry is similar but has several shorter sword-
shaped leaves with no cavities in addition to the erect hollow ones. Petals greenish-
yellow. Rare. Wet places. c and ne Ala.

DROSERACEAE: Sundew Family

Sundew   *Drosera leucantha* Shinners

Members of this genus have stalked glands on the leaves. These glands exude a clear
sticky secretion which aids in the insect-catching ability of the leaf.

In this species the leaves are basal, the blades much wider than the petioles, and the
scape is very finely glandular hairy. Occasional. Moist places, in thin pinelands or open;
Fla into se La, ne Ala, and adj Tenn, C.P. of SC, and c and ce NC. Mar-May. *D. brevifolia* Pursh.

In *D. capillaris* Poir. the scape is glabrous and the leaf blades longer than wide.
Common. Similar places; Fla into e Tex, se Tenn, C.P. of Ga, and se Va. Mar-Aug. In
D. rotundifolia L. the leaf blades are wider than long. Rare. Sphagnum bogs and seep-
age places; nw SC into ne Ga, ne Ill, Mont, Cal, Alas, and Greenl. June-Aug.

Sarracenia psittacina × 1/4

Sarracenia minor × 1/4

Sarracenia alata × 1/6

Drosera leucantha × 1

Woods Stonecrop; Sedum   *Sedum ternatum* Michx.

Perennial to 15 cm tall, forming mats, the flowerless branches prostrate or spreading, and with about 6 broad flat crowded leaves at their tips. Lower leaves whorled, not as wide. Leaves below flower clusters spatulate. Petals white. Stamens dark red. Occasional. On rocks, often calcareous, rich woods; n SC into n Ala, cw Ark, ne Mo, s Mich, and w Mass. Apr-June.

  S. nevii Gray is similar but all leaves are alternate and glaucous. Leaves below flowers are slender or absent. Rare. On limestone or shale rocks; sw NC into n Ala, cn Tenn, ne WVa, and c NC. May-June. *S. glaucophyllum* R. T. Clausen.

Lime Stonecrop   *Sedum pulchellum* Michx.

Winter annual to 45 cm tall. Plants green, succulent. Leaves on flowering stems numerous, alternate, sessile, narrow, often almost as thick as wide, auricled at base. Petals rose-colored to white. Anthers dark red. Carpels separate, loosely ascending. Leaves of certain European species have been used in salads and as a potherb. Some of our species may also be usable. Occasional. Shallow soil on and in crevices of limestone rocks; nw Ga into e Tex, se Kan, cw Mo, and w Va. Apr-May.

  S. pusillum Michx. is also an annual. Leaves green, succulent, thick, spatulate to obovate or elliptic, and not auricled at base. Rare. Granitic rock outcrops; cs NC into ce SC, and in Pied. of Ga w to vicinity of Atlanta. Mar-Apr.

Diamorpha; Elf-orpine   *Diamorpha smallii* Britt.

Winter annual to 10 cm tall. Plants reddish, succulent. Leaves alternate, fleshy, the blades obtuse and nearly circular. Petals 4 or 5, white. Stamens 8 or 10. Carpels 4 or 5, united at base for one-third to one-half of their length. Carpels slow to lose their seeds. Occasional. Forms spectacular dense colonies in and around depressions on granitic outcrops, sometimes on exposed sandstone rocks; Pied. and outer part of Blue Ridge Mts. of NC, SC, and Ga; ne Ala, nw Ga, and the adj. part of Tenn. Mar-May. *D. cymosa* (Nutt.) Britt. *Sedum smallii* (Britt.) Ahles.

SAXIFRAGACEAE : Saxifrage Family

Mountain Saxifrage   *Saxifraga michauxii* Britt.

Perennial with basal leaves only. Sometimes with bracts similar to small leaves in the lower parts of the inflorescence. Blades oblanceolate to spatulate-oblong. Sepals reflexed in fruit. Petals unequal in size, 3 are large and cordate and with a pair of yellow spots, the other 2 smaller and lanceolate. Fruit with distinct longitudinal veins. Tender young leaves of this and other species have been used in salads. Common. Moist rocks and slopes; n Ga into cn Tenn, ne WVa, and w Va. Mar-Nov.

  S. micranthidifolia (Haw.) Steud. also has relatively long leaves, the blades oblong to lanceolate or oblanceolate. Sepals reflexed in fruit. Filaments thickened above. Rare. Seepage slopes and moist rocks; nw SC into ne Ga, e Tenn, se Pa, and c Va. Mar-June.

Sedum ternatum × 2/5

Sedum pulchellum × 1

Diamorpha smallii × 1⅓

Saxifraga michauxii × 1/4

Early Saxifrage   *Saxifraga virginiensis* Michx.

Perennial with basal leaves only. Leaf blades ovate to oblong, crenate or shallowly dentate. Sepals erect to spreading when flower is open. Petals equal in size. Stamens 10. Hypanthium partly fastened to the ovulary, which is 2-celled. Common. Rock exposures, hillsides, thin woods; ce Ga into ne Ark, se Man, NB, and Va. Feb-May.

Two species have relatively wider leaves and the hypanthium free from the ovulary. *S. careyana* Gray has filiform filaments and a fruit body under 3.5 mm long. Rare. Moist rocky places and slopes; nw Ga into e Tenn, w NC, and w Va. May-June. *S. caroliniana* Gray has filaments slightly broadened above and fruit bodies over 3.5 mm long. Rare. Rocks and wet slopes; ne Tenn into nw NC, e Va, and adj Ky. May-June.

Foamflower; False-miterwort   *Tiarella cordifolia* L.

A perennial with most, if not all, leaves basal. The flowers are in racemes, and white or pink tinged, except for the 10 yellow anthers. Common. Rich woods; sw Ga into Miss, Mich, and NS. Mar-June. *T. wherryi* Lak.

The leaves of *Mitella diphylla* L., Miterwort, and some species of *Heuchera*, Alumroot, are similar. The Miterwort (n Ga into Miss, e Mo, Minn, and Me) has only 5 stamens, a very slender raceme, and beneath it two opposite leaves rather than a single leaf or none. Alumroots, which are widely distributed, have only 5 stamens and have panicles instead of racemes.

Alumroot   *Heuchera villosa* Michx.

Perennial with all leaves from a rhizome, the blades simple, sharply lobed, the terminal lobe triangular. Calyx with fine soft hairs, the tube at flowering under 3 mm long. Occasional. Shaded cliffs and ledges; c Ala into se Mo, cs Ind, c WVa, c Va, and nw SC. June-Oct.

H. parviflora Bartl. also has a calyx with fine soft hairs but the leaf blades are nearly circular in outline. Occasional. Similar habitats; e Pied. of Ga into ne Ala, s Ill, cw and ce WVa, and nw SC. July-Oct. In *H. americana* L. the calyx is very short glandular hairy, and the teeth and lobes of the leaves are obtuse. Common. Rich or rocky woods; sw Ga into ne Tex, ce Mo, se Mich, s Ont, Conn, and NC. Apr-June. In *H. longiflora* Rydb. the calyx is also glandular hairy but the tube is 3 mm or more long. Rare. Rocky woods; cw NC into c Tenn and s WVa. Apr-June.

Grass-of-Parnassus   *Parnassia asarifolia* Vent.

Instead of being a grass, as the name might indicate, it is related to Foamflower. Plants to 20 cm tall, each flowering stem with one nearly circular leaf, the other leaves basal, petioled, and with kidney-shaped blades. The petals have short stalks. The 5 fertile stamens are separated by shorter sterile ones. Occasional. Wet or moist places, in shade or open; ne Ala into e Tex, e Ky, ce WVa, and nw SC. Aug-Nov.

Two other species are similar but have the sterile stamens longer than the fertile: *P. grandifolia* DC. which has pointed sterile stamens. Rare. Tex into se Mo; n Fla; nw SC into e Tenn, s WVa, and cw Va. Aug-Nov. *P. caroliniana* Michx. which has rounded sterile stamens. Rare. Fla into s Miss; also in se NC. Aug-Nov.

Saxifraga virginiensis × 3/4

Tiarella cordifolia × 1/3

Heuchera villosa × 1/6

Parnassia asarifolia × 1/2

Goat's-beard
Aruncus dioicus (Walt.) Fern.

Members of this family usually have stipules and many stamens, and have a hypanthium and superior or inferior ovularies.

This species has male and female flowers on separate plants. Both kinds of flowers are almost white, the staminate flowers being the more conspicuous. Plants are erect, to 2 m tall, and bear a few large compound leaves and a large pyramid-shaped panicle of flowers. Occasional in rich woods; n Ga into Okla, Ia, se NY, and n SC. May-June.

This species closely resembles *Astilbe biternata* (Vent.) Britt. (False Goat's-beard), a member of the *Saxifragaceae*, which may be identified by the 3-lobed terminal leaflet and by having 2 carpels and 10 stamens. The terminal leaflets of *Aruncus* have no lobes, and it has 3–4 carpels and 15 or more stamens.

Indian-physic
Gillenia trifoliata (L.) Moench

A much branched herbaceous perennial sometimes 1 m tall. The alternate leaves have 3 leaflets and 2 narrow stipules 6–8 mm long with the largest lobe about 1 mm wide. The narrow, white, usually unequal petals are conspicuous. Fruits are small follicles. Common. Rich woods, frequently on slopes; Pied. of Ga into Miss, se Ky, s Ont, Mass, and nw SC; sw Mo. Apr-June.

G. stipulata (Muhl.) Baill. has much longer stipules, the largest lobe 10 mm or more wide, and the lower leaves more dissected than the upper. Occasional. Rich woods; n Ga into e Tex, se Kan, sw NY, e Va, and c NC. May-June.

Cinquefoil; Fivefingers
Potentilla canadensis L.

Our members of this genus have palmately compound leaves. The five sepals are interspersed with 5 sepal-like bracts. Each flower produces several separate achenes.

This species is a perennial from a short rhizome to 2 cm long and 8 mm thick. Stems soon becoming prostrate. Leaflets 5. First flower usually from node above the first well-developed internode. Common. Open well-drained places; Ga into Ark, Mo, Ky, ne O, sw Ont, and w NS. Mar-May.

P. simplex Michx. is similar but coarser, the stems more erect at first and then arching and often rooting at tip, and the first flower usually from the node above the second well-developed internode. Common. Open, dry to moist places; Ga into e Tex, Minn, and sw NB. Apr-June.

Rough-fruited Cinquefoil
Potentilla recta L.

Plants with several stems from a perennial base. Leaves with 7–9, rarely 5, leaflets, the lower leaves abundant and on long hairy petioles. Flowers abundant, 1.5–2.5 cm wide, on erect stalks in a broad terminal cluster. Petals showy, usually pale yellow, broadly notched at apex. Seed-like fruits with low curved ridges. Common in a variety of open habitats; Fla into Tex, Minn, and Nfld. Apr-July, occasionally to Sept.

P. intermedia L. is similar but has larger leaves with only 5 leaflets, flowers 8–10 mm wide, and petals about as long as the sepals. Rare. Mich to Nfld and south in mts to NC. *P. argenta* L., of a similar distribution, but more frequent, is smaller, and the leaflets are densely white tomentose beneath.

Aruncus dioicus × 1/4

Gillenia trifoliata × 1/8

Potentilla canadensis × 1

Potentilla recta × 1/8

Three-toothed Cinquefoil   *Potentilla tridentata* Ait.

Perennial to 30 cm tall from decumbent thin woody stems; leaflets 3, with 3 (rarely 5) teeth at tip; petals white, the flowers resembling those of strawberry, but the fruits are dry. Most other species of *Potentilla* have yellow petals. Rare. Rock crevices and balds of high mts; Ga into NC, Tenn, WVa, Pa, ND, Mack. Dist. of NW Terr, and Greenl. Also in open, rocky, or gravelly places north of our area. June-Aug.

   P. norvegica L. is another species with 3 leaflets but plants are stout, to 90 cm tall, usually an annual or biennial, and the petals yellow. Ga into Cal, Alas, and Greenl. May-frost. *P. monospeliensis* L.

Barren-strawberry   *Waldsteinia parviflora* Small

A perennial much like a strawberry except the flowers have yellow petals and the fruits are dry. Leaves and flower clusters from rootstocks at the ends of creeping rhizomes. Leaflets 3 per leaf, each usually longer than wide. The petals are about as long or shorter than the sepals and are 1–1.5 mm wide. Attractive as a wildflower in woodland gardens. Occasional. Rich woods, usually deciduous and on slopes; cw SC into nw Ala, se Ky, cs Va, and c NC. Apr-June.

   In *W. lobata* (Baldw.) T. & G. the leaves are simple, though shallowly lobed. Rare. Pied. and adj mts of Ga. Apr-May. In *W. fragarioides* (Michx.) Tratt. the leaflets are about as wide as long and the petals are 2.5–6 mm wide and prominently longer than the sepals. Occasional. Moist or dry woods; cn NC into Ky, cs Mo, cs Ind, O, ne Minn, s Ont, and s NB. Mar-June.

FABACEAE: Bean Family

Sensitive-brier   *Schrankia microphylla* (Soland. ex Smith) Macbr.

Our members of this family have a 1-carpelled pistil. Fruit commonly a 1-celled pod splitting along 2 sides, but some are indehiscent and 1-seeded or transversely divided into 1-seeded joints.

   This species is a perennial with prostrate to weakly arching stems. Leaves, stems, and fruits with numerous prickles. The many leaflets "go to sleep" when disturbed; the veins beneath are obscure. Flowers perfect or unisexual, in heads. Fruits with prickles on the ribs. Common. Open drier places; Fla into e Tex, Ky, and Va. May-Sept.

   S. uncinata Willd.—*S. nuttallii* (DC.) Standl.—is very similar, having raised lateral veins on the underside of the leaflets. Ala into e and nc Tex, SD, and Ill. *Desmanthus illinoensis* (Michx.) MacM. has similar leaves but the plants are erect and the flowers are white or greenish and in smaller heads. Pied. of SC and nw Ga into NM, ND, and O.

Potentilla tridentata × 2/3

Waldsteinia parviflora × 1/2

Schrankia microphylla × 2

Wild Senna   *Cassia marilandica* L.

Species of this genus have pinnately compound leaves with an even number of leaflets. Stamens 5 or 10. Petals 5, slightly unequal.

This species is an erect little-branched perennial to 2 m tall. Leaflets 5–10 pairs, over 25 mm long, oblong to elliptic, mucronate. Stipules falling early. Upper 3 stamens lacking normal anthers. Fruit straight or curved, 5–10 cm long, 8–11 mm wide, about 3 mm thick, with small appressed hairs or none, the segments of fruit longer than wide. Occasional. Usually moist places, thin woods or open; Fla into e Tex, cn Kan, Ind, sw Pa, and ce Va. July-Aug. *C. medsgeri* Shafer.

C. *hebecarpa* Fern. is similar but the fruit has spreading hairs and the segments are as wide as tall. Rare. Pied. of Ga into s Wisc and NH. July-Aug.

Partridge-pea   *Cassia fasciculata* Michx.

Annual to 1.2 m tall, erect to nearly prostrate. Leaflets 6–26 pairs, to 18 mm long. Flowers 10–30 mm wide. Fruit to 9 mm long. Common. Open places, usually disturbed; Fla into s and c Tex, e SD, s Pa, and Mass. June-Sept. *Chamaecrista fasciculata* (Michx.) Greene.

C. *deeringiana* Small & Penn., which also has large flowers, is a perennial from long horizontal roots. Rare. Rocky and sandy soils, open pinelands and scrub oak; Fla into s Ala and w C.P. of Ga. June-Aug. Two species have smaller flowers, less than 10 mm wide. C. *nictitans* L. has stems that are glabrous or with small incurved hairs. Common. Open places, usually disturbed; c Fla into e Tex, e Kan, Mass, and s Vt. June-Oct. C. *aspera* Muhl. has larger and spreading hairs. Occasional. Sandy soils; pen Fla, coastal Ga, s SC. June-Oct.

Coffee-weed; Sickle-pod   *Cassia obtusifolia* L.

Erect annual to 1.5 m tall. Leaflets 2–3 pairs, mostly 3–6 cm long and 2–4 cm wide, broadly obtuse, an elongate gland between or just below the two lower leaflets. Flowers on pedicels over 10 mm long. Upper 3 or 4 stamens lacking normal anthers, the 3 lowest with very large anthers. Fruit 15–45 mm long, very slender, usually strongly curved, 4-angled or nearly so. Important as the alternate host of the tobacco etch virus disease. Recently proved to be toxic when eaten in considerable amounts. Common. Waste places, cultivated land, pastures; Fla into e Tex, cw Mo, Ill, s Mich, and se Pa. June-frost.

Some books incorrectly refer to this species as *C. tora* L., which is an Old World species having flowering pedicels under 10 mm long, fruiting pedicels under 15 mm long, and differences in the seeds. Rare if present in the Southeast.

Coffee Senna   *Cassia occidentalis* L.

Erect ill-scented annual to 2 m tall. Leaflets 3–6 pairs, 3–9 cm long, 1.5–3 cm wide, chiefly acuminate. Stipules falling early. A gland near base of petiole. Upper 3 stamens much reduced. Fruit linear, 7–14 cm long, 5–10 mm wide, straight or slightly curved, the margins thickened. Reported to be weakly toxic. Roasted and ground seeds have been used as a coffee substitute. Seed extracts are reported to have an antibiotic activity. Occasional. Waste places and cultivated land; Fla into s Tex, s Ind, Tenn, NC, and e Va. July-frost. *Ditremexa occidentalis* (L.) Britt. & Rose.

Cassia marilandica × 1/9

Cassia fasciculata × 1/2

Cassia obtusifolia × 1/2

Cassia occidentalis × 1/3

Thermopsis *Thermopsis villosa* (Walt.) Fern. & Schub.

Perennial to 1.6 m tall, unbranched or with a few short vegetative branches. Leaves palmately compound with 3 leaflets. Stamens 10, separate. Calyx persistent. Pods hairy, compressed, not inflated, sessile or nearly so, erect. Sometimes used as an ornamental. Occasional. Thin woods or in open; mts of Ga and Ala, Blue Ridge of Tenn and NC, c Tenn. May-July. *T. caroliniana* M. A. Curtis.

Members of this genus are often mistaken for species of *Baptisia* which may be recognized by their stipitate ovary and fruits, and inflated fruits.

Bush-pea *Thermopsis fraxinifolia* M.A. Curtis

Perennial to 90 cm tall, with several to numerous zig-zagging branches. Bracts usually shorter than pedicels. Calyx persistent, the tube glabrous or nearly so. Stamens 10, separate. Ovary and pods sessile or nearly so. Occasional. Roadsides, thin woods, or in open, usually dry; mts of NC, SC, and Ga. Apr-July.

T. mollis (Michx.) M. A. Curtis is similar but has bracts longer than pedicels and the calyx tube with small fine hairs. Thin woods and open, drier places; mts Ga into ne Ala, e Tenn, c Va, and Pied. of NC. *T. hugeri* Small. Apr-June.

Yellow False-indigo *Baptisia tinctoria* (L.) R. Br.

Members of this genus are perennials, have 10 separate stamens, stalks on the ovularies and fruits, and inflated fruits. Some species have been reported poisonous when eaten but information on this subject is lacking for most.

This species is bushy-branched, to 1 m tall. Leaflets mostly less than 4 cm long, black when dried. Flowers about 10 mm long, in terminal racemes. Pod almost black at maturity. Plants used locally as a dye. Common. Thin woods, dry places; n Fla into La, se Ont, and sw Me; se Minn. Apr-Aug.

B. lecontei Torr. & Gray is similar but the leaflets do not dry black and the lower flowers of each raceme have a pair of small bracts on their stalks. Occasional. Dry sandy soils, thin pinelands and scrub; cs Ga into n pen Fla. Apr-June.

Cream Wild-indigo *Baptisia bracteata* Ell.

Plants to 60 cm tall, loosely branched, and having soft spreading grayish hairs. Flowers on pedicels mostly less than 1.5 cm long in drooping, one-sided racemes with persistent bracts 5 mm wide or wider. Petals cream-colored. Occasional. Dry thin woods; ne Ala into Pied. Ga and SC; cw NC. Apr-May.

B. leucophaea Nutt. is similar but with stiffer hairs and the flowers on pedicels mostly over 1.5 cm long. Common. Sandy soils; e La into e half of Tex, se Minn, sw Mich, nw Ind, and w Ky. In *B. cinera* (Raf.) Fern. & Schub. the racemes are usually erect and have bracts less than 3 mm wide and which drop off soon after the petals drop. Occasional. Sandy soils, scrub and thin woods; cw SC into se Va and C.P. of NC; c NC.

Thermopsis villosa × 1/10   Thermopsis fraxinifolia × 1/4

Baptisia tinctoria × 2/5   Baptisia bracteata × 1/3

White Wild-indigo   *Baptisia alba* (L.) R. Br.

Plants to 1.2 m tall, with few to many divergent branches. Leaflets 20–35 mm long. Flowers 12–18 mm long, in 1 to several terminal racemes. Pods cylindrical, brown, not over 11 mm thick, divergent to erect. Common. Dry thin woods, low pinelands; e half of n Fla into Pied. of Ga, and cs and e Va. Apr-July. *B. albescens* Small.

Another similar species is *B. leucantha* T. & G. with flowers 2–3 cm long and black pendent fruits 8–25 mm broad. Thin woods, prairies, dry places; cs Ala into e Tex, se Ont, O, and e Tenn; cn Fla into c Pied. of Ga, and cn and ce NC. *B. pendula* Larisey.

Blue Wild-indigo   *Baptisia australis* (L.) R. Br.

Glabrous glaucous plants to 160 cm tall, bushy branched, the upper branches ascending and the lower ones spreading. Racemes one to several, erect or nearly so, with a few to 35 flowers. Petals blue. Fruits thin-walled, plump, 3–6 cm long, and with a long persistent claw-shaped style. An attractive and easily grown plant. Occasional. Thin woods and borders, limestone glades; n Ga into ne Ala, ce Ind, sw NY, c Md, and cn NC; also cn Tex into se Neb, cw Ill, and ne Ark; escaped elsewhere. Apr-May. *B. minor* Lehm.

This species is divided into two varieties by some. *B. australis* var. *australis* has leaflets from 4–8 cm long and the stipes on the fruit about twice as long as the calyx. In var. *minor* (Lehm.) Fern. the leaflets are 1.5–4 cm long and the stipes about as long as the calyx. A few persons treat these as species.

Pineland Wild-indigo   *Baptisia lanceolata* Walt.

Plants to 90 cm tall, widely and bushy-branched. Leaflets spatulate to oblanceolate, mostly 4 cm or more long. Flowers single in axils of outer leaves or also 2–4 in short terminal racemes, standard 15 mm long or longer. Pod subglobose to ovoid, 15–22 mm long. Common. Dry sandy hills and open sandy pinelands; sw Ala into cw SC and n Fla. Mar-May.

Two other species are similar. *B. nuttalliana* Small with obovate-cuneate leaflets and pods 5–13 mm long. Common. Woodlands, sandy soils; cs La into e and c Tex, se Ark, and cw Miss. Apr-May. *B. elliptica* Small has broadly elliptic leaflets. It may be only a variety of *B. lanceolata*. Occasional. Dry sandy pinelands; sw Ga into nw Fla and sw Ala. Apr-May.

Baptisia alba × 1/8

Baptisia australis × 2/5

Baptisia lanceolata × 1/5

Showy Crotalaria   *Crotalaria spectabilis* Roth

Members of this genus have 10 united stamens, the anthers alternately of 2 sizes, and sessile inflated fruits.

This species is an annual, to 1.5 m tall. Leaves simple, glabrous, mostly 6–20 cm long. Stipules and bracts at base of flower stalks ovate, 5 mm long or longer. Any part of the plant, especially the seeds, is poisonous when eaten. Growing plants are reported to reduce or eliminate nematodes from the soil. Occasional. Fields, roadsides, orchards; Fla into e half of Tex, c Mo, Tenn, NC, and se Va; absent in Blue Ridge. Mar-Oct.

C. retusa L. is similar but the stipules and bracts are narrow and under 2 mm long. Rare. Fla; e Tex; se NC. July-Sept.

Rabbit-bells   *Crotalaria rotundifolia* (Walt.) Gmel.

Perennial to 40 cm tall from a prominent taproot. Stems erect, several to many, with appressed hairs; or decumbent and with appressed or spreading hairs. Leaves simple, upper surface hairy. Plants poisonous. Sandy areas, pinelands, thin woods; Fla into se La, c Ala, c Ga, and se Va; also ne Ga and c NC. Mar-Nov.

Other similar species are: *C. sagittalis* L. which is erect to strongly ascending and has spreading hairs on the stems. Upper surface of leaf hairy. Dry places in thin woods or open; Ala into e Tex and Kan, c Minn, sw Mich, e Ky, Tenn, NC, cs Va, e WVa, s Vt, and Mass. May-Oct. *C. purshii* DC. with glabrous upper surface of leaf. Sandy areas, pinelands, thin upland woods; n Fla into se La, s Ga, and se Va. Apr-Aug.

Lady Lupine   *Lupinus villosus* Willd.

Our species of this genus are perennials with 10 united stamens, the anthers alternately of 2 sizes, the fruits sessile and flattened, and possibly poisonous.

Plants to 50 cm tall, from a deep woody taproot. Stems mostly decumbent, a few to many in a dense clump. Leaves evergreen and simple, which is unusual for lupines since almost all have deciduous palmately compound leaves. Standard purple to reddish with a deep reddish purple spot. Pods shaggy with hairs 4–5 mm long. Common. Sandhills and thin woods on dry sandy places; coastal Miss into n Fla, lower C.P. of Ga, and se NC. Mar-May.

L. diffusus Nutt. is similar but the standard is blue with a white spot and the fruits have appressed hairs about 2 mm long. Occasional. Similar habitats; coastal Miss into Fla, e C.P. of Ga into s C.P. of NC. *L. westianus* Small is a shrub with a single stem at the base but soon branching, the branches becoming erect. Rare. Sandhills and dunes; c and nw Fla.

Sundial Lupine   *Lupinus perennis* L.

This species grows to 70 cm tall from creeping underground stems. Leaves palmately compound, with 7–11 leaflets. Petals rarely white. Pods with short to long hairs. Thin woods and in open sandy soils; se Tex into c Ga, n Fla, ne NC, c Va, s Me, and w into ne WVa, n O, n Ill, and ce Wisc. Mar-June, sometimes Aug-Sept.

The more slender plants with the upper calyx-lip deltoid and with 2 lanceolate lobes, instead of being half-orbicular with 2 deltoid lobes, have been separated by some as a species (*L. nuttallii* Wats.), and others as a variety or subspecies (*gracilis*). Some authors recognize no subspecific categories. The slender form is reported from se Tex into n Fla, C.P. of Ga, and ce SC.

Crotalaria spectabilis × 1/2

Crotalaria rotundifolia × 1/4

Lupinus villosus × 1/7

Lupinus perennis × 1/4

Rabbit-foot Clover   *Trifolium arvense* L.

Members of this genus have compound leaves with 3 finely serrate or dentate leaflets and united uniform-sized stamens. The corolla withers and persists concealing the ripened pod.

This species is an annual, when in flower unlike any other clover. The clusters of flowers are soft and simulate a rabbit's foot. The stems branch freely and are topped by numerous heads in vigorous plants. If mature heads are eaten by livestock, they may cause intestinal irritation. Common. Dry fields and roadsides, waste places; natzd., Fla into e Tex, Minn, Que, and Me; also scattered westward. Apr-Aug.

Low Hop Clover   *Trifolium campestre* Schreb.

Flowers usually 20–40 per head, each flower stalked. Terminal one of the three leaflets on a stalk much longer than those of the other two leaflets. Petioles usually shorter than the leaflets. Although weedy, plants are valuable as soil builders. Common. Natzd. In lawns, fields, roadsides, and waste places; Fla into e Tex, se ND, and NS; also in scattered localities westward, especially on the Pacific slopes. Apr-Oct. *T. procumbens* L.

There are two other species which are natzd. and of similar appearance and distribution: *T. agrarium* L. which is less common and may be identified by its sessile terminal leaflets. *T. dubium* Sibth. which usually has only 3–15 flowers per head.

Red Clover   *Trifolium pratense* L.

Perennial with several stems from a strongly developed taproot. Stipule tips triangular and abruptly awned. Flower heads globose, sessile. Flowers over 1 cm long and sessile. Common. In fields, roadsides, other open places, extensively cultivated; nearly throughout temperate N.A. Apr-Sept.

T. reflexum L., Buffalo Clover, also has large globose heads but the flowers are stalked, the standard brighter red, and the wing and keel petals almost white to pink. Occasional. Thin woods; Fla into e Tex, e Kan, Ill, and Va. Apr-Aug. In *T. incarnatum* L., Crimson Clover, the petals are scarlet or deep red (rarely white) and the flower heads are peduncled and, except at first, cylindrical. Overripe Crimson Clover can be dangerous to horses. Its short stiff hairs may become impacted in the digestive tract. Occasional. Frequently cultivated and escaped, especially in the South. Natzd. from Eurasia. Apr-June.

Summer-farewell   *Petalostemum caroliniense* (Lam.) Sprague

Members of this genus have pinnately compound leaves with an odd number of leaflets, and 5 stamens, an unusual number for the Bean Family. The keel and wing petals are attached to the united bases of the stamens. The fruits are 1–2–seeded pods which usually do not split open.

This species is a perennial to 1.2 m tall. Leaflets 3–11. Flowers in heads with bracts at their bases, the lower bracts brownish and broadly ovate to orbicular. Petals white. Common. Dry sandy places, pinelands and scrub; Fla into se Miss, ce Ga, and se NC. Aug-Oct. *P. pinnatum* (Gmel.) Blake. *Kuhnistera pinnata* (Gmel.) O. Ktze.

Trifolium arvense × 1½

Trifolium campestre × 1½

Trifolium pratense × 3/4

Petalostemum caroliniense × 1/2

Purple-tassels   *Petalostemum gattingeri* Heller

Perennial to 50 cm tall, with several to many decumbent to erect stems. Leaflets 5–7. Bracts at base of flower heads long pointed from broad bases. Calyx loosely hairy. Petals rose-purple. Rare. Rocky calcareous open areas of cedar glades; nw Ga into n Ala and c Tenn. May-June.

    P. purpureum (Vent.) Rydb. is similar but the bracts at the base of the flower heads are acuminate from narrower bases and the calyx is appressed-hairy. Petals violet to rose-purple. Common. Prairies, dry hills; cw Ala into c La, n NM, s Alba, s Man, and e Ind. June-July.

White-tassels   *Petalostemum albidum* (T. & G.) Small

Perennial to 1 m tall. Leaflets 3–7, scattered, 5–10 mm long. Calyx glabrous on outside and not strongly 10-ribbed. Petals white. Occasional. Dry sand and pinelands; Fla into se Ala and e and s C.P. of Ga. Aug-Sept.

    Other similar species are: *P. candidum* (Willd.) Michx. which has a strongly 10-ribbed calyx and broader and longer (9–30 mm) leaflets. Petals white. Common. Dry places, prairies, upland woods; cw Ala into Tex and n Mex, s Alba, and e Ind. Apr-Aug. *P. carneum* Michx. which has more abundant leaves, 5–9 leaflets, and rose to deep pink petals. Occasional. Habitat similar; se Ga into Fla and s Ala. June-Aug.

Goat's-rue   *Tephrosia virginiana* (L.) Pers.

Members of this genus are perennials with deep roots. The leaves are pinnately compound with an odd number of leaflets. Lateral veins of the leaflets parallel and running from midrib to margin. Stamens 10 and all united.

    This species is stiffly ascending to erect, 20–70 cm tall. Variable in amount and character of hairs. Leaflets 15–25. The inflorescence is terminal. Fruit 35–55 mm long, 4–5.5 mm wide, straight or curved slightly downwardly. The roots have been shown to contain various amounts of rotenone, which is an insecticide and fish poison, but not poisonous to mammals. Common. Dry places, in thin pine or hardwood stands, or in open; Fla into e half of Tex, cn Kan, cw Wisc, and s NH. Apr-July. *Cracca virginiana* L. *C. mohrii* Rydb.

Rusty Tephrosia   *Tephrosia hispidula* (Michx.) Pers.

Plants with 1 to many decumbent to erect stems to 50 cm long from a prominent taproot. Leaves ascending, leaflets 9–23, usually acute. Petioles shorter than the length of the lowermost leaflet. Stems, petioles, and sometimes other parts bearing mostly appressed ashy to brownish hairs. Inflorescences of 1–3 flowers, erect to curving, appearing to be opposite leaves. Occasional. Dry to moist pinelands and savannahs; c Fla into se Ga and c C.P. of NC; w Fla. May-Aug. *Cracca hispidula* (Michx.) O. Ktze.

    Similar species include: *T. spicata* (Walt.) T.& G. which has mostly spreading hairs and inflorescences of 2–20 flowers. Common. Dry usually sandy soils, thin woods, or in open; Fla into sw La, se Ky, NC, and se Va. Mar-Aug. *T. florida* (F. G. Dietr.) C. E. Wood which has the petioles of the lower leaves 1–4 times as long as the lowermost leaflets. Occasional. Fla into se La, sw Ga, and s C.P. of NC. May-Aug.

Petalostemum gattingeri × 1/4

Petalostemum albidum × 1/3

Tephrosia hispidula × 1

Tephrosia virginiana × 4/5

Pencil-flower   *Stylosanthes biflora* (L.) B.S.P.

Perennial with 1 to several prostrate to erect stems from a stout rootstock. Fruit in two sections, the lower one usually aborting and becoming stipe-like. Common. Dry soil, thin woods and barrens; c Fla into e Tex, se Kan, c Ill, Ky, s Pa, and ce NJ. May-Sept.

Those plants that are prostrate to slightly ascending have been recognized by some as *S. riparia* Kearn. Recent studies, however, indicate that there is only one indivisible species.

Bladder-pod   *Glottidium vesicarium* (Jacq.) Harper

Annual to 4 m tall. Leaves evenly pinnate. Flowers 8–15 mm long, in racemes shorter than the leaves. Petals yellow, tinged with red, the wings sometimes mostly dark pink. Fruit tapered at both ends; the body flattened; seeds 2, rarely 1 or 3; at maturity the firm outer layer separating from a thin soft layer enclosing the seeds. Seeds are poisonous with consumption as low as 0.05 percent of body weight causing death. Cattle sometimes choose the fruits as food. Hundreds from a single herd have been killed under special circumstances. Occasional. Low areas in open places; Fla into e third of Tex, se Okla, ce Ga, and e half of NC. July-Sept. *Sesbania vesicaria* (Jacq.) Ell.

Florida Beggarweed   *Desmodium tortuosum* (Sw.) DC.

Our species of this genus have 3 leaflets, stipule-like structures just below each leaflet, and loments as fruits, i.e., they break apart into joints which readily cling to passing objects. Young seeds are tasty and not reported to be poisonous.

This species is an annual to 3.5 m tall with slender and spreading branches. Constrictions between the 3–7 loment joints are equally deep on both edges, the joints oval to suborbicular. Leaves with 3 leaflets to 13 cm long. Petals purple, 5–7 mm long. All species are valuable as forage and soil builders, and fruits are eaten by birds. Common. Fields, roadsides, waste places; Fla into se Tex, s Pied. of Ga, and s C.P. of NC. June-Oct.

D. viridiflorum (L.) DC., a perennial to 2 m high, has similar loments but the top constrictions are shallow. Common. In similar habitats; Fla into e Tex, s Ark, NC, and Del. June-Sept.

Beggar's-ticks   *Desmodium cuspidatum* Muhl. ex Willd.

Stout erect perennial to 1.5 m tall. Flowers to 12 mm long, in conspicuous clusters at ends of spreading branches. Leaflets glabrous beneath or with a few small straight hairs. Bracts beneath lower flowers over 6 mm long. Joints of loment 3–7, large, 7–11 mm long. Occasional. Open places, thin upland woods, and rich woods; n Fla into ne Tex, e Kan, s Minn, s Mich, and s NH. July-Sept.

Three species have trailing stems. They occur in various dry habitats. *D. rotundifolium* DC. with orbicular leaflets 3–7 cm long. Common. n Fla into se Tex, La, c Mo, s Mich, s Ont, and s Vt. *D. ochroleucum* M. A. Curtis with terminal leaflet ovate, 4–7 cm long. Rare. n Ga into e Ky, w Va, Del, and c NC. *D. lineatum* DC. with terminal leaflet ovate to suborbicular, 1–3 cm long. Occasional. Fla into e Tex, C.P. of Ga, and se Md.

Stylosanthes biflora × 3/4

Glottidium vesicarium × 1/2

Glottidium vesicarium × 1/80

Desmodium tortuosum × 3/5

Desmodium cuspidatum × 1/5

Narrow-leaved Lespedeza   *Lespedeza angustifolia* (Pursh) Ell.

Members of this genus have pinnately 3-foliate leaves, the leaflets entire; fruits indehiscent, 1-seeded, and not adherent. All species provide fruits for birds and nutritious
forage.

Erect to ascending perennial to 1 m tall. Leaflets narrow. Flowers in dense racemes
1–3.5 times longer than the leaves at their bases. Common. Usually moist places in
thin pinelands or savannahs; n Fla into se Miss, ce Ga, and e Mass; rarely inland to c
Tenn. Aug-frost.

Two species have similarly clustered flowers: *L. capitata* Michx. in which the dense
racemes are shorter than to 1.5 times longer than the leaves. Common. Disturbed areas,
dunes, upland prairies, and wet places in C.P.; nw Fla into e and n Tex, cn Neb, Minn,
and c Me. July-Oct. *L. hirta* (L.) Hornem. which has leaflets half as wide as long.
Common. Well drained open areas, fields, pinelands, scrub; c Fla into e third of Tex
and Okla, c Mich, and s Me. Aug-Oct.

Korean Lespedeza; Korean Clover   *Lespedeza stipulacea* Maxim.

Annual to 40 cm tall, rarely taller, with few to many prostrate, spreading, ascending, or
erect branches. Stems with small upwardly appressed hairs. Stipules 3–4 mm wide.
Apex of fruit rounded, with a very short point. Important in soil improvement and
hay-production. Molded hay has caused poisoning in the same manner as for White
Sweet Clover. Fruits are eaten extensively by wild birds. Common. Fields, roadsides,
and other open places; n Fla into e Tex, Ia, Ill, and NS. July-Sept.

L. striata (Thunb.) H. & A., Japanese Clover or Japanese Lespedeza, is quite similar but the stems have the hairs downwardly appressed and the stipules are under 2 mm
wide. Apex of fruit acuminate to a distinct point or beak. Often continues growth after
L. stipulacea stops. Also important to soil and birds, and for hay. Common. Similar
habitats; Fla into Tex, Kan, s half of Ill, and NJ. July-Oct.

Slender Lespedeza   *Lespedeza intermedia* (Wats.) Britt.

Perennial with 1 to several stiffly erect to somewhat arching stems to 1 m tall. Leaflets
glabrous above, about one-third as wide as long. Common. Dry places, in thin woods
and open; nw Fla into se La, e Okla, s half of Mich, s Ont, s Me, and s tip of SC.
July-Oct.

Two other common species are similar in appearance and habitats: *L. stuevii* Nutt.
with terminal leaflets averaging over one-third as wide as long and with fine appressed
to erect hairs above. n Fla into e half of Tex and Kan, se Va, se Pa, and e Mass. Aug-
Oct. *L. virginiana* (L.) Britt. with terminal leaflets averaging less than one-third as
wide as long and with sparse fine appressed hairs above. n Fla into e half of Tex and
Kan, s Wisc, Pa, and s NH. Aug-Sept.

Creeping Lespedeza   *Lespedeza repens* (L.) Bart.

Prostrate perennial with several to many well-spaced thin branches, the ends sometimes
ascending. Stems with sparse and very short appressed hairs. Keel petals about equaling
wings. Common. Dry open places, roadsides, thin woods, sandy pinelands; n Fla into
e Tex, se Kan, sw Wisc, s Ind, and ce NY. Apr-Oct.

Two species are similar: *L. violacea* (L.) Pers. which has weakly ascending stems,
and keel petals usually longer than the wings. Common. Dry open places, roadsides,
thin woods, prairies; c Ga into ne Tex, s Mo, s Wisc, and Mass. July-Sept. *L. procumbens* Michx. which bears spreading hairs. Common. Similar places; n Fla into e and
cn Tex, s Wisc, O, and s NH. May-Sept.

Lespedeza stipulacea × 1

Lespedeza angustifolia × 1/2

Lespedeza repens × 1/2

Lespedeza intermedia × 3/5

Bigflower Vetch   *Vicia grandiflora* Scop.

Climbing annual to 60 cm tall. Leaves with tendrils on the ends. Flowers 2 or rarely 1, 3, or 4, short stalked in the axils of the upper leaves. Petals yellow, 2–3.5 cm long. The seeds of several species of *Vicia* have been used as food but this should be done with caution since some are reported to be poisonous. Occasional. Roadsides, fields, other open places; Fla into Miss, e Tenn, NC, and Del. Mar-June.

Other species with short stalked axillary flowers are: *V. angustifolia* L. with linear leaflets and purplish petals 1–1.8 cm long. Common. In similar habitats; Fla into e Tex, Minn, and NS; Cal to BC. Mar-June. *V. sativa* L. with oblong to obovate leaflets and purplish or rarely white petals 1.8–3 cm long. Rare. In similar habitats; Pied. of Ga into ne Tex, Ia, and Nfld. Apr-June.

Smooth Vetch   *Vicia dasycarpa* Ten.

Annual or rarely perennial with tendrils on ends of leaves. Flowers short stalked, 10–30 in peduncled elongate axillary racemes. Pedicels attached at side of base of calyx. Raceme glabrous or with short appressed hairs. Longest calyx lobe 1–2 mm long. Common. Fields, roadsides, waste places; nearly throughout the contiguous 48 states. Apr-Sept.

V. villosa Roth is similar but has spreading hairs and the longest calyx lobe 2–5 mm long. Common. Similar in habitat and distribution. Apr-Sept. In *V. cracca* L. the pedicels are attached near the center of the base of the calyx. Rare. In similar habitats; NC into e Tenn, Minn, BC, s Que, and Nfld. May-July.

Woods Vetch   *Vicia hugeri* Small

Slender trailing or climbing perennial to 70 cm long, with tendrils on ends of leaves. Leaflets 8–20, linear, pointed. Flowers 5–7 mm long and 8–13 in each raceme. Pods with one seed. Occasional. Open woods; ce Ala into nw SC. Apr-June.

Other species with racemose flowers and white or blue-tinged petals include *V. caroliniana* Walt. which has flowers 8–12 mm long and 7–20 per raceme, white to blue-tinged petals with the keel blue tipped, and pods with 5–8 seeds. Common. Rich woods; n Fla into ne Tex, se Mo, c Wisc, c NY, Pa, and NC. Mar-June. *V. acutifolia* Ell. which has 4–6 linear leaflets, flowers 7–8 mm long and 4–10 per raceme, and pods with 4–8 seeds. Common. Sandy moist soils in open, se SC into ne and pen Fla. Feb-June.

Everlasting Pea   *Lathyrus latifolius* L.

Perennial with decumbent to high-climbing broadly winged stems. Leaves with a pair of blades and a branched well-developed terminal tendril. Flowers 15 mm or longer, in axillary racemes. Petals commonly purple, or red, pink, or white. Style strongly flattened. Ovary and fruit glabrous. The seeds are poisonous. Occasional. Roadsides and waste places, open situations; Pied. of Ga into e Tex, Mo, cs Me, and NC. May-Sept.

Two other species also have two blades on each leaf, with the tendrils and flowers smaller and the flowers fewer. *L. hirsutus* L. has a hairy ovary and fruit. Rare. Central C.P. of Ga into e and cn Tex, ce Mo, and Va. Apr-July. *L. pusillus* Ell. is an annual and the smallest of the species. The flowers are 12 mm long or shorter and the ovary and fruit glabrous. Rare. Similar distribution. Apr-July.

Vicia grandiflora × 2/3

Vicia dasycarpa × 2/3

Vicia hugeri × 1/2

Lathyrus latifolius × 1/2

Butterfly-pea   *Clitoria mariana* L.

Perennial from a deep narrow taproot. Stems to 1 m long, little branched, spreading or sometimes twining. Leaves compound, with 3 entire leaflets. One to several flowers open at a time, persisting longer than a day. Flowering even during drought when few other attractive plants are in flower. Calyx tube much longer than the lobes. The standard petal is 25 mm or more long, about 2× as long as the wing and keel petals, and different from most legumes in that the standard petal is below the others. Fruit with a stipe, dehiscent, several-seeded, the seeds sticky. Common. Dry places, thin woods or open; Fla into c Tex, s Mo, s O, and s NY; Ariz. May-Sept. *Martiusia mariana* (L.) Small.

Climbing Butterfly-pea   *Centrosema virginianum* (L.) Benth.

Twining perennial from a tough elongated root. Leaflets 3. Calyx tube shorter than the lobes and hidden by conspicuous bracts. Petals lasting one day. Standard petal 25–35 mm long, about twice as long as the wing and keel petals. Fruit sessile, flattened, many-seeded, 7–14 cm long, with a long persistent style. Common. Drier places, thin woods or open; Fla into c Tex, Ark, and s NS. Mar-Sept. *Bradburya virginiana* (L.) O. Ktze.

Cardinal-spear; Coral Bean   *Erythrina herbacea* L.

Perennial to 1.2 m tall. Leaves alternate with 3 leaflets which are hastate to widely deltoid and occasionally prickly beneath. Stipules are curved spines. Inflorescence of one or more terminal spike-like racemes. Calyx red, tubular. Corolla scarlet, the standard to 53 mm long, folded so that the entire flower appears long and narrow. Wing and keel petals 13 mm or less long. Fruit to 21 cm long, constricted between the few to many brilliantly scarlet seeds which hang on after the pod splits open. Occasional. Open woods, sandy soils; Fla into s tip of and ne Tex, se SC, and se NC. Apr-July.

In the warmer parts of the range of the species, aboveground stems often live over a number of winters. This has led some persons to believe that there is another species, *E. arborea* (Chapm.) Small, but this is not supported by more thorough studies.

Groundnut; Indian-potato   *Apios americana* Medic.

Perennial twining vine with tuberous enlargements on the roots. These may be 6 cm in diameter and are edible, either raw, boiled, fried, or roasted. When eaten raw an unpleasant rubber-like coating is left in the mouth, a quality lost in roasting or frying. When well prepared the tubers can be one of our best wild foods. Seeds have also been used as food. The leaves have 5 or 7 ovate to lanceolate pinnately arranged leaflets. The flowers are as many as 30 in a tight cluster but do not open all at once. The petals are brownish purple to reddish purple. The fruits are 6–12 cm long and about 6 mm thick when mature and usually have 8–10 seeds. Common. Moist places in woods or open; Fla into c Tex, se ND, and NS. June-Sept. *A. tuberosa* Moench, *Glycine apios* L.

Clitoria mariana × 2/3

Erythrina herbacea × 2/5

Centrosema virginianum × 1¼

Apios americana × 1½

Galactia   *Galactia elliottii* Nutt.

Our members of this genus are perennials and vines with prostrate or trailing stems, one species having erect stems only. Leaves once-pinnate, the leaflets entire and odd numbered. Each flower has a pair of very small bracts at or near the top of the pedicel. Pod few to many seeded.

This species is a twining, climbing perennial vine often with a long horizontal rootstock and some tuberous roots. Leaflets 7 or 9. Flower clusters are long-peduncled and axillary. Petals sometimes tinged with red. Fruits 3–5 cm long, 6–13 cm wide, densely covered with short appressed hairs. Common. Open sandy areas, usually low; Fla into the coastal region of Ga and s SC. May-Sept.

Trailing Milk-pea   *Galactia minor* Duncan

A perennial with largest leaflets 12–16 mm long. Hairs on stem very small and pointed toward the tip. Flowers 15–18 mm long, often single or uncommonly to 3 on each peduncle. Common. Sandy soils in open, or in thin pine or scrub oak woods; n Fla into C.P. of Ga. July-Sept.

G. regularis (L.) B.S.P. is also trailing whereas most other species are twining. The largest leaflets 15–40 mm long, hairs on stem very small and sometimes scanty but turned away from stem tip, flowers 3 to 7 on each peduncle, and flower clusters shorter to longer than the leaves. Common. In similar habitats; Fla into Miss, C.P. of Ga, and c Md. May-Aug.

Dollar-weed   *Rhynchosia reniformis* DC.

Our members of this genus have resinous dots on the foliage, entire blades, 9 stamens united and 1 separate, and 1–2–seeded fruits.

This species is an erect perennial to 22 cm tall. Leaves unifoliate or a few at tip trifoliate. Common. Sandy soils, pinelands, thin woods, open places; c Fla into se Tex, c Ala, ce Ga, and c C.P. of NC. Apr-Sept. *R. simplicifolia* (Walt.) Wood.

R. michauxii Vail has similar unifoliate leaves but the stems are elongate and trailing or twining. Occasional. Similar habitats; Fla. Mar-Sept.

Erect Rhynchosia   *Rhynchosia tomentosa* (L.) H. & A.

Erect little-branched perennial 15–85 cm tall. Leaves mostly with 3 leaflets. Corolla equal or shorter than the calyx. Common. Dry places, thin woods, pinelands; c Fla into c La, se Ky, NC, s Md, and s Del. May-Sept. *R. erecta* (Walt.) DC.

Other species with 3-foliate leaves have trailing or twining stems. Species with similar, but generally broader, ovate to ovate-rhombic leaflets: *R. difformis* (Ell.) DC. with flower clusters on peduncles 1–35 mm long. Occasional. Fla into e Tex, ce Ga, and se Va. May-Aug. *R. latifolia* Nutt. with flower clusters on peduncles 3–30 cm long. Common. Woodlands, prairies, alluvial woods, rocky places; e third of Tex into c Okla, s Mo, w Ky, and c Miss. May-Aug.

Galactia elliottii × 2/5

Galactia minor × 1⅓

Rhynchosia reniformis × 1/3

Rhynchosia tomentosa × 1/3

Wild-bean   *Strophostyles umbellata* (Willd.) Britt.

Trailing or sometimes twining perennial vine. Leaves with 3 leaflets. Flowers 9–15 mm long, nearly sessile at top of axillary peduncles. Bract at base of calyx half as long, or less, as the glabrous (or nearly so) calyx-tube. Keel petals strongly curved and beaked. Seeds of this genus are probably edible. We know of no report of their being poisonous. Occasional. Fields and thin woods, often sandy soils; n Fla into e Tex, Mo, se NY. June-Sept.

S. helvola (L.) Ell. is similar but is an annual. The bract at the base of the calyx equals or exceeds the calyx tube. Fields, roadsides, thin woods, low places between dunes; Fla into e and cn Tex, e SD, sw Que, and s Me. In *S. leiosperma* (T. & G.) Piper the flowers are 5–8 mm long and the calyx-tube is quite hairy. Ala into se and cn Tex, ne Colo, s Wisc, and cw Ind. July-Oct.

GERANIACEAE: Geranium Family

Wild Geranium; Cranesbill   *Geranium maculatum* L.

Perennial to 60 cm tall from a dark thick rhizome. Basal leaves with long petioles, the upper ones sessile or short petioled. Petals 15–25 mm long, rose-purple, rarely white. Stamens 10. Ovulary 5-carpelled. Fruit with a thick base and a beak 19–25 mm long, hence the name "Cranesbill." Base of fruit splitting apart and coiling upwardly at maturity. Common. Rich woods, meadows; SC into sw Ga, e Okla, s Man, and s Me. Apr-June.

Carolina Cranesbill   *Geranium carolinianum* L.

Annual to 55 cm tall. Petals 4–6 mm long, pale pink. Pedicels about as long as the calyx. Sepals with subulate tips 1 mm long or longer. Stamens 10. Carpels with hairs over 0.6 mm long. Common. Dry places, thin woods, fields, waste places; nearly throughout the contiguous 48 states. Mar-June.

Similar species include: *G. dissectum* L. which has dark purple petals and carpel hairs under 0.6 mm long. Apr-July. Rare. Similar places; ce NC into Miss, ne Tex, s Mich, and Mass. *G. columbianum* L. which has pedicels over 2 cm long. Occasional. Similar places; n Ga into se Ind, and NY. May-Aug. *G. pusillum* L. with awnless sepals and finely hairy carpels. Unusual in having only 5 stamens. Rare. Similar places; mts of NC into e Ky, WVa, and NJ. May-Sept. *G. molle* L. also with awnless sepals but with glabrous carpels. Rare. Similar places; n SC into c Tenn, e Mo, NY, and cn NC. Apr-Aug.

OXALIDACEAE: Wood-sorrel Family

Yellow Wood-sorrel   *Oxalis stricta* L.

Perennial to 50 cm tall from long slender rhizomes. Leaflets 1–2 cm broad. Stems decumbent to erect, with small whitish appressed hairs. Flowers 7–11 mm long, in 1–4 flowered umbels. Common. Woods, waste places; Fla into e Tex, ND, several states in the west, s Que, and s Me. May-frost.

In *O. grandis* Small the flowers are larger, over 12 mm long. The leaflets are 2–5 cm broad and with narrow, reddish or purplish margins. Occasional. Rich woods; n Ga into n Ala, se Ill, ne O, c Md. *O. recurva* Ell. also has large flowers (13–18 mm long) but the leaflets are only 0.5–1.4 cm broad. Occasional. Thin woods, dry sandy or rocky places; Fla into e Tex, Ky, s WVa, and c Va.

Strophostyles umbellata × 1/2   Geranium maculatum × 1/2

Geranium carolinianum × 1   Oxalis stricta × 1½

Violet Wood-sorrel   *Oxalis violacea* L.

Stemless perennial, the leaves and scapes all from a bulbous base. Sepals and pedicels glabrous, with calloused orange tips. All species of *Oxalis* have sour watery juice and if eaten in excess may cause poisoning. Small amounts chewed or added to salads are probably safe. Occasional. Rich woods, rocky places, pinelands, prairies; Fla into e Tex, e ND, and Conn. Mar-May and Aug-Oct.

   O. corymbosa DC. is similar but the sepals and pedicels are hairy. Rare. Commonly cultivated and escaped locally. Fla into se Tex, cw SC, and se Va. *O. martiana* Zucc. *O. acetosella* L. is also stemless but lacks a bulbous base and is creeping by slender rhizomes. Flowers often one per peduncle, petals are mostly white, veined with pink. Rich woods; nw Ga into high mts of Tenn and NC, n in the mts to e O, s Ont, ne Minn, and s Nfld. June-Sept. *O. montana* Raf.

POLYGALACEAE: Milkwort Family

Bachelor's-button   *Polygala nana* (Michx.) DC.

Members of this genus have flowers in racemes or spikes. Flowers are perfect and irregular with three small sepals and two larger petal-like ones called the wings. The corolla resembles those of some legumes, as do the stamens which are united by their filaments and to the petals. Polygalas are easily separated from the legumes by the 2-carpelled ovulary and fruit.

   This species is a biennial to 15 cm tall. Leaves succulent. Pedicels winged. Largest sepals with cusps at least 1 mm long. Flowers turn to a dark bluish green when dried. Common. Wet pinelands, or low open areas; se Tex into nw Ga, nw Fla, c SC, and pen Fla; Rhea Co., Tenn. Mar-June. *Pilostaxis nana* (Michx.) Raf.

Candyweed   *Polygala lutea* L.

Glabrous biennial with succulent leaves. Stems decumbent to erect, to 50 cm tall. Cusp on largest sepals less than 1 mm long. Racemes light to dark orange, turning pale yellow upon drying. Pedicels winged. Common. Wet pinelands and savannahs, bogs; Fla into s La, C.P. of Ga, and Long Island, NY. Apr-Oct. *Pilostaxis lutea* (L.) Small.

Large-flowered Polygala   *Polygala grandiflora* Walt.

Perennial to 50 cm tall. Stems usually unbranched, one to several, with appressed or spreading hairs. Leaves alternate, oblanceolate to linear-oblanceolate, 1.5–5 cm long. Flowers 6–7 mm long, the largest sepals as long as wide. Common. Sandy soils, pinelands, fields; Fla into se La, C.P. of Ga and SC, and sw C.P. of NC. Apr-Sept.

   P. polygama Walt. is similar but the flowers are a little smaller, about 4 mm long, and the largest sepals about twice as long as wide. Small flowers that never open are found on horizontal branches at the base of the plant. Common. Usually in dry sandy or rocky soils, thin woods, pinelands; Fla into e Tex, se Tenn, NC, Va, s Man, and Me. Apr-July.

Oxalis violacea × 1/2

Polygala nana × 1/2

Polygala lutea × 1/3

Polygala grandiflora × 1

Senega-root   *Polygala senega* L.

Perennial to 50 cm tall. Stems usually unbranched, one to several from a thick crown and stout root. Leaves alternate. Flowers white, in dense racemes, persisting until fruits mature, then not densely crowded. The roots of the plant were formerly used medicinally, first by the Seneca Indians for snakebite and later by early American herbalists to induce salivation for croup, asthma, and lung diseases. Occasional. Dry places, thin woods, rocky soils, often calcareous; n Ga into Ark, s Alba, c Sask, and NB. Apr-Aug.

   P. boykinii Nutt. has similar white spikes of flowers but the spikes are longer and narrower, and most of the leaves are whorled. Occasional. Pinelands, woods, sandy to clay and often calcareous soils; Fla into se La, cw Ala, and se Ga. Mar-Aug.

Tall Milkwort   *Polygala cymosa* Walt.

Glabrous biennial to 1.2 m tall. Leaves in a basal rosette, linear, to 8 cm long. Stems usually one. Racemes numerous in terminal cymes. Flowers turning greenish yellow to dark green on drying. Seeds glabrous. Common. In shallow water of cypress ponds, swamps, depressions; Fla into se La, C.P. of Ga, se NC, and locally to Del. May-Aug. *Pilostaxis cymosa* (Walt.) Small.

   P. baldwinii Nutt. also has numerous racemes in a terminal cyme but the flowers are white or nearly so, the plants only to 60 cm tall, and the lower leaf blades spatulate to obovate. Rare. Low pinelands and swamps; Fla into se La; sw Ga. June-Aug. *Pilostaxis baldwinii* (Nutt.) Small.

Short Milkwort   *Polygala ramosa* Ell.

Glabrous biennial to 50 cm tall. Leaves elliptic to spatulate. Stems usually one, rarely to 4 as seen in the picture. Racemes several to numerous in terminal cymes. Flowers yellow, turning to dark green on drying. Seeds hairy. Common. Wet pinelands and savannahs, swamps, pond margins; Fla into se Tex, C.P. of Ga, ce NC, and scattered locally north to s NJ. May-Aug. *Pilostaxis ramosa* (Ell.) Small.

Drum-heads   *Polygala cruciata* L.

Erect annual to 35 cm tall. Stems freely branched above. Leaves mostly whorled. Flowers in dense racemes, 10 mm or more broad, sessile or sometimes with peduncles to 35 mm long. Bracts remaining on the raceme after the fruits fall. Wings acuminate. Common. Wet places, pinelands, savannahs, bogs; Fla into e Tex, c Tenn, c WVa, n O, e Neb, Minn, and s Me. June-Oct. *P. ramosior* (Nash) Small.

   P. brevifolia Nutt. is similar but most of the leaves are opposite or whorled and the wings are acute. Rare. Wet places, pinelands, and savannahs; Fla into se Miss; C.P. of NC; NJ. June-Oct. In *P. sanguinea* L. the leaves are alternate and the wings are 3 mm or more wide, ovate to oval, and obtuse to mucronate. Occasional. Open places, woods, prairies, meadows; ne SC into Tenn, ne Tex, Minn, and NS. June-Aug.

Polygala cymosa × 1/2

Polygala senega × 1/3

Polygala cruciata × 1/2

Polygala ramosa × 2/5

Polygala *Polygala curtissii* Gray

Annual to 40 cm tall, usually freely branched above. Leaves alternate, linear. Flowers in dense racemes about 10 mm broad, the bracts persistent as subulate hooks on the racemes after the fruits fall. Wings elliptic over 3 mm long. Common. Open places, often sandy or rocky, thin to normal woods; upper C.P. of Ga, ce Ala, c Tenn, s WVa, and Del. June-Nov.

P. mariana Mill. is similar but the racemes are 9 mm or less broad and the bracts falling from the racemes. Common. Open places, usually moist, pinelands, savannahs; n Fla into se Tex, cw Ala, se Ga, ne NC, and s NJ. June-Oct.

EUPHORBIACEAE: Spurge Family

Tread-softly; Spurge nettle *Cnidoscolus stimulosus* (Michx.) Engelm. & Gray

Erect perennial to 1 m tall from a long root. Sepals white, the petals none. The fruits have three hard seeds. Stems, leaves, and female flowers bearing long stiff sharp hairs with a caustic irritant which on contact produces a painful irritation and in some persons a severe reaction. Common. Sandy areas, including thin woods; Fla into se Va, Pied. of Ga, and e La. Mar-Sept. *Jatropa stimulosa* Michx.; *Bivonea stimulosa* (Michx.) Raf.

Queen's-delight *Stillingia sylvatica* Garden ex L.

Perennial, usually with several stems from the enlarged rootstock. Male flowers in a yellowish terminal spike, the female flowers few and at its base. Fruits 3-lobed, 3-carpelled, and 3-seeded. A western species of the genus has been shown to be poisonous and this species may be. Common. Sandy soils in open or thin woods; C.P.—se Va into Fla and Tex; then w into NM and n into Kan. Apr-July.

S. aquatica Chapm. is similar but with narrower leaves and is shrubby. Occasional. Depressions, usually in water; se SC into coastal Ala. Apr-Sept.

Flowering Spurge *Euphorbia corollata* L.

Our members of this genus are perennials with milky juice. All have single-sex flowers. Both sexes are borne in cups (cyathia) usually with 4 or 5 petal-like lobes, the whole resembling a flower. The male flowers consist of a single stamen and the female of a single 3-carpelled pistil. The fruits contain 3 seeds, one in each cavity, and split open. Plants of all species are probably poisonous. The juices may cause skin irritation, and plants when eaten may cause severe poisoning. Spurges often contaminate hay.

This species is an erect perennial with symmetrical leaves, cyathia with white petal-like lobes, which are over 1 mm wide. Common. Thin dry woods, fields, roadsides, along railroads; occasionally in moist places; Fla into se and c Tex, Minn, and s Me. May-Sept.

Polygala curtissii × 2/3

Cnidoscolus stimulosus × 3/5

Stillingia sylvatica × 3/4

Euphorbia corollata × 1/3

Painted-leaf; Wild Poinsettia   *Euphorbia cyathophora* Murr.

Annual to 60 cm tall, usually glabrous, with alternate midstem leaves, and small to large red patches on the upper leaves. The cyathia lack petal-like lobes and usually have only one gland, about 1 mm long, the depression in its top oblong. Seed not angular in cross section. Occasional. Various natural habitats in the open, waste places; Fla into Ariz and e SC; adventive into e SD, Minn, and Va. Apr-Oct. *E. heterophylla* L. of most books; *Poinsettia heterophylla* (L.) Small.

    E. heterophylla L. is similar but never has red patched leaves, the depression in the top of the gland is circular, and the seeds have two lateral angles. Rare. Open areas; Fla into s Tex. June-Oct. *E. dentata* Michx. resembles the above two species but the leaves are mostly opposite and none has red patches. Rare. Dry open places, thin woods; SC into Ariz, Wyo, Minn, and NY. July-Oct.

Prostrate Spurge   *Euphorbia supina* Raf.

Prostrate annual. Stems finely hairy on all sides. Leaves with very small teeth near tip. Peduncles under 6 mm long. Common. Cultivated areas, waste places, crevices of roads and sidewalks; Fla into Tex, ND, s Que, and Me. May to freezing.

    E. prostrata Ait. (*E. chamaesyce* L.) is similar but the stem is hairy in a line on one side only. Rare. Similar habitats; Fla into Tex, Mo, and Va. Three prostrate species have entire leaves and glabrous stems: *E. cordifolia* Ell. has leaves twice as long as wide or shorter. Occasional. Open pine-oak woods of sandhills; c C.P. of NC into Fla and s tip of Tex. June-Oct. In *E. ammannioides* H.B.K. the leaves are more than twice as wide as long and the fruits are about 2 mm long. Occasional. Sand dunes along the coast; se Va into Fla and Tex. In *E. polygonifolia* L. the fruits are 3–3.5 mm long. Occasional. Dunes and beaches; Ala into Fla and NB.

BUXACEAE: Box Family

Allegheny-spurge   *Pachysandra procumbens* Michx.

Perennial with elongated rhizomes. Stems to 30 cm tall, often decumbent at base. Leaves clustered near the upper end of the stem, evergreen for one winter, dropping after the plant flowers the following spring. The stamens and pistils are in separate flowers, the flowers in spikes arising from lower portions of the stem, the staminate flowers crowded in the upper parts of the spike, with a few or no pistilate flowers at the base. Corolla absent, stamens 4. Rare. Rich woods usually calcareous soils of ravines or slopes; nw Fla into se La, Miss, c Ky, and nw SC. Mar-May.

    There are 3 other species in the genus native to Japan and/or China. One, *P. terminales* Sieb. & Zucc., is used as an ornamental in the Southeast and occasionally persists. The flowers are in terminal spikes.

Euphorbia cyathophora × 1

Euphorbia supina × 1

Pachysandra procumbens × 1/2

Jewelweed; Touch-me-not   *Impatiens capensis* Meerburg

A succulent annual to 2 m tall, heavily glaucous, thus repelling water. Water drops usually readily roll off the leaves but sometimes stand on horizontal areas and appear like jewels in reflected light. Some flowers conspicuous, orange-yellow spotted with brown, on slim usually drooping pedicels. Sepals 3, colorful, one of them forming a prominent sac with a curled spur at the base. Other flowers very small, these primarily producing the fruits. Fruits usually drooping, 5-carpelled, green and coiling elastically into five sections when finally mature, often projecting the seeds considerable distances, thus the second common name. Common. Wet places, usually in woods; SC into e Tex, Alba, Alas, and Nfld. May-frost. *I. biflora* Walt.

In *I. pallida* Nutt. the flowers are light yellow to cream colored. Occasional. Wet places, usually in woods; n Ga into ce Okla, s Sask, and NS. June-Sept.

MALVACEAE: Mallow Family

Sida   *Sida rhombifolia* L.

Annual or southward a biennial to 1.2 m tall, the stems very tough. Flowers solitary in the leaf axil, on peduncles several times longer than the petioles. Common. Waste-places; natzd., Fla into se and e Tex, e Tenn, NC, and se Va. Annuals and biennials in June-Oct; biennials again in Apr-May.

S. spinosa L. has sharp projection at the base of most leaf petioles, often with 2 or more flowers in each axil. Common. Open places; natzd., Fla into e Tex, e Neb, s Wisc, s Pa, and Mass. June-frost. *S. elliottii* T. & G. has narrow leaves, about 3–6 mm wide, and longer petals. Rare. Open areas, usually sandy soil; Fla into Miss, se Mo, Tenn, and Va. July-Oct. *S. carpinifolia* L. f. has shorter peduncles (under 1 cm). Rare. Waste places, open areas, thin woods; se SC into Fla and s Miss. May-Oct.

Smooth Marsh-mallow   *Hibiscus militaris* Cav.

Glabrous perennial to 2 m tall. Leaves serrate, unlobed, or with divergent basal lobes. Petals pink with a purple eye, to 8 cm long. Seed pod glabrous or nearly so. Seeds covered with dense reddish brown hairs. Occasional. Marshes and other open places along streams; Fla into e and cn Tex, s Minn, c O, se Pa, cs Ky, se Ala, C.P. of SC, and e Va. June-Sept.

H. grandiflorus Michx. also has lobed leaves but the lobes are usually larger and not as divergent. The blades are soft hairy beneath. Petals pink with a purple to red center, 12–15 cm long. Seed pod to 5.5 cm long, coarsely hairy outside. Rare. Marshes, ditches, other wet places in open; Fla into s Miss; coastal Ga. July-Aug.

Swamp Rose-mallow   *Hibiscus moscheutos* L.

Perennial to 2 m tall. Leaves soft hairy beneath, glabrous above, unlobed or the lower ones shallowly lobed. Petals white, or less often pink but always with a purple to reddish center, 10–12 cm long. Seed pod glabrous. Occasional. Open swamps, fresh and brackish marshes; Fla into e Tex, Tenn, s Ind, and Md. May-Sept.

H. lasiocarpus Cav. is similar but the leaves are grayish stellate hairy above and the seed pod is hairy. Occasional. Open swamps and marshes; Fla into e and nw Tex, c Ill, Pied. of Ga, and ne NC. June-Oct. *H. incanus* Wendl.

Impatiens capensis × 1/2

Sida rhombifolia × 1

Hibiscus militaris × 1/3

Hibiscus moscheutos × 1/3

Pineland Hibiscus; Comfort-root   *Hibiscus aculeatus* Walt.

Perennial to 2 m tall. Stems and leaves rough with short stout hairs. Leaves with 3–5 palmate lobes or clefts. Corolla with a purple eye, otherwise cream-colored at first, turning to deeper yellow, and finally pink as the petals wither. Petals 5–6 cm long. Common. Low open pinelands; upland bogs; Fla into se La, c C.P. of Ga, and ce NC. June-Sept.

In *H. coccineus* Walt. the plant is glabrous; the leaves have 5–7 narrow, palmate, and often cleft lobes. The corolla is crimson to deep red. Rare. Open swamps and fresh or brackish marshes; c and n Fla into s Ala; se Ga. June-Sept.

H Y P E R I C A C E A E : St. John's-wort Family

Spotted St. John's-wort   *Hypericum punctatum* Lam.

Members of this genus are herbaceous or woody plants with entire opposite leaves. The blades ordinarily have internal glands visible with transmitted light; lens is usually needed to see them. Some species cause sensitivity to light when eaten.

This species is an erect perennial to 1 m tall. Leaves, stems, sepals, and often the petals conspicuously marked with black dots or short streaks. The uppermost stem leaves are oblong and usually rounded at the tip. Petals 4–7 mm long, stamens in 3–5 clusters. Common. Moist to dry places, fields, thin woods, roadsides; Fla into nc Tex, Minn, s Que, and Me. June-Sept.

H. pseudomaculatum Bush is similar but the leaves are ovate to somewhat triangular and more pointed at tip, and the petals over 7 mm long. Rare. Similar habitats; Fla into e Tex, sw Mo, s Ill, ce Tenn, and cw SC. June-Sept.

Pineweed; Orange-grass   *Hypericum gentianoides* (L.)B.S.P.

Annual to 50 cm tall. Leaves subulate, usually less than 5 mm long, appressed. Flowers sessile or nearly so. Stamens in clusters, fastened together at their bases. Mature capsule to 55 mm long, over twice as long as the sepals. Common. Fields, pastures, and roadsides, usually in sandy or poor soils; Fla into e and c Tex, s Wisc, se Ont, and s Me. July-Oct. *Sarothera gentianoides* L.

In *H. drummondii* (Grev. & Hook.) T. & G. the leaves are linear-subulate, 6–18 mm long, and ascending. The sepals are 4–7 mm long, about as long as the fruit. Occasional. Dry sandy or clay soils, in open, pastures, fields, thin woods; n Fla into se and c Tex, se Kan, s Ind, w Pa, w NC, and se Va. July-Sept. *Sarothera drummondii* Grev. & Hook.

C I S T A C E A E : Rockrose Family

Sun-rose   *Helianthemum carolinianum* (Walt.) Michx.

Hairy perennial to 30 cm tall, with ascending to erect stems from wiry often tuberous-thickened roots. Lower surface of the leaf blades hairy but the epidermis not hidden. Outer 2 sepals narrow, the other three broad. Petals lasting a day or less, 8–20 mm long. Stamens separate. Styles united. Ovulary with three parietal placentas. Seeds 80–135. Occasional. Dry sandy soils, roadsides, thin woods; Fla into e Tex, s Ark, C.P. of Ga, and ce NC. Mar-May. *Crocanthemum carolinianum* (Walt.) Spach.

Eight other species occur in the se United States. Their flowers are less conspicuous and the epidermis of the lower leaf surface is hidden by matted hairs.

Hibiscus aculeatus × 1/2

Hypericum punctatum × 3/5

Hypericum gentianoides × 3/5

Helianthemum carolinianum × 3/5

Field-pansy   *Viola rafinesquii* Greene

Annual, 4–30 cm tall. Stems slender, erect or decumbent at base, single or branched. Sepals one-half to two-thirds as long as petals. Petals white to blue or reddish-purple, the lower three petals with purple veins. All of the violets are said to be emetics, and many are laxative. The English have used a syrup of violets made from the flowers in the treatment of consumption. Occasional. Fields, pastures, roadsides, thin woods; cw SC into ce and cn Tex, c Kan, se Neb, e Pa, and cw NJ. Mar-May.

V. arvensis Murr. is similar but the stems not as slender, the sepals as long as or longer than the petals, and the petals yellowish with purple veins. Rare. Scattered localities, e SC into n Miss, n Mich, and Me. Mar-June.

Spear-leaved Violet   *Viola hastata* Michx.

Perennial to 25 cm tall from an elongate brittle whitish rhizome. Leaves 2–5 near the top of the stem, elongate and with a protruding lobe at each side of the base of the blade. Occasional. Rich deciduous woods; upper Pied. of Ga into ne Ala, e and cw Va, and c SC; n WVa into cn O and c Pa. Mar-May.

Two other stemmed violets have yellow corollas. In *V. pubescens* Ait. (*V. pensylvanica* Michx; *V. eriocarpa* Schwein.) the rhizome is short, dark, and scaly. The leaf blades are cordate and about as wide as long. Common. Rich deciduous woods; n Ga into ne Tex, s Man, NB, and cn SC. In *V. tripartata* Ell. (*V. glaberrima* Ging.) the rhizomes are slender, knotted, and dark. The leaf blades are entire to deeply 3-lobed. Common. Well-drained areas in deciduous woods; sw Ga into ne Miss, ne Tenn, cn NC, and cn SC; w WVa into s O and sw Pa. Mar-May.

Long-spurred Violet   *Viola rostrata* Pursh

Perennial to 25 cm tall from a prominent rhizome. Stems tufted, erect or nearly so. Corolla lilac-purple with a narrow and curved spur that is 7–20 mm long. Occasional. Rich woods; nw SC into n Ala, e Ky, e Wisc, sw Que, c NH, and Conn. Mar-May.

Two other species with aboveground stems and purplish flowers but with shorter and broader spurs are: *V. walteri* House which has prostrate stems that root at the nodes. Spur 3–5 mm long. Occasional, but locally common or absent. Rich woods, often well-drained places; n Fla into e Tex, cw Va, and c NC; cs O. Mar-May. *V. conspersa* Reichb. with erect tufted stems. Spur 4–5 mm long. Rare. Moist places, meadows, woods; cn Ala into O, se ND, s Que, NS, and w NC; nw SC. Mar-May.

Lance-leaved Violet   *Viola lanceolata* L.

Perennial without aboveground stems. Petals white. In subs. *vittata* (Greene) Russell which is illustrated the leaf blades are linear, being 6–15 times as long as broad. Common. Wet sandy soils, in thin woods or open. Fla into se Tex, C.P. of Ga, and se Va; se Okla and nw Ga. Mar-May.

In subs. *lanceolata* the leaves are lanceolate, being 3.5 to 5 times as long as broad. Rare. Sandy soils, open areas; nw Fla into e Tex, e Minn, and NS. Mar-May.

Viola rafinesquii × 1½

Viola hastata × 1/4

Viola rostrata × 1

Viola lanceolata × 2/3

Primrose-leaved Violet   *Viola primulifolia* L.

Perennial without aboveground stems, glabrous or hairy. Petals white. Leaf blades
ovate, 1.5 to 2 times as long as broad. Common. Wet places, swamps, savannahs, margins of water; Fla into e Tex, se Okla, Tenn, Ind, e Pa, and NS. Mar-May.

 V. blanda Willd. also has white petals but the leaf blades are as long as broad, or
shorter than broad, and their bases cordate. The lower pair of petals is glabrous. Moist
places in woods or open, often at water edge; nw SC into n Ala, s Ind, sw Que, and s
Me. Apr-June. *V. pallens* (Banks) Brainerd is very similar to *V. blanda* but the lower
pair of petals has a small tuft of hairs on the inside. Occasional. Wet places in thin
woods or open; nw SC into n Ga, WVa, Minn, Alas, and Lab. Apr-May. *V. macloskeyi*
Lloyd subsp. *pallens* (Banks) Baker.

Three-lobed Violet   *Viola triloba* Schwein.

Perennial with thick horizontal rootstock and no aboveground stem. Leaves hairy, as
wide as long or wider, with 3–5 broad lobes. Some petals hairy. Common. Dry or moist
places, woods; n Fla into e Tex, c Okla, Mich, s Vt, and Mass. Mar-May.

 Other similar species are: *V. palmata* L. which has 5–9 long linear lobes on the
blade. Occasional. Similar habitats; n Ga into Mich, Vt, Mass, and c C.P. of NC. *V.
septemloba* Le Conte which has glabrous leaves with 5–9 narrow deep lobes. Occasional, rare out of lower C.P. Low pinelands, swamps, shallow soils on limestone; Fla
into se La, Ga, c Tenn, cs Va, and Conn. *V. esculenta* Ell. which also has glabrous
leaves but with 3–5 broad moderately deep lobes. Occasional. Moist to dry places in
swamps, on slopes, in thin or dense woods; Fla into se Tex, cw Miss, se Ga, NC, and
se Va; locally ne Miss into nw Ga. Mar-Apr.

Florida Violet   *Viola floridana* Brainerd

First recognized at localities in Florida, hence its name, but now known from seven
states. Perennial with a thick horizontal rootstock. Some petals hairy. Leaf blades cordate not lobed, glabrous above and below. Occasional. Rich woods, often in swamps;
Fla into La, Miss, SC, and ce NC. Mar-Apr.

 Other similar species include: *V. affinis* Le Conte which has very short stiff hairs on
the upper surface of the basal lobes of the leaf, and the petioles and peduncles about
equal. Common. SC into n Ga, Ark, Ind, ne Ill, Wisc, w Vt, and Mass. *V. cucullata*
Ait. which has peduncles longer than the petioles, otherwise much like *V. affinis*.
Common. NC into Tenn, Mich, e Minn, s Ont, and Nfld. *V. sororia* Willd. which has
leaf blades hairy on both surfaces. Common. Moist places, meadows and woods; c Fla
into e Tex, e ND, sw Que, and se Me.

Bird-foot Violet   *Viola pedata* L.

A stemless perennial with a vertical rootstock. Leaves glabrous, with 3 principal divisions, these palmately divided into 5–11 narrow lobes. Pedicels longer than the leaves.
Plants often in tight circular clusters having as many as 30 flowers open at once. Flowers large, corolla 3–4.5 cm broad, the petals without hairs. Plants with the upper two
petals dark purple, as seen in the picture, are less common than those having five light
purple petals. Some books consider the two kinds as separate varieties, the former being
var. *pedata* and the latter var. *lineariloba* DC. Common. Roadside banks, thin woods,
open places, often rocky, well-drained places, sw Ga into e Tex, e Kan, ce Minn, se
NH, and NC. Mar-May.

Viola primulifolia × 3/5

Viola triloba × 3/4

Viola floridana × 2/5

Viola pedata × 2/3

Piriqueta   *Piriqueta caroliniana* (Walt.) Urb.

Perennial to 50 cm tall, spreading by sprouts from the roots. The petals become easy to knock off before the day is over. Flowers heterodistylous, i.e., one kind of flower with the stamens longer than the pistil, as in the picture, and in the other kind the pistil the longer. The species varies considerably in shape of leaves and in amount and kind of hairs on the stem and leaves. Some forms have been treated as species or varieties but present information is insufficient to make sound conclusions. Occasional. Sandy soil in open or in thin woods; Fla into sw Ga and sw SC. Apr-Sept.

PASSIFLORACEAE: Passion-flower Family

Passion-flower, May-pop   *Passiflora incarnata* L.

Climbing or trailing tendril-bearing perennial. Leaves deeply 3-lobed. Sepals and petals 5 each, behind the prominent purple-marked elongate fringes of the crown. Stamens 5, the filaments united into a tube which surrounds the long stalk of the ovary. Stigmas 3 on underside of the tips of the 3 spreading styles. Fruit fleshy, when ripe yellow and edible, ellipsoid, to 7 cm long, the many seeds fastened to inside of outer wall. There are forms with completely white petals and crown. These and the common form are used as ornamentals. Common. Fields, roadsides, thin woods; Fla into e Tex, e Okla, s Ind, sw Pa, and se Va. May-Aug.

   P. lutea L. has similar-shaped, but much smaller and greenish-yellow flowers. Leaves only shallowly lobed, and fruit to 15 mm long and black. Common. Woods and thickets; Fla into e and c Tex, se Kan, c Ind, and se Pa. June-Sept.

CACTACEAE: Cactus Family

Prickly-pear   *Opuntia compressa* (Salisb.) Macbr.

The large flat stem segments hold together tightly. Leaves are small, fleshy, pointed, fastened below the light colored tufts of tiny spines, and fall early. Because these spines can penetrate the skin easily, extreme caution should be used in handling the plant. The fruit is reddish when ripe and may be eaten if the tufts of tiny spines are removed. This and the species below could be called shrubs because the stems remain alive above ground from year to year. Occasional. Dry open areas, often sandy or rocky; Fla into e Tex, Mont, s Ont, and Mass. Apr-June.

   O. drummondii Grah. has smaller stem segments which break apart easily and have numerous large spines. Common. Sandy soils in open or in thin woods; Fla into s Miss, s Ga, and coastal NC.

Piriqueta caroliniana × 2/3

Passiflora incarnata × 1/2

Opuntia compressa × 1/3

Smooth Meadow-beauty   *Rhexia alifanus* Walt.

This is our only genus of this large mostly tropical family of about 4000 species, three-fourths of which are American. The 13 species are confined to the United States except one which also occurs in the West Indies. Species of this genus are perennials with opposite leaves, an urn-shaped hypanthium which is fused around the ovary and continues above it, asymmetrical petals, and 8 stamens with anthers opening by pores at the apex.

This species is a sparingly branched perennial to 1.2 m tall and has a completely hairless stem, prominently curved anthers, and a glandular-hairy hypanthium. The leaves are mostly lance-ovate to elliptic or lanceolate, to 75 mm long at mid-stem where they are the largest. The petals are spreading and to 25 mm long. Common. Sandy and peaty soils of low pinelands, bogs, and savannahs; n Fla into se Tex and C.P. of Ga and NC. May-Sept.

Pale Meadow-beauty   *Rhexia mariana* L.

This species also has prominently curved anthers. Hypanthium with some hairs, the neck as long as or longer than the body, lobes narrowly triangular to acute or acuminate. Petals 12–25 mm long, white to pale lavender, the exposed parts in bud with no hairs. In two varieties the midstem is winged-angled and with 4 approximately equal faces, and the hypanthium is 10–13 mm long. In the other variety the 4 faces at mid-vein are prominently unequal and the hypanthium only 6–10 mm long. Common. Low pinelands, bog margins, and ditches; Fla into e Tex, se Okla, Mo, sw Ind, se Ky, NC, cs Va, and se NY. May-Oct.

There are two similar species with unequal faces at midstem. In *R. cubensis* Griseb. the hypanthium is 10–14 mm long and has scattered glandular hairs. Occasional. Fla into s Miss, s Ga, and se NC. In *R. nashii* Small the hypanthium is 10–20 mm long and smooth. Occasional. Wetter habitats; Fla into s and c Miss, se Ga, and se Va.

Common Meadow-beauty   *Rhexia virginica* L.

Stems to 1 m tall, spongy-thickened near the base, wing-angled and 4 nearly equal faces at midstem, glandular hairy or with only a few hairs at the nodes. Leaves ascending, lanceolate to ovate or elliptic. Hypanthium lobes acute to acuminate, the neck shorter than the body. Anthers curved. The sweetish and slightly acid young leaves are good in salads. Common. Wet places, thin pinelands or in open; Fla into e Tex, O, c Wisc, and cs Me. June-Oct.

R. aristosa Britt. also has similar stems but the leaves are mostly lanceolate and the hypanthium lobes aristate. Rare. Peaty soils of low open pinelands, bogs, savannahs, and cypress stands; ne Ala into se NC; Del and se NJ. *R. salicifolia* Kral & Bostick is similar to *R. aristosa* but the leaves are mostly linear-spatulate, oblong, or elliptical, and the blades are spreading but turned vertical. Rare. Sandy shores of lakes and depressions between dunes; nw Fla into cs Ala.

Yellow Meadow-beauty   *Rhexia lutea* Walt.

Perennial to 40 cm tall with a stout woody taproot or rootstock. Stems hairy. Leaves oblong, linear, or spatulate. The hypanthium is 6–7 mm long with a narrow neck. Anthers about 2 mm long and almost straight. Petals yellow, broadly ascending at pollen-shedding. Common. Low pinelands and savannahs, seepage areas, bogs; n Fla into se Tex, se Ga, and ce NC, May-July.

Two other species have stout taproots or rootstocks, ascending petals, almost straight anthers about 2 mm long, and ovate to suborbicular leaves. *R. petiolata* Walt. with acuminate-aristate sepal lobes and lavender-rose petals. Occasional. Fla into se Tex, c Ala, se Ga, and se Va. June-Sept. In *R. nuttallii* James the sepal lobes are blunt to acute and the petals lavender-rose. Occasional. Low pinelands, bogs; Fla into se Ga. June-July.

Rhexia alifanus × 2/3

Rhexia mariana × 1⅓

Rhexia virginica × 1/3

Rhexia lutea × 2/3

Primrose-willow   *Ludwigia decurrens* Walt.

Annual to 2 m tall, usually with several ascending branches. Leaves lanceolate, sessile. Stems with narrow wings. Petals 6–12 mm long. Stamens 8. Fruit about twice as long as broad. Common. Open wet places, shallow water; Fla into e Tex, se Kan, s Ind, cw WVa, Tenn, NC, and se Va. July-Oct. *Jussiaea decurrens* (Walt.) DC.

Two related species have creeping and floating stems and can be bad weeds, often forming dense floating mats. The fruits are elongated but the stems are not winged and there are 5 sepals and petals. In *L. peploides* (H.B.K.) Raven the stems and leaves are glabrous. Rare. Fla into Tex, se Kan, Mo, cw Ind, and w Ky; scattered from Ga into NJ. *Jussiaea diffusa* Forskl.; *J. repens* L. In *L. uruguayensis* (Camb.) Hara the stems and leaves are hairy and the petals 12–20 mm long. Rare. Fla into Tex, sw Mo, Miss, Ga, and se NY.

False-loosestrife   *Ludwigia linearis* Walt.

Perennial to 80 cm tall. Leaves linear, alternate. Sepals narrowly deltoid. Petals 4, longer than the sepals. Stamens 4. Fruit sessile, narrowly obconical. Common. Wet pinelands, swamps, bogs, edge of ponds; Fla into se Tex, c Tenn, nw and sw Ga, c SC, and s NJ. June-Sept.

L. linifolia Poir. is similar but the sepals are nearly linear and the capsule narrowly cylindrical. Rare. Wet places in pinelands, swamps, and in open. Fla into s Miss, s Ga, and se NC. June-Sept. There are over 25 species of *Ludwigia* in the Southeast. Few have conspicuous flowers, some have opposite leaves, others have no petals, and some are entirely prostrate. All occur in moist to wet habitats. Usually the scars left by the petals are easily seen on the top of the fruits.

Showy Evening-primrose   *Oenothera speciosa* Nutt.

Members of this genus have 4 petals and 8 stamens. The hypanthium is peculiar in that it not only surrounds and adheres to the sides of the ovulary but is prolonged into a tube beyond the ovulary.

This species is an erect to spreading perennial to 70 cm tall. Leaves oblong-lanceolate to linear, the wider ones irregularly dentate or narrowly lobed, especially near the base. Flower buds nodding. Petals white to dark pink. Anthers 1.2–2 mm long. Fruit an ellipsoid to subglobose capsule. This species is hardy and drought-resistant and makes a showy ornamental. Occasional. Dry places, fields, roadsides, wasteplaces, prairies; Fla into Tex, cn Kan, Ill, Tenn, and Va. Mar-July.

O. triloba Nutt. is unusual in having no aboveground stems, the leaves and flowers arising from a stout rootstock. Fruit 20–35 mm long. Occasional. Dry often calcareous soils, open places; n Ala into cs Tex, cn Kan, c Tenn, se Ind, and se Tenn. Apr-May.

Ludwigia decurrens × 2/5

Ludwigia linearis × 1¼

Oenothera speciosa × 2/5

Sundrops   *Oenothera tetragona* Roth

Variable perennial to 80 cm tall. Leaves narrowly ovate or elliptic, to lanceolate or narrowly linear. Flower buds erect, petals 1–2 cm long, anthers 4–8 mm long. Capsule ellipsoid to nearly oblong, with a short stalk, glabrous or with erect hairs. Common. Dry
to wet often rocky places, thin woods or in open; SC into La, cw Mo, s Mich, and NS.
Apr-Aug.

O. *fruticosa* L. is quite similar but hairs are always present on the capsule and are
slightly ascending to appressed-ascending. Common. Similar habitats; Fla into Miss, e
Okla, s Mich, and NS. In var. *subglobosa* (Small) Munz the hairs on the capsule are
curled and appressed and under .25 mm long. Occasional. Around granitic outcrops;
Pied. of Ga. O. *linifolia* Nutt. is an annual with linear-filiform stem leaves. Petals 3–4
mm long. Rare. Dry rocky places, sandy barrens; Fla into e Tex, se Kan, s Ill, and n
Ala; cs NC. Apr-July.

Evening-primrose   *Oenothera biennis* L.

A biennial to 2 m tall, usually branching only near the top. Petals 1–2.5 cm long. Capsules nearly cylindric. Seeds horizontally arranged. Occasional. Fields, roadsides, waste
places, prairies; throughout most of the United States. June-Oct.

In O. *grandiflora* Ait. the petals are 3–6 cm long. Rare. Woods and waste places;
C.P. of Ala; scattered escape from cultivation elsewhere. Two other species have cylindrical fruits. In O. *laciniata* Hill plants usually branch from near the base, are rarely
over 70 cm tall, flowers sessile in the axils of leaves, bases of leaves deeply cut, and seeds
ascending in the capsules. Common. Fields, gardens, waste places; Fla into Tex, ND,
and Me. Mar-July. O. *humifusa* Nutt. is similar to the latter species but the upper stems
and leaves are closely and densely hairy, and leaves at base of the flowers are entire or
obscurely toothed. Occasional. Coastal sands; Fla into La and NJ. Apr-Oct.

HALORAGACEAE: Water-milfoil Family

Parrot-feather   *Myriophyllum brasiliense* Camb.

Most often seen as a bright green mass covering the surface of water. Parts of the plant
are usually submerged and in some habitats are reddish, as in the picture. All leaves
are similar, feather-like, and whorled. A native of South America. Commonly used in
aquaria. Common. Fla into Va and c Tex; more local north into c Mo, Tenn, and e
NY. Seldom flowering.

The leaves of other species are mostly submerged. Those of M. *heierophyllum*
Michx. are the most similar to M. *brasiliense* and are distinguished from it by being
smaller, thicker, and serrate above-water. Occasional. Any fresh water; Fla into NM,
se ND, w Ont, sw Que, and Mass. Apr-July.

Oenothera tetragona × 4/5

Oenothera biennis × 1/5

Myriophyllum brasiliense × 2/5

Rattlesnake-master *Eryngium yuccifolium* Michx.

Perennial to 1.8 m tall, the flowers many in each of 3–30 heads. The narrow parallel-veined leaves suggest it is a monocot instead of a dicot, and the flowers in heads that it is a member of a family other than the AMMIACEAE. Plants were once thought to be effective in the treatment of snakebite and were used as an emetic. Occasional. Thin woods, meadows, and prairies; Fla into e Tex, se Neb, Minn, O, Ky, Va, and NJ. June-Aug.

E. synchaetum (Gray) Rose is sometimes separated, usually as a variety, on the basis of narrower leaves and having marginal bristles of the leaves in clusters of 2–5 instead of single. Pinelands and prairies; C.P.—SC into Fla and e Tex; also Ark into s Mo. *E. aquaticum* L. also has narrow leaves but they are pinnately-veined. Occasional. Wet pinelands, fresh and brackish marshes; Fla into s Ala, s Ga, and se NJ. June-Oct.

Creeping Eryngium *Eryngium prostratum* Nutt.

Creeping perennial. Leaf blades simple, sometimes broadly lobed. Flowers many, in heads 5–7 mm long which are solitary in leaf axils. Corolla blue. Common. Pond and lake margins, wet places in thin woods or open; Fla into coastal and e Tex, cs Mo, w Ky, Ala, nw Ga, sw NC, and se Va. May-Oct.

E. baldwinii Spreng. is similar but the stem-leaves have narrow blades or segments, the flowering heads are less than 5 mm long, covered with minute swollen projections. Both species are often hidden or nearly so, by larger herbs, especially grasses. Occasional. Wet pinelands or savannahs, edges of swamps; Fla into cs Ga and se La. May to frost.

Meadow-parsnip *Zizia aptera* (Gray) Fern.

Perennial to 70 cm tall, the lower leaves simple, ovate to suborbicular, rarely 3-parted. Terminal leaflet of upper leaves entire near the base. Fruit ribbed and smooth. Common. Dry to moist situations in open or woods; cn Fla into n Ark, Ia, BC, and RI. Mar-July.

In *Z. aurea* (L.) W.D.J. Koch the lower leaves are compound, leaflet blades with 5–10 teeth per cm. Occasional. Moist habitats in open or in woods; n Fla into e Tex, Sask, and Me. *Z. trifoliata* (Michx.) Fern. is similar to the latter species, but with coriaceous leaves instead of membranaceous and the blades with 2–4 teeth per cm. Occasional. Rich woods; n Fla into e Tenn, WVa, Va, and c SC.

Mock–bishop-weed *Ptilimnium capillaceum* (Michx.) Raf.

Glabrous annual to 85 cm tall. All leaves 2–3 times pinnately compound, the divisions very narrow. Inflorescences of compound umbels with a whorl of short filiform leaves at the base. Larger plants with 25 or more umbels. Petals white. Fruit broadly ovoid to nearly orbicular, slightly flattened, with a small conic structure on the tip, corky-thickened marginal ribs, and no spines. Common. Ditches, edges of ponds and lakes, marshes, swamps, and other wet places; Fla into cs Tex, se Okla, se Mo, cw Ga, cs NC, and se Mass. Apr-Aug.

In *P. costatum* (Ell.) Raf. the leaf segments are more crowded, the primary lateral divisions appearing whorled. Rare. In similar habitats; c Pied. of Ga into cs Tex, and sw Ill; se NC. July-Sept.

Eryngium yuccifolium × 1/3

Eryngium prostratum × 2

Zizia aptera × 1⅓

Ptilimnium capillaceum × 1/5

Angelica   *Angelica venenosa* (Greenway) Fern.

Perennial to 150 cm tall from a deep stout taproot. Leaves 1–3–divided. Leaflets serrate, several to many and broad, the petioles prominently winged toward their bases. At least the upper part of the stem, the peduncles, and the pedicles are very finely hairy. The snow-white flowers are in compound umbels without bracts. Fruits about as broad as long, finely hairy, flattened, with three ridges on each flattened side and two wings on each of the edges. Reported many years ago to be poisonous but was probably confused with *Cicuta*, Water Hemlock, which is poisonous. Angelica is not listed as poisonous in current poisonous plant books. In *Cicuta* the veins of the leaflets end at the notches; in *Angelica* they do not. Common. Thin upland woods, and dry places in open; Fla into Miss, e Okla, s Mich, sw Mass, and e Conn. June-Aug.

Wild Carrot; Queen-Anne's-lace   *Daucus carota* L.

Erect, usually branched, hairy biennial to 2 m tall from a strong taproot. Leaves pinnately dissected, often so deeply as to appear compound, the segments narrow. Inflorescence a compound umbel, rounded when in flower but concave later and when in fruit, with a whorl of narrowly once-pinnate leaves at the base. Wings of fruit each with 12 or more prickles. The cultivated carrot is a race of this species. Wild carrot is edible when young but the root, especially the center, soon gets tough. It is a bad weed of some crops, in gardens, lawns, and pastures. Common. Throughout the United States and s Canada. May-Sept.

   D. pusillus Michx. is similar but an annual, smaller. Leaves more finely dissected, those in the whorl at the base of the umbels twice-compound. Spines on the wings of the fruit 10 or less each. Occasional. Open places; Fla into Cal, BC, Mo, Ala, SC, and se Va. Apr-June.

ERICACEAE: Heath Family

Spotted-wintergreen; Pipsissewa   *Chimaphila maculata* (L.) Pursh

Glabrous perennial to 25 cm tall. Leaves evergreen, alternate to nearly whorled, thick, with a whitish band along the midrib, mostly widest toward the base. Fruit an erect 5-carpelled capsule. Although the stems are herbaceous in texture they live over the winter. The plants can therefore be considered as shrubs. For nearly a century this plant was an official drug, and it is still gathered by mountain herb-gatherers for use in relieving disturbances of the urinary system. Common. SC into c C.P. of Ga, n Ala, Mich, s Ont, and s NH. May-July.

   In *C. umbellata* (L.) Bart. the leaves lack the whitish band and most leaves are widest toward the apex. Occasional. Dry woods; c NC into ne O, ne Ill, Minn, and Gaspe Pen. May-July.

Pine-sap   *Monotropa hypopithys* L.

This plant may be rather pretty long after flowering, as may be seen in the photograph taken in October when the fruits were maturing. Younger plants may be yellow, tawny, pink, or red. The plants contain no chlorophyll and live on organic matter, probably with the aid of fungi. Flowers are drooping and petals are separate. Occasional. Upland woods; n Fla into ne Cal, BC, and Nfld. May-Oct. *Hypopitys americana* (DC.) Small, *H. lanuginosa* (Michx.) Nutt.

   Monotropsis odorata Ell., which has a spicy odor, is somewhat similar but smaller, the petals united, and the fruits nodding instead of erect. Rare. Woods; n Ga into n Ala, c WVa, and Md. Mar-June.

Angelica venenosa × 1/3

Daucus carota × 2/5

Chimaphila maculata × 3/5

Monotropa hypopithys × 1/3

Trailing-arbutus   *Epigaea repens* L.

Stems trailing, hairy, perennial. Leaves evergreen, elliptic to elliptic-ovate, hairy on both surfaces, sometimes nearly glabrous when old. Corolla white to pink, with a tube 6–10 mm long and spreading lobes about as long. Fruit with many small seeds. Common. Sandy or rocky, usually dry acid soils of woods; nw Fla into s Ala, cs and nw Ind, ce Minn, Man, Sask, Nfld, and NC. Feb-May.

DIAPENSIACEAE: Pixie Family

Shortia; Oconee-bells   *Shortia galacifolia* T. & G.

One of our rarest wildflowers. This low perennial is vegetatively similar to *Galax*, but the leaves are prominently and pinnately veined. The bell-shaped white to pink corolla is 2–2.5 cm long and is distinctive. Shortia was discovered by André Michaux in the "montagnes de Carolinie" on 8 Dec. 1788. John Torrey and Asa Gray named it in 1842 on the basis of a specimen collected by Michaux which Gray found in the museum of the Jardin des Plantes, Paris. Gray, Charles Sargent, and others searched long for Shortia, but it was not rediscovered until 1877 when 17-year-old George Hyams found it in McDowell Co., NC. This is the only North American species of the genus, but there are around 10 species in Japan, Formosa, and China. Rare. Rich mountain woods of only seven counties in Ga, SC, and NC; transplanted elsewhere. Mar-Apr.

Galax   *Galax aphylla* L.

The shiny, leathery, cordate leaves of this evergreen perennial may be 15 cm wide, size being dependent on the chromosome number of the plant as well as environmental conditions. Individual plants may have twice as many chromosomes as others. Leaves of the former may reach 15 cm wide, those of the latter reaching a width of only 10 cm. The small flowers are on a leafless stem to 50 cm tall. Petals are white or sometimes light pink or light blue. The leaves turn reddish to bronze in winter and are often used in Christmas decorations. Common. Moist to dry woods chiefly in the mountains; n Ga and n Ala into Ky, Md, se Va, and n SC. Apr-July.

PRIMULACEAE: Primrose Family

Fringed Loosestrife   *Lysimachia tonsa* (Wood) Kunth

Members of this genus are perennials usually with opposite or whorled and entire leaves. Petals united at base. Stamens 5 fastened to corolla base. Seeds many, placentation central.

In this species, plants are erect, leaves lanceolate to ovate-lanceolate, those of midstem opposite, the petioles with hairs only near the base, and flowers on long pedicels in leaf axils. Occasional. Dry thin woods, bluffs; cw Ga into e and cn Ky and cn NC. May-Aug.

L. ciliata L. is similar but the petioles are hairy from stem to blade. Common. Moist woods, shaded stream banks; Miss into Neb, ne NM, Wash, BC, Lab, NS, and cs SC. May-Sept. In *L. quadrifolia* L. the leaves are lanceolate to ovate and whorled, and the petals entire and red at base. Common. Moist or dry thin woods or in open; cw SC into ne Ala, n Ind, ne Ia, Wisc, se Me, and NC. May-July.

Epigaea repens × 1

Shortia galacifolia × 1

Galax aphylla × 2/5

Lysimachia tonsa × 1

Shooting-Star   *Dodecatheon meadia* L.

Perennial to 60 cm tall with thick fleshy roots. Leaves all basal, entire, elliptic-lanceolate to oblanceolate, 10–30 cm long, and up to 8 cm wide. Flowers few to many in a terminal umbel. Young pedicels erect, flowers nodding when fully opened, the fruits on erect pedicels. Petals united at the base, the lobes turned backward. Ovary 1-celled with central placentation. Occasional. Rich woods, meadows, prairies; cs SC into n Ala, e Tex, se Kan, s Wisc, and DC. Mar-May.

LOGANIACEAE: Logania Family

Indian-pink   *Spigelia marilandica* L.

Erect perennial to 70 cm tall with 4–7 pairs of sessile leaves. Fruit 4–6 mm long and 6–10 mm broad, with 2 distinct lobes. Seeds few. Extracts of the roots, which contain an alkaloid, have been used in medicine to get rid of intestinal parasites. Misuse has caused poisoning. Common. Rich woods; Fla into e Tex, se Okla, sw Ind, nw Ga, and to e SC. Apr-June.

GENTIANACEAE: Gentian Family

Marsh-pink   *Sabatia dodecandra* (L.) B.S.P.

Perennial to 100 cm tall, with slender to robust rhizomes. Branches alternate. Upper leaves wider than diameter of stem. Flowers pedicelled. Corolla lobes 8–13, pink or rarely white. Occasional. Var. *dodecandra* usually occurs in brackish habitats; cw and nw Fla; SC into Conn. June-Sept. Var. *foliosa* (Fern.) Wilbur occurs on river banks and beside ponds and streams; Fla into se Tex and lower C.P. of SC. June-Sept.

    S. bartramii Wilbur is similar but the upper leaves are narrower than the stem. Occasional. Moist open places, savannahs, pinelands, ditches, often in water; Fla into se Miss and s Ga. June-Sept. *S. calycina* (Lam.) Heller also has many similar characteristics but is shorter, to 50 cm tall, and has only 5–7 corolla lobes. Occasional. Edge of marshes, lowland hardwoods, ditches; Fla into se Tex, sw Ga, and se Va. June-July.

Rose-pink Sabatia   *Sabatia angularis* (L.) Pursh

Erect biennial to 90 cm tall without rhizomes. Branches opposite. Lower part of stem strongly 4-angled. Pedicels usually 15–35 mm long. Corolla pink, rarely white. Common. Usually moist open places, pinelands, roadsides, wooded ravines, granitic outcrops; nw Fla into e Tex, e Kan, sw Mich, Conn, and SC. July-Aug.

    S. brachiata Ell. is similar but smaller (to 60 cm tall) and the lower part of the stem is terete. Occasional. Dry places, fields, savannahs, open pine and oak woods; La into se Mo, NC, and se Va. June-July. *S. quadrangulata* Wilbur also has many similar characteristics but is smaller, to 60 cm tall, the petals are white, and the pedicels are less than 5 mm long. Occasional. Wet to dry places, fields, savannahs, thin woods; nc and nw Fla into c Pied. of Ga, cs and ce Va. June-July.

Dodecatheon meadia × 1/5

Spigelia marilandica × 1½

Sabatia dodecandra × 1

Sabatia angularis × 1/4

Narrow-leaved Sabatia   *Sabatia brevifolia* Raf.

Annual to 60 cm tall with alternate branches. Calyx about one-half or less as long as the corolla, the lobes bristle-like to subulate and less than 8 mm long. Corolla white. Common. Savannahs, pinelands, sandy uplands, occasionally in moist places; sw Ala into Fla and se SC. Aug-Oct.

Two species have pink flowers and are otherwise similar. *S. stellaris* Pursh has calyx lobes linear to almost filiform and more than 8 mm long. Common. Salt marshes and nearby meadows, inland in Fla; s La into Fla and s Mass. June-Aug. *S. campanulata* (L.) Torr. is a perennial and the calyx and corolla are nearly equal. Common in C.P., rare to occasional elsewhere. Bogs, savannahs; La into Fla, s Ga, and se Mass; n Ga into ne Ala, c Tenn, and w NC; scattered localities in Ark, Ind, and Ky. June-Aug.

Upland Sabatia   *Sabatia capitata* (Raf.) Blake

Perennial to 60 cm tall, usually with few branches. Flowers sessile and with many petals. The basal and stem leaves are similar in shape, the upper ones usually over 10 mm and always over 5 mm wide. Calyx lobes linear, erect. Rare. Thin hardwoods, hillsides, ridges, occasionally in moist lowland woods; c and ne Ala into nw Ga and adj. Tenn. June-Aug.

S. gentianoides Ell. is similar but usually unbranched and with the basal leaves broad, the upper leaves narrowly linear, and under 5 mm wide. Calyx lobes subulate, the tips usually reflexed. Occasional. Bogs, wet meadows, savannahs, ditches; se and ce Tex into Fla, s Ga, and e NC. Aug-Oct.

White Sabatia   *Sabatia difformis* (L.) Druce

Erect perennial to 1 m tall, with a gnarled stout branched rhizome. Upper stem angular, branches opposite. Flowers with long pedicels. Corolla lobes over 7 mm long. Common. Usually moist savannahs and pinelands; C.P.—Fla into se Ala and NC. May-Aug.

S. macrophylla Hook. is similar but the stems are terete and corolla lobes are to 7 mm long. Occasional. June-July. In var. *macrophylla* calyx lobes are erect or only slightly curved at tip, equaling or less than the calyx-tube in length. Savannahs, pine barrens, flatwoods, swampy places; cn Fla into se La and cw Ga. In var. *recurvans* (Small) Wilbur the calyx lobes are strongly curved backward and exceed the calyx-tube. Savannahs, pine barrens, seepage areas; ne Fla into C.P. of Ga.

Pennywort   *Obolaria virginica* L.

A purplish-green fleshy perennial to 20 cm tall. Roots brittle. Stem simple or with a few erect branches. Leaves opposite. Flowers dull white or tinted with light purple, 7–15 mm long. Stamens separate and of equal size. Seeds very small, less than 1/4 mm long and about 1600 per capsule. Rare. Rich woods, usually moist places; c Ala into nw Miss, s Ind, NJ, and NC; nw Fla; se La. May-June.

Sabatia brevifolia × 1/3

Sabatia capitata × 1/2

Sabatia difformis × 1/3

Obolaria virginica × 1

Pale Gentian   *Gentiana villosa* L.

Glabrous perennial to 60 cm tall. Leaves in 5–12 pairs. Flowers in a terminal cluster with 2 to 6 leaves at their bases, sometimes other flowers in the upper 1–6 pairs of leaf axils. Calyx lobes linear, mostly longer than the tube. Corolla greenish-white, often tinged with purple, the lobes with an obliquely triangular appendage on the lower edge of one side of each lobe. Anthers sometimes united. Occasional. Rich woods; nw Fla into se La, Ky, s O, and se Pa. Sept-Dec.

    G. alba Muhl. is similar but has deltoid-ovate to ovate-lanceolate calyx lobes. Occasional. Moist woods, prairies, and meadows; n Ark into c Minn, Pa, and ne NC. Sept-Oct. *G. flavida* Gray. In *G. decora* Pollard the calyx lobes are very narrow, pointed, and shorter than the tube. Rare. Rich woods and openings; nw SC into ne Ga, ne Tenn, and c WVa. Sept-Nov.

Soapwort Gentian   *Gentiana saponaria* L.

Glabrous or finely hairy perennial to 65 cm tall. Leaves in 7–15 pairs, resembling those of *Saponaria*, thus the name. Flowers in terminal clusters, with leaves at their bases, sometimes other flowers in the upper 1–10 pairs of leaf axils. Calyx lobes shorter than to about as long as the tube. Corolla purple or blue, or if lighter colored then with purple or blue lines. Appendages centrally located between the corolla lobes and with 2 erect lobes. Anthers united. Common. Moist, often open places; nw Fla into e Tex, se Okla, c Tenn, Ill, se NY, and Va. Sept-Nov.

    G. catesbaei Walt. has similar flowers but the calyx lobes are longer than the tube. Common. Moist places, thin woods, pinelands; cn and ne Fla into NJ. Sept-Nov.

Stiff Gentian   *Gentiana quinquefolia* L.

Annual to 80 cm tall. Stem and branches wing-angled. Flowers in terminal clusters, rarely single, the pedicels short to as long as the flowers. Corolla lobes with no appendages between them. Anthers not united. Common. Rich woods, road banks, moist open places; cn Ga into e Tenn, WVa, s Ont, w NY, mts of Va, and nw SC. Aug-Nov.

Columbo   *Swertia caroliniensis* (Walt.) O. Ktze.

Stout biennial or triennial to 3 m tall. Leaves in whorls of 3–9, lanceolate to oblanceolate, to 45 cm long. Flowers in a pyramidal panicle sometimes with smaller clusters from the leaf axils below. Flowers occasionally occupying the top third of the plant. Sepals, petals, and stamens 4 each. Corolla 20–35 mm broad, light greenish-yellow, often marked with small purple-brown dots, each petal bearing a large fringed greenish gland. Fruit a flattened, 1-celled capsule; the seeds large, flat, and fastened to the outer wall in two rows. Rare. Rich woods, dry open places often in calcareous habitats; nw SC into se La, se Mo, Ind, s Wisc, s Ont, w NY, O, and c Tenn. May-June. *Frasera caroliniensis* Walt.

Gentiana saponaria × 2/5

Gentiana villosa × 2/5

Swertia caroliniensis × 2/3

Gentiana quinquefolia × 1

Floating-heart   *Nymphoides aquaticum* (Walt.) O. Ktze.

Perennial from a thick rhizome. Leaf blades floating, nearly circular, 5–20 cm in diameter, veins prominent, undersurface pebbly and purple. What seem to be long petioles are mostly stems, on the upper end of which develop an umbel of flowers and one leaf with a short petiole. After flowering, tubers to 2 cm long and 4 mm broad usually develop and hang downward under the umbel. Occasional. Ponds, lakes, and slow streams; Fla into e Tex, C.P. of Ga, and s half of C.P. of NC; scattered localities north to Del. Apr-Sept.

N. cordatum (Ell.) Fern. has ovate, usually smaller leaf blades which are not purple-pebbly beneath. The tubers are much elongated and very slender. Occasional. Fla into La, C.P. of Ga, Conn, NY, and Nfld; locally into Minn, Wisc, and s Ont. Apr-Aug. *N. lacunosum* (Vent.) O. Ktze. of some books.

APOCYNACEAE: Dogbane Family

Blue-star   *Amsonia tabernaemontana* Walt.

Perennial to 1.1 m tall, little branched or unbranched, the stems glabrous, leaves alternate, juice milky. Corolla finely hairy on outside. Pods erect, 2 per pedicel, about 3 mm wide and to 13 cm long, each splitting on one side. Seeds cylindrical and packed into one row. Common. Rich deciduous woods; Fla into ne Tex, e Kan, sw Ind, and s Va. Mar-May.

A. rigida Shuttlw. is similar but has no hairs on the outside of the corolla, and the leaves are usually shorter and more abundant. Rare. Moist situations in thin woods or in open; n Fla into s and ne Miss, s Ala, and s Ga. The corolla is also glabrous outside in *A. ciliata* Walt. but the leaves are only 1–5 mm wide although 3–8 cm long. Common. Sandy areas in thin woods or in open; c NC into C.P. of Ga, Fla, and cs and cn Tex; then north into s Mo.

Dogbane   *Apocynum androsaemifolium* L.

Perennial to 9 cm tall, juice milky. Leaves spreading or drooping. Corolla 5–10 mm long, bell-shaped, the lobes spreading or curved backward. The fruit of any one flower consisting of a pair of slender pods 12–22 cm long which split along one side. Members of this genus are reported to be poisonous when eaten. Common. Open areas and thin woods; mts of Ga into e Tenn, WVa, O, c Ind, ne Okla, Colo, c Tex, s Cal, Alas, and NS. June-Sept.

A. cannabinum L., which is similar, has spreading or ascending leaves, a cylindrical corolla 2–5 mm long and with erect or only slightly divergent lobes. Fla into s Cal, Wash, c Alba, Que, and Vt. May-Aug.

Nymphoides aquaticum × 1/10

Amsonia tabernaemontana × 4/5

Apocynum androsaemifolium × 1/9

Red Milkweed *Asclepias lanceolata* Walt.

Members of this genus are perennials and the juice is milky except in two species. The flowers are in umbels and are complicated, although some characteristics are easily understood and are quite helpful in identification to species. Flowers consist of an outermost calyx with 5 small reflexed lobes, usually hidden by the 5 reflexed lobes of the corolla, which is red in the accompanying photograph. The orange structures above the red corolla are hoods which together form the crown. The crown may be elevated on a column as seen in the photograph. Each hood contains a cavity from which a needle-like horn may protrude. (Horns are visible in the picture of *A. perennis.*) In most species the fruits are erect and on deflexed pedicels. Seeds, except in one species, bear a tuft of silky hairs. Several species are known to be poisonous when eaten raw; it is likely that most, if not all, species are toxic. Young fruits and shoots of some species are reported to be excellent for food when boiled and the first water discarded.

This species may grow to 120 cm tall. The stem is erect and rarely branched. The leaves are narrowly lanceolate and in 3–6 pairs. There are 1–6 umbels, corolla red, crown usually orange, and horns hidden. The fruits are erect on deflexed pedicels. Occasional. Wet savannahs and pine barrens, fresh or brackish marshes; Fla into se Tex, c C.P. of Ga, and coastal NC into NJ. May-Sept.

A. rubrua L. has similar flowers, except the corolla is sometimes purplish-red. The leaves are lanceolate. Occasional. Bogs, marshes, low pine barrens; nw Fla into e Tex, c upper C.P. of Ga, and se NY; e Pied. of Ga. June-Aug.

White Milkweed *Asclepias variegata* L.

Stem unbranched, to 1 m tall. Leaves broad, in 2–5 pairs. Peduncles 1–7 cm long, pedicels 1–2 cm long. Corolla lobes 7–8 mm long. Crown 4–7 mm wide. The horns are exposed but are turned in toward the top center of the flower. Mature fruits erect on deflexed pedicels. Common. Upland woods; cn Fla into e Tex, ce Okla, ne O, Md, s Conn, and SC. Apr-June.

Curly Milkweed *Asclepias amplexicaulis* Sm.

Plants with a single stem, to 1 m tall. Leaves sessile, clasping the stem, in 4 to 6 pairs, wavy margined, thus the common name. The single umbel, rarely 2 or 3, is on a stout peduncle 10–60 cm above the uppermost leaves. Crown 5–8 mm broad and prominently darker than the corolla. Fruits erect on deflexed pedicels. Occasional. Thin woods, open and often sandy places, usually dry habitats; n Fla into e Tex, Okla, Ia, c Wisc, O, Md, e Pa, c Vt, and Mass. May-June.

Aquatic Milkweed *Asclepias perennis* Walt.

Sometimes growing to 50 cm tall, the stems slender, usually branching only from the base. All leaves opposite, lanceolate. Peduncles thin, 2–5 cm long. Pedicels 5–15 mm long. Umbels 1 to few. Horns longer than the hoods. Crown 2–3 mm wide. Mature fruits drooping. Seeds without hairs. Common. Wet woods, especially in swamps and along rivers; Fla into se Tex, s Ind, w Tenn, c Ala, and C.P. of SC. May-Sept.

Asclepias lanceolata × 1

Asclepias variegata × 1/2

Asclepias amplexicaulis
× 1/2

Asclepias perennis × 3/5

Whorled-leaf Milkweed   *Asclepias verticillata* L.

Stem usually simple, sometimes branched near the top, to 80 cm tall. Leaves very narrow, whorled. Umbels 2–14 from the upper nodes. Peduncles slender, 15–25 cm long. Corolla lobes 3.5–4.5 mm long, the crown 3–5 mm wide. The horns are prominently exposed. Fruits erect, on erect pedicels. Common. Dry thin woods, sandhills, rocky places; Fla into e Tex, ND, se Man, cw Wisc, and Mass. May-Sept.

In *A. cinera* Walt. also the leaves are quite narrow but they are opposite and are longer, 5–9 cm. The umbels are 1–4, terminal or axillary from the upper nodes, on slender peduncles 5–22 mm long. Corolla and crown lavender to almost white, the horns protruding from the hoods. Fruits erect on erect peduncles. Occasional. Pinelands, sandy ridges, sometimes in moist open places; n Fla into lower half of C.P. of Ga and sw SC.

Poke Milkweed   *Asclepias exaltata* L.

Plants with a single stem, to 150 cm tall. Leaves opposite but otherwise much like those of Pokeweed. Pursh named the plant *A. phytolaccoides*, apparently because of this similarity. Umbels 2–7 from the upper nodes. Peduncles slender, 3–9 cm long. Longest pedicels 3–6 cm long. Horns prominently longer than the hoods. Fruits 12–14 cm long. Occasional. Deciduous woods, meadows; nw SC into ne Ala, c Wisc, s Me, and Mass. June-Aug.

A. syriaca L. is similar but the leaves are of an oblong type and finely hairy beneath instead of mostly lanceolate and glabrous beneath. The flowers are heavily fragrant. This is our only species with small conical structures on the fruit surface. Young fruits and shoots are commonly used for food in some areas after boiling and throwing off the first water. Occasional. Open, usually dry places; nw Ga into nw Kan, cn Neb, e SD, se Man, Mich, NB, and ne NC.

Butterfly-weed; Chigger-weed   *Asclepias tuberosa* L.

Plants roughish-hairy. Stems 1 to several from a thick root; erect, ascending, or decumbent; usually branching at the top into 2–5 parts, these sometimes elongated and spreading and each bearing 1–6 umbels. The sap is not milky. Leaves abundant, alternate, linear to elliptic, obovate, oblanceolate, or hastate. Corolla and crown usually orange but varying to yellow or red. Either the crown or the corolla may be darker than the other. Common. Dry places, thin woods or open; Fla into n Mex, Ariz, s Utah, se Neb, cw Minn, s NH, and Mass. May-Aug.

This highly variable species has been divided into intergrading subspecies. The leaves of subspecies *tuberosa* are typically obovate to oblanceolate; of subspecies *rolfsii* hastate; of subspecies *interior* lanceolate to ovate and deeply cordate; and of subspecies *terminalis*, which is out of our area, lanceolate to ovate and obtuse to truncate at base.

Weak-stemmed Milkweed   *Asclepias michauxii* Dcne.

Stems to 40 cm long, usually decumbent, 1 to several from a thick elongated root. Sap not milky. Leaves mostly opposite, numerous, very narrow, 5–12 cm long. Umbels one per stem, terminal, usually with less than 20 flowers. Corolla lobes 4–6 mm long. Crown 5–8 mm wide. Fruits erect on erect peduncles. Occasional. Sandy pinelands; Fla into se La, C.P. of Ga, and sw SC. Apr-June, occas. into Sept.

A. longifolia Michx. has similar leaves but 8–14 cm long. Stems erect, to 70 cm, and usually with 3 or more umbels, the largest with 25–35 flowers. Crowns only 2–3 mm wide. Fruits erect but on deflexed pedicels. Rare. Savannahs, wet pinelands; Fla into e Tex, C.P. of Ga and NC, and s Del. May-July. *A. hirtella* (Penn.) Woods. is also similar but generally larger. The largest umbels have over 50 flowers. Occasional. Thin woods and open places; nw Ga into se Ark, e Okla, Ia, Mich, and WVa.

Asclepias verticillata × 3/5

Asclepias exaltata × 1/7

Asclepias michauxii × 1/2

Asclepias tuberosa × 1/4

Fragrant Milkweed   *Asclepias connivens* Baldw.

Erect unbranched perennial to 95 cm tall. Leaves opposite, sessile or nearly so, blades narrowly lanceolate to oblong-elliptic. Inflorescences terminal, or terminal and lateral in the upper 1–5 nodes. Flowers very unusual: large, the corolla lobes 12–15 mm long, hoods 7–9 mm long and converging over the stigma. Fruits erect on declined pedicels, long and narrowly elliptical. Rare. Low pinelands and savannahs, margins of cypress swamps; Fla into se Miss; s half of C.P. of Ga. June-Aug. *Anantherix connivens* (Baldw.) Feay.

    A. virides Walt. has equally large and showy flowers but the petals are spreading with ascending tips. The hoods are much smaller, deflexed at their bases, the tips rounded and ascending. Rare. Dry pinelands, thin woods on hillsides, cedar glades, prairies; Fla; se Ga; Ala into e Tex, se Neb, s Ill, nw Ga; e Ky into se O and nw WVa. Apr-Aug. *Asclepiodora viridis* (Walt.) Gray.

Swamp Milkweed   *Asclepias incarnata* L.

Stems to 1.5 m tall. Leaves numerous, ovate-elliptic to linear-lanceolate, petioled, pubescent beneath, 1–3 cm wide. Hoods 3–4 mm long. Corolla and crown pink to rose-purple. Fruits erect on erect pedicels. Reported as edible when treated like *A. syriaca.* Common. Moist open places, edge of water; c Pied. of Ga into e Tenn, Ky, nw Ark, Kan, se Man, s Ont, Me, s NS, and ce NC, also in scattered localities to the s and w. July-Sept.

    There are two subspecies: subspecies *incarnata* is essentially glabrous to weakly fine hairy and usually much branched, whereas subspecies *pulchra* is generally conspicuously hairy and infrequently branched to simple. *A. purpurascens* L. is similar but the leaves are 4–8 cm wide and the hoods 5–7 mm long. Rare. Wet or dry places in thin woods or open; cn Tenn into se Okla, c Ia, ce Wisc, s NH, and se Va; mostly absent from Appalachian Mts. June-July.

Four-Leaved Milkweed   *Asclepias quadrifolia* Jacq.

Stem unbranched, to 50 cm tall. Leaves thin and opposite. The middle internode obviously shorter than those above or below, most often reduced until the two middle pairs of leaves appear whorled, thus the common name. Peduncles 15–35 mm long. Pedicels 15–30 mm long. Crown 5–8 mm wide. Corolla lobes about 5 mm long. Horns shorter than the hoods. Fruit erect. Common. Upland woods; nw SC into ne Ala, cs Ky, c Ind, O, NY, and Mass; c Ark into cs Okla, ne Mo, se Minn, and c and s Ill. Apr-June.

Green Milkweed   *Asclepias obovata* Ell.

Stems usually unbranched, to 55 cm tall, densely hairy as are the leaves. Umbels 1–8 in the upper nodes, sessile or nearly so. Pedicels stout, 8–10 mm long. Petals greenish-yellow, thus the common name. Horns shorter than the hoods. Crown 6–8 mm wide. Rare. Sandy pinelands and ridges; cn Fla into se Tex, C.P. of Ga, and se SC; c Ark. June-Sept.

    In *A. tomentosa* Ell. the pedicels are about 2 cm long, and the horns longer than the hoods. Rare. Sandy soils, open places; sw into n Fla; c SC into c NC; e Tex. In *A. viridifolia* Raf. the crown is only 2–3 mm broad, and the plant usually taller and not as hairy. Hoods and corolla lobes about equal in length. Occasional. Mostly in prairies but also dry fields, roadsides, and rocky places; Pied. of Ga, into ne Mex, e Wyo, cn ND, s Ont, Md, e Pa, and sw Mass. June-Aug.

Asclepias incarnata × 1/2

Asclepias connivens × 3/5

Asclepias obovata × 1/2

Asclepias quadrifolia × 2/3

Sandhill Milkweed *Asclepias humistrata* Walt.

Stems stiff and spreading 1 to several from a deep narrowly fusiform root. The spreading habit; 5–10 close pairs of broad, sessile, clasping leaves; and abundant milky juice make this species distinctive. Other prominent features include the tan-colored flower buds, a nearly white crown, and erect fruits on deflexed pedicels. Plants often grow in very hot and dry places without wilting. Common. Sandhills, dry oak woods, pine barrens; Fla into se La, C.P. of Ga, and c and ce NC. Mar-July, occas. into Sept.

Spiny-pod *Matelea carolinensis* (Jacq.) Woods.

As the common name suggests, fruits of this opposite-leaved perennial twining vine are spiny although not especially sharp. Fruits are pointed and contain many seeds which at their tips bear a conspicuous tuft of long hairs. Petals are 10–15 mm long and spreading. Occasional. Woods and thickets on slopes; Ga into Miss, c Tenn, WVa, and Del. Apr-Oct.

M. flavidula (Chapm.) Woods. is similar except the petals are yellow to green. Rare. Similar habitats; e SC into nw Fla. *M. floridana* (Vail) Woods. has maroon or green petals, 4–8 mm long. Rare. Similar habitats; n Fla. *M. decipiens* (E. J. Alex.) Woods. has maroon, ascending petals up to 16 mm long. Occasional. Similar habitats; Ga into e Tex, s Mo, s Ind, and NC. *M. obliqua* (Jacq.) Woods. has rose petals that are 4 to 6 times longer than wide. Occasional. Similar habitats with limy soil; n Ga into se Mo, se Pa, and w NC. Apr-Oct. *M. baldwyniana* (Sweet) Woods. has white or cream ascending petals. Similar habitats with limy soil; w Ala into e Okla and s Mo.

Trailing Spiny-pod *Matelea pubiflora* (Dcne.) Woods.

Prostrate perennial. Flowers in small axillary umbels which often blend with the ground cover. Upper surface of petals hairy. Pods much like those of *M. carolinensis*. Rare. Sandhills and scrub oak areas; Fla into s C.P. of Ga. Apr-Oct.

M. alabamensis (Vail) Woods. has similar pods but the stems are twining, and the petals are light green with a prominent network of dark green veins on the inner surface. Rare. Woods and thickets on slopes; sw Ga and se Ala. Apr-Oct. One species, *M. gonocarpa* (Walt.) Shinners, has smooth pods with five wings and angles. The petals are spreading and yellow, green, brown, or black in color. Petals often are two colors with the darker color being toward the center of the flower. Occasional. Woods and thickets on slopes and upper terraces of lowland woods; Fla into e Tex, s Mo, and e Va. May-Aug. *M. suberosa* (L.) Shinners.

Asclepias humistrata × 1/2

Matelea carolinensis × 2/3

Matelea pubiflora × 1/2

Stylisma   *Stylisma patens* (Desr.) Myint

A prostrate or spreading vine with no tendency to twine. Flowers usually solitary. Sub-species *angustifolia*, shown in the picture, has glabrous sepals and narrow leaves; in subspecies *patens* the sepals are hairy. Common. Dry sandy soils, rarely sandy loams; C.P.—NC into c Fla and s Miss. May-Sept.

 S. humistrata (Walt.) Chapm. is similar but the flowers are mostly 2–4 together, the sepals glabrous, and the stem tips have a tendency to twine. Common. Sandy soils in open or in woods; se Va into n Fla, e Tex, and s Ark. *S. villosa* (Nash) House is like the previous species and can be identified by its hairy sepals. Occasional. Dry sandy soils; pen Fla and C.P. of Tex. *S. aquatica* (Walt.) Raf. (C.P.—se NC into ne Fla, also La into se Tex and se Ark) has pink, maroon, lavender, or red corollas.

Jacquemontia   *Jacquemontia tamnifolia* (L.) Griseb.

Erect or reclining and usually twining annual. Plants, especially the inflorescence, tawny hairy. Leaf blades entire, cordate-ovate to elliptic-ovate, 5–12 cm long, the upper ones increasingly smaller. Flowers in heads on long axillary peduncles equal to or longer than the adjacent leaves; style 1; stigmas 2, flattened, elliptic or oblong; ovulary 2-celled; fruit 4-seeded. Occasional. Fields, gardens, roadsides, waste places; Fla into e Tex, Pied. of Ga, e NC, and se Va. June-frost. *Thyella tamnifolia* (L.) Raf.

Low Bindweed   *Calystegia spithamaea* (L.) R. Br.

Members of this genus are perennial twining vines, the calyx is concealed by 2 large bracts, and the fruits are 1-celled. This species has 1–4 flowers which are from the axils of the lower and/or medial leaves only. Occasional. Thin woods, open areas, often in sandy or rocky soils; cn Fla into cw Mo, Minn, s Ont, s Que, sw Me, and ne SC. May-July. *Convolvulus spithamaeus* L.

 C. sepium (L.) R. Br. is similar but flowers are more abundant and come from axils of leaves along a greater part of the stem. The stem and leaves are glabrous to short hairy. Occasional. Fields, roadsides, waste places, thin woods; Fla into s Tex, Ore, BC, and Nfld. Apr-July. *Convolvulus sepium* L.; *C. americanus* (Sims) Greene; *C. repens* L. The leaves are felty hairy in *Calystegia sericata* (House) Bell. Rare. Thin woods or in open, usually on slopes; n Ga, nw SC, and sw NC. June-July. *Convolvulus sericatus* House.

Common Morning-glory   *Ipomoea purpurea* (L.) Roth

Our species of this genus are twining vines, the calyx is not hidden by bracts, and the 1 stigma 2-lobed in some species. The mature fruits are dry, 2–4 celled, and 2–6 seeded.

 This species is an annual with one main stem from a taproot. Leaves unlobed. Pedicels with reflexed hairs. Sepals acute or acuminate, the points shorter to slightly longer than the base, glabrous or hairy. Corolla funnel-shaped, and purple, red, bluish, white, or variegated. Stigma 3-lobed. Mature fruit usually 3-celled and 6-seeded. Common. A weed of fields, fencerows, waste places; Fla into Ariz, Wisc, and NS. June-frost.

Stylisma patens × 2/3

Jacquemontia tamnifolia × 1/2

Calystegia spithamaea × 1/3

Ipomoea purpurea × 2/5

Fiddle-leaf Morning-glory   *Ipomoea stolonifera* (Cyrillo) Poir.

Glabrous, trailing, fleshy perennial. Stems rooting at the nodes. Most leaf blades lobed near base, sometimes deeply so. Flower stalks about as long as the leaves. Occasional. Coastal dune areas; se NC into Fla and Mex. June-Oct.

Another Morning-glory, *I. pes-caprae* (L.) Sweet, the Railroad-vine, is also found in coastal dune areas. The leaf blades are fleshy, nearly orbicular, and up to 11 cm wide. The corolla is purple and up to 8 cm wide. Rare. Ga into Fla and Tex. June-Oct.

Red Morning-glory   *Ipomoea coccinea* L.

Glabrous annual. Leaves ovate, the tip acuminate, basal lobes rounded or with 1–3 angular projections. Calyx 6–8 mm long. Corolla with a long tube. Stamens and pistil longer than the tube. Seeds 4. Occasional. Fields, thickets, roadsides, waste places; Fla into Ariz, cw Ill, s Mich, s Pa, and se Mass. May-Oct. *Quamoclit coccinea* (L.) Moench.

I. hederifolia L. is similar but some or all leaves are 3-lobed on most plants and the calyx 4–5.5 mm long. Rare. Fla into se Tex, C.P. of Ga, and se SC. *Quamoclit hederifolia* (L.) G. Don. *I. quamoclit* L. has similar flowers but the leaves are pinnately divided into many narrowly linear segments about 1 mm wide or less. Rare. Fla into e Tex, Mo, Miss, C.P. of SC, and se Va. June-Nov. *Quamoclit vulgaris* Choisy.

Ivyleaf Morning-glory   *Ipomoea hederacea* (L.) Jacq.

Hairy annual from a taproot. Leaves usually lobed, sometimes resembling those of English Ivy, hence its common name. Pedicels with reflexed hairs. Sepals prominently hairy at the base, with long tapering tips that are spreading or curved backward. Corolla funnel-shaped, light blue when fresh, then turning to light purple; or rarely white. Stigma 3-lobed. Mature fruit 3-celled and 6-seeded. Common. Weed of fields, fencerows, wasteplaces; Fla into Ariz, c Kan, e ND, and NY. July-frost.

Wild Potato-vine   *Ipomoea pandurata* (L.) Mey.

Leaves and calyx glabrous or nearly so, anthers 5–7 mm long, and the corolla always with a reddish purple center. Stems arise from a deep vertical perennial tuberous root that sometimes weighs as much as 30 lbs. Indians are reported to have roasted pieces of the root for food, but caution should be taken as the fresh root is said to be purgative. Starch extracted from the root is probably safe. Common. A troublesome weed, fields, roadsides, waste places, in open; Fla into c Tex, e Kan, s Ont, se NY, and e Mass. June-Sept.

In *I. macrorhiza* Michx. leaves are felty hairy beneath, the corolla is smaller, 5–8 cm long, and lacks the reddish purple center, and the sepals are prominently but finely hairy. Rare. Sandy open places; Fla to s Miss and coastal SC. June-Aug.

Ipomoea stolonifera × 1/3

Ipomoea coccinea × 1

Ipomoea hederacea × 1/3

Ipomoea pandurata × 1/4

Coastal Morning-glory   *Ipomoea trichocarpa* Ell.

Perennial from a branched root. Leaves usually lobed. Pedicels glabrous. Sepals ciliate on margin and hairy at base. Corolla funnel-shaped, 28–55 mm long, pink to purple or rarely white. Anthers 1.5–3.2 mm long. Stigma 2-lobed. Mature fruit 2-celled and 4 seeded. Common. Open places; roadsides, fencerows, thickets, abandoned fields; Fla into e Tex, C.P. of Ga, and se NC. May-Oct.

    I. lacunosa L. is similar but the flowers are only 15–23 mm long and the corolla is white. Common. Similar places; Fla into c Tex, e Kan, cw Ill, s O, and s NJ. Aug-frost. *I. sagittata* Cav. has narrowly sagittate leaves, anthers are 5–7 mm long, the corolla 55–75 mm long and rose-lavender. Common. Bogs, fresh and brackish marshes, interdune areas, occasionally in dry habitats; along and near the coasts of Fla into Tex and NC. May-Sept.

POLEMONIACEAE : Phlox Family

Hairy Phlox   *Phlox amoena* Sims

Perennial to 30 cm tall. Flowering stem with 5–9 pairs of oblong-elliptic to linear and hairy to nearly glabrous leaves. Inflorescence compact, stamens shorter than the glabrous corolla tube. Corolla pink to reddish or bluish purple. Common. Dry places, deciduous or mixed woods, rocky places; n Fla into e Miss, s Ky, and c Pied. of NC. Mar-June.

    P. floridana Benth. is similar but is taller, to 80 cm, there are more than 9 pairs of glabrous leaves on the flowering stems, and the inflorescence is not as compact. Occasional. Thin pinelands, scrub oak, sandy places; cw and nw Fla into se Ala and cs Ga. June-Sept. In *P. pilosa* L. the leaves are linear to narrowly lanceolate, the flowers loosely arranged, the calyx lobes subulate, and the corolla tube usually finely glandular hairy. Common. Thin woods, sandy pinelands, sandy scrub; Fla into e Tex, ce ND, w NY, and Conn, but mostly absent from the Appalachian Mts. Apr-June.

Blue Phlox   *Phlox divaricata* L.

A perennial with spreading basal shoots. Flowering stems to 50 cm tall, with a few well separated pairs of oblong to lanceolate or narrowly ovate leaves. Flowers loosely arranged, on glandular hairy branches. Corolla blue to purple, often with a reddish purple eye, stamens shorter than the tube. Occasional. Rich deciduous woods; cn Fla into e Tex, e SD, sw Que, nw Vt, ne and sw NC, and ne C.P. of Ga. Mar-Apr.

    Other species with loosely arranged flowers and a few well-separated pairs of leaves on the flowering stem are: *P. ovata* L. with oblanceolate to elliptic or obovate leaf blades and stamens projecting beyond the corolla tube. Occasional. Thin deciduous woods or in open; cn SC into n Ala, e Ind, se Pa, and Pied. of NC. May-June. *P. stolonifera* Sims with abundant creeping stems, obovate to spatulate leaf blades, and stamens longer than the finely glandular hairy corolla tube. Rare. Deciduous woods especially stream terraces; cn SC into ne Ga, e edge Tenn, s O, c Pa, and sw Va. May-June.

Ipomoea trichocarpa × 3/4

Phlox amoena × 1/6

Phlox divaricata × 2/5

Smooth Phlox *Phlox glaberrima* L.

Perennial to 1.5 m tall with 7–23 nodes. Leaves 4–20 cm long, the lateral and marginal veins indistinct, the margins entire. Inflorescence a corymb, broader than long. Calyx cylindrical or nearly so. Corolla tube glabrous. Stamens projecting beyond the corolla tube. Most of the tall Phloxes make excellent garden plants. Occasional. Moist or wet places in woods, meadows; Pied. of Ga into ne Ark, se Wisc, sw O, s Va, and ce NC. Apr-Aug.

Two other species are similar but the leaf margins are very finely serrate and ciliate and the lateral veins are prominent. *P. amplifolia* Britt. has an open broad inflorescence with glandular-pubescent bracts and glabrous corolla tube. Rare. Hardwoods; n Ala into c Mo, s Ind, and cw NC. July-Sept. In *P. paniculata* L. the inflorescence is compact, glabrous, and the corolla tube usually hairy. Occasional. Rich moist places in thin woods or open; n Ga into c Ark, ne Kan, c NY and ce and sw NC. July-Oct.

Annual Phlox *Phlox drummondii* Hook.

This species has a great variety of cultivated forms differing especially in color and shape of the corolla. Many of these have escaped and have become established in numerous places. Different forms are often found in close proximity, as seen in the picture, which was taken from directly above the plants. All plants are annuals with the upper leaves mostly alternate. Stems, leaves, calyx, and the corolla tube bear glandular hairs. Common locally. Open areas, usually sandy and well drained; native to Tex but escaped eastward into Fla and se Va, and northward at least into se Mo. Mar-June.

Thick-leaf Phlox *Phlox carolina* L.

This species is one of several tall Phloxes. Plants are often hard to name, partly because they often hybridize. This species is a perennial to 1 m tall with 6–25 nodes. Leaves 4–12 cm long, the lateral and marginal veins indistinct, the margins entire. Inflorescence a somewhat cylindrical corymb with the lower branches peduncled. Calyx cylindrical or nearly so. Corolla tube glabrous. Stamens projecting beyond the corolla tube. Common. Thin deciduous or mixed woods or open places, wet or dry; sw Ga into Miss, ne Tex, se Mo, s Ind, sw Va, e Md, and SC. May-Oct.

P. maculata L. is similar but to 1.5 tall with 18–35 nodes; leaves 7–15 cm long and 10–50 mm wide; inflorescence cylindrical, to 40 cm long, the lower branches few if any, longer than the upper. Stamens just inside rim of the corolla tube. Occasional. Moist places, thin woods or in open; nw SC into se Mo, se Minn, sw Que, sw Conn, and ce NC. June-Sept.

Jacob's-ladder *Polemonium reptans* L.

Glabrous to hairy perennial with one to several, loosely clustered, ascending to erect, branching stems to 50 cm tall. Leaves alternate, pinnately compound. Leaflets 3–8 pairs and a terminal one. Petals united. Carpels 3. Common. Rich, moist woods; cn NC into Ky, nw Ga, e Okla, se Minn, and s NH. Apr-May.

Phlox glaberrima × 1/2

Phlox drummondii × 1/2

Polemonium reptans × 1

Phlox carolina × 1/4

Baby Blue-eyes   *Nemophila triloba* (Raf.) Thieret

A tender annual with spreading stems which branch mostly from the base. Lower leaves long-petioled, parted or deeply cleft into 3–5 divisions. Flowers and fruits solitary in leaf axils but usually turned toward the other side of the stem. Petals united. Stamens with two small scales at base. Ovulary one-celled, with 2 placentas and 4 ovules. Fruit a capsule with 1 or 2 seeds. Occasional. Moist woods; n Fla into e Tex, ne Ark, c Tenn, and se Va; probably absent from the higher Appalachians. Mar-May. *N. microcalyx* (Nutt.) F. & M.

Waterleaf   *Hydrophyllum canadense* L.

Rhizomatous essentially glabrous perennial to 70 cm tall with fibrous roots. Upper leaves with 5–7 palmate lobes, the lower ones often partly or wholly pinnately compound. Flower buds in short coiled clusters which straighten after the flowers open. Petals united. Filaments prominently long hairy. Young parts of this and other species are probably edible raw or cooked. Rare. Rich woods; n Ga into ne Ark, e Mo, s Ont, and sw Vt; c NC. May-June.

   H. appendiculatum Michx. is similar but is a biennial and finely hairy. Rare. Tenn into ne Ark, ce Kan, se Minn, s Ont, and sw Pa. Two species have pinnately compound leaves. In *H. virginianum* L. there are 3–7 leaf segments and the plant is glabrous to slightly hairy. Occasional. Rich, usually moist woods; c NC into n Ark, s Man, and s NH. In *H. macrophyllum* Nutt. larger leaves have 9–13 segments. Stems are conspicuously hairy. Rare. Rich moist woods; n Ala into se Ill, n WVa, and cw NC.

Phacelia   *Phacelia bipinnatifida* Michx.

Members of this genus are hairy, annual or biennial herbs, the leaves are pinnately lobed to divided, and the flower buds are in coiled clusters which straighten after all flowers open.

   This species is an upright biennial to 60 cm tall, corolla lobes are not fringed, the lower two-thirds of the filaments are hairy, stem and branches of the inflorescence have a few to many small glandular hairs, and fruiting pedicels are recurved. Occasional. Rich woods, often in rocky places; cn Ga into n Ala, ne Ark, c Ill, c Ind, s WVa, and e NC. Mar-May.

   P. ranunculacea (Nutt.) Const., in contrast, has weak stems to 25 cm long, the corolla 2–4 mm broad, and the filaments are glabrous. Rare. Rich often alluvial woods; e Tenn into ne Ark, se Mo, s Ill, and sw Ind; c NC; DC and vicinity.

Fringed Phacelia   *Phacelia purshii* Buckl.

Weak stemmed branched annual to 50 cm tall. Stems and pedicels with appressed hairs. Leaves pinnately lobed or divided. Corolla lobes fringed across their ends. Stamens 5. Carpels 2. Fruit 1-celled. Seeds minute and numerous. Occasional. Moist places in woods or open; cn Ga into n Ala, se Mo, ce Ill, ne O, ne WVa, and cw NC. Apr-May.

   P. fimbriata Michx. is similar but the hairs on the stem and pedicels are spreading and the petals are usually cream or white and have longer fringes. Rare, sometimes abundant locally. Rich mountain woods; sw NC into ce Tenn and WVa.

Nemophila triloba × 4/5

Hydrophyllum canadense × 3/5

Phacelia bipinnatifida × 1/3

Phacelia purshii × 1¼

Phacelia   *Phacelia dubia* (L.) Trel.

This species, as do most others of the genus, often grows in showy masses. An annual with weak, usually much branched, stems to 40 cm long. Stem and branches of the inflorescence are hairy but with few glands. Pedicels spreading to ascending. Marginal hairs of the sepals not spreading. Corolla blue to white, the lobes entire. Occasional, though abundant locally. Usually thin woods, fields, sterile soils, on and around granitic outcrops; cs SC into nw C.P. of Ga, c Tenn, c O, sw Pa, and NC. Mar-May.

P. *maculata* Wood is similar but the marginal hairs on the sepals are spreading. Occasional. On and around granitic rocks, fields, sandy margins of creeks. Pied. of Ga and adj. Ala into cn SC and adj. NC. Apr-May.

Tall Hydrolea   *Hydrolea corymbosa* Ell.

Erect slender perennial to 70 cm tall, with few spines, if any. Leaves elliptic to elliptic-lanceolate, alternate, entire. Flowers at top of the stem. Petals light violet to purplish pink, united at the bases. Stamens fastened to the corolla tube. Styles 2, separate and much longer than the ovulary, which is glandular-hairy and 2-celled. Fruit a capsule with many small seeds. Common locally. Aquatic habitats; sw and cs Ga, adj Fla and southward. July-Sept. *Nama corymbosum* (Macbr.) O. Ktze.

H. *ovata* Nutt. is also erect but stouter, to 1 m tall, and armed with spines. Leaves are ovate. Flowers to 28 mm wide and at the top of the stem. Locally abundant in aquatic habitats; sw Ga into e Tex, cs Mo, and cw Ala. June-Sept. *Nama ovatum* (Nutt.) Britt.

Hairy Hydrolea   *Hydrolea quadrivalvis* Walt.

Perennial with succulent, hairy, spiny stems ascending from a creeping or decumbent base. Flowers 1–8 in short axillary clusters. Petals united at their bases. Stamens 5, attached to corolla tube. Styles 2, separate. Ovulary and fruits 2-celled. Fruits dry, splitting into 2 halves. Seeds small, many, longitudinally ribbed. Occasional. Swampy woods, edges of ponds and lakes, marshes, stream banks; Fla into se La, c Miss, C.P. of Ga, and se Va. June-Sept.

H. *uniflora* Raf. is similar but is not hairy. Occasional. Similar habitats; ce Miss into La, e Tex, se Mo, and s Ill. June-Sept. *H. affinis* Gray; *Nama affine* (Gray) O. Ktze.

Phacelia dubia × 1/3

Hydrolea corymbosa × 4/5

Hydrolea quadrivalvis × 1/2

Bluebells; Virginia-cowslip   *Mertensia virginica* (L.) Pers.

Stems tender, ascending to erect, to 70 cm tall, usually several from the perennial root. Leaves simple, alternate, mostly rounded at apex. Flowers hanging like bells, the buds pink. Corolla tube densely hairy inside base. Stamens 5, anthers yellow. Fruit 4 ovoid nutlets. About 40 species occur beyond the Southeast, to the west and north. Occasional; locally abundant, especially in mid part of range. Rich woods, often in moist places, sometimes in open; nw Ga into ne Ark, se Minn, se Me, c Va, and Tenn; c NC. Mar-Apr.

Turnsole; Indian Heliotrope   *Heliotropium indicum* L.

Erect coarse branching annual to 1 m tall, stems and leaves hairy. Corolla blue. Inflorescences coiled at first, as in the small plant photographed, but straightening as the flowers open. Fruits with 2 diverging lobes, in spikes which may become over 15 cm long. Occasional. Usually in moist rich soils of woods and fields, ditches; Fla into cs Tex, se Kan, c Ill, ne and Pied. of Ga, and se Va; locally northward. June-frost. *Tiaridium indicum* (L.) Lehm.

Our other species with similar though larger flowers, to 6 mm broad, and 2-lobed fruits is *H. amplexicaule* Vahl. It is a perennial from a strong root, the stems often decumbent and spreading, and leaves 2-6 times as long as broad. Rare. Fla into s Miss, Pied. of Ga, and ce NC. Mar-Sept. *H. anchusaefolium* Poir. *Cochranea anchusaefolia* (Poir.) Guerke.

Puccoon   *Lithospermum carolinense* (Walt.) MacM.

Perennial to 80 cm tall. Stems erect, simple or with one to several branches, from a prominent taproot. Roots with a reddish-purple content, once used as a dye for cloth. Leaves with rough hairs. Inflorescence coiled when flowers are in bud. Fruiting calyx lobes 9–15 mm long. Corolla 15–25 mm wide at end. Corolla rich yellow to orange-yellow. Occasional. Dry soils, especially sandy ones, thin woods or in open; sw and cw SC into nw Fla, c and n Tex, sw Ont, w NY, cw Ill, e Tenn, and s Ala; Mex; some western states. Mar-June. *Batschia caroliensis* (Walt.) Gmel.

L. canescens (Michx.) Lehm. is similar but the hairs on the leaves are soft, the fruiting calyx lobes 6–8 mm long, the corolla 10–15 mm wide. Occasional in the Southeast; common in the Northwest. Dry places, often sandy; prairies, open woods; nw Ga into e Okla, e Kan, s Sask, sw Ont, c Va, and Tenn. Apr-May.

Mertensia virginica × 2/5

Heliotropium indicum × 1

Lithospermum carolinense × 2/5

Moss Verbena   *Verbena tenuisecta* Briq.

The flower of many Verbenas resembles that of Phloxes except that it is slightly irregular. Also, the fruit is an aggregate of 4 nutlets held tightly by the calyx.

This species is probably the best known. It is abundant along roadsides, producing conspicuous expanses of flowers. The stems branch abundantly and are prostrate or decumbent, root at the nodes, and are largely unaffected by mowing. The leaves are opposite, deltoid in outline, and deeply and narrowly segmented. The corolla is lavender to purple, or white. It can probably serve as an ornamental much more than is generally appreciated, seemingly free of pests and diseases. Common. Roadsides, fields, waste places; Fla into s and se Tex, Pied. of Ga, and se NC. Feb-frost. *Glandularia tenuisecta* (Briq.) Small.

Stiff Verbena   *Verbena rigida* Spreng.

Erect perennial from coarse elongate rhizomes, often forming large patches which are conspicuous when in flower. The stems and especially the leaves are rough-hairy. Leaves lanceolate to oblanceolate, coarsely serrate, clasping the stem. The flowers overlap in dense short stiffly erect spikes, rarely to 6 cm long, the axis with short-stalked glands. This makes a hardy, drought-resistant ornamental. Occasional. Waste places, roadsides, fields, pastures; Fla into e Tex, Pied. of Ga, and e NC. Mar-Oct.

Narrow-leaved Verbena   *Verbena simplex* Lehm.

Erect to ascending perennial to 60 cm tall. Stems glabrous to sparingly hairy. Leaves serrate, linear to oblanceolate, to 1 cm wide, narrowly cuneate at the base. Flowers and later the fruits overlapping, in slender spikes, usually 1 spike at tip of each stem or branch. Corolla 5–6 mm wide. Occasional. Dry places, thin woods or in open; nw Ga into e Okla, Minn, sw Que, w NH, and cn SC; absent from s Appalachian Mts. May-Sept. *V. angustifolia* Michx.

Stylodon carneus (Medic.) Moldenke looks like a large edition of *V. simplex*. It has leaves 1.2–3 cm wide, the stems are hairy and the flowers are not continuous on the spike. The fruit is one unit with a cap. Occasional. Sandy soils, usually dry places, in thin woods or in open; Fla into s and se Tex, C.P. of Ga, and c and se NC. Apr-July. *S. caroliniensis* (Walt.) Small; *V. carnea* Medic.

Lippia   *Lippia nodiflora* (L.) Michx.

Perennial, usually with prostrate or decumbent rooting stems. Leaves opposite, blunt- or round-tipped, and with 1–7 teeth on each side above the middle. Flowers many in a tight head which is longer than broad as the seeds become mature. Common. Sandy, usually moist and open habitats; se Va and mostly along the coast into Fla, Tex, and Mex; n into se Mo. Apr-frost.

The similar *L. lanceolata* Michx. has taller ascending to erect stems, and acute leaves with 5–11 teeth on each side to below the middle. Wet places; occasional along the coast from s NJ into Fla and Tex; more scattered into s Cal and from Tex n into Neb, Minn, Ont, and c Pa. June-frost.

Verbena rigida × 2/5

Verbena tenuisecta × 1⅓

Lippia nodiflora × 1

Verbena simplex × 1/2

Blue-curls   *Trichostema dichotomum* L.

Members of this family have opposite simple leaves, usually square stems, petals united
and irregular, ovulary superior, style arising from the central depression of the 4 lobes
of the ovulary, fruit usually 4 nutlets nestled in the persistent calyx tube.

This species is an annual to 80 cm tall. Leaves to 7 cm long, less than 5 times as
long as wide, the lower ones often falling during dry periods. Lower lip of the corolla
narrow but prominent and drooping. The 4 stamens are strongly arched and bluish,
thus the common name. Common. Dry places in open, or thin woods; Fla into e Tex,
Ill, s Mich, and Me. Aug-frost.

T. setaceum Houtt. is quite similar but with narrower leaves, more than five times as
long as wide. Occasional. Fla into e Tex, se Mo, s O, and Conn. *T. lineare* Nutt. Aug-
frost.

Wood-sage; Germander   *Teucrium canadense* L.

Erect rhizomatous perennial to 150 cm tall. Leaves lanceolate to ovate-lanceolate. Flowers in 1 or more terminal spikes. Corolla purplish, pink, or cream-colored. Upper 4
lobes of the corolla nearly equal, oblong, turned forward, so that there seems to be no
upper lip. The lower lip very prominent. Anther-bearing stamens 4. Ovulary 4-lobed,
not deeply 4-parted as in most mints. Fruit of 4 nutlets which are fastened at their
sides. Often confused with *Stachys*, which has a distinctly 2-lipped corolla. Occasional.
Moist to wet places in thin woods or open, prairies; Fla into Tex, BC, and NS. June-
Aug. *T. nashii* Kearn.; *T. virginicum* L.

Heart-leaf Skullcap   *Scutellaria ovata* Hill

In members of this genus the calyx is enlarged when in fruit and has a helmet-like
protuberance on the upper side.

This species is a perennial to 1.4 m tall. Largest leaves with petioles one-fourth as
long as blade or longer; blades 4–5 cm long; ovate to ovate-lanceolate with cordate
bases. Racemes 1 to many, the axis glandular-hairy, and the lower bracts sessile. Calyx
glandular-hairy. Occasional. Dry to wet habitats in woods or marshes; se NC into Fla,
s and e Tex, Minn, n O, and Md. May-Aug.

S. saxatilis Ridd. also has all leaves with cordate bases, but they are thinner, usually
smaller, and often deltoid. The racemes are one-sided and the lower bracts are petioled.
Rare. Usually rocky places, in woods or in open; ce Tenn into ne NC, WVa, s Ind, e
O, and Del. May-Sept.

Hairy Skullcap   *Scutellaria elliptica* Muhl.

Perennial to 75 cm tall. Stems hairy, sometimes finely so, with 2–7 nodes below the inflorescence. Upper leaves crenate to crenate-serrate, the first pair below the inflorescence
less than 3 times as long as wide. Corolla 12–21 mm long, blue to violet to rarely
white. Common. Usually in deciduous woods on slopes; Ga into se Tex, s Mo, sw
Mich, se NY. May-July.

S. incana Biehler is similar but is taller and often has more racemes of flowers below
the terminal one. Occasional. Pied. of Ga into e Okla, Ind, sw NY, NJ, and NC. June-
Aug.

Trichostema dichotomum × 1/2

Teucrium canadense × 1/2

Scutellaria ovata × 1/2

Scutellaria elliptica × 2/5

Narrow-leaved Skullcap   *Scutellaria integrifolia* L.

Perennial to 75 cm tall, upper leaves linear-lanceolate to narrowly elliptic, more than 3 times as long as broad. The bases of lower leaves obtuse, often cordate. Racemes 1–7, or rarely many. Corolla 13–28 mm long. In var. *integrifolia* lower internodes have small hairs which curve upward and usually inward. Common. Open, usually wet situations, rarely in thin woods; Fla into e Tex, Ark, s O, and Mass. Apr-July. In var. *hispida* Benth. the lower internodes have prominent divergent hairs and few or no small incurving hairs. Occasional. Fla into e Tex, Ark, cw Tenn, C.P. of Ga, and se Va. Apr-July.

In *S. multiglandulosa* (Kearn.) Small the lower leaf bases are less than 90°, usually broadly cuneate, and there are spreading glandular hairs on the lower internodes. Rare. Dry soil, usually sandy. Ga, upper C.P. into e Pied. May.

Large-flowered Skullcap   *Scutellaria montana* Chapm.

Perennial to 50 cm tall. Upper leaves crenate to crenate-serrate, the first pair below the inflorescence less than 3 times as long as wide. Corolla 25 mm long or longer. Perhaps not distinct from *S. elliptica*. Rare. In deciduous woods or in open; n Ga into e Tenn, n Ala, and n Miss. May-July.

S. parvula Michx. is small, growing to 35 cm tall, has flowers in the axils of leaves only, and bears underground tubers. The stem is simple or branching from the base. The upper leaves are narrowly ovate-lanceolate to ovate, to 17 mm long, and entire to shallowly toothed. Occasional. Various habitats, but usually in the open; n Fla into e and nc Tex, e ND, c Me, and n SC. Apr-June.

False Dragon-head   *Physostegia virginiana* (L.) Benth.

Perennial to 1.5 m tall, the stem single but sometimes with short branches at the top. Leaves in 13–22 pairs, the lower ones often falling early, the blade margins of the larger leaves with sharp teeth. Flowers few to many in 1–7 spikes. Corolla from almost white to rose purple, 1.8–3 cm long. Common. Moist to mesic situations in open or woods; n Ga into c Tex, ND, s Ore, s Me, and SC. May-Oct. *P. angustifolia* Fern., *Dracocephalum virginianum* L.

In *P. purpurea* (Walt.) Blake (*Dracocephalum denticulatum* Ait.), the leaves have rounded teeth or are undulate. Fla into s Miss, s Ga, and se Va. Apr-Aug. *P. intermedia* (Nutt.) Engelm. & Gray has corollas less than 1.8 cm long. Fla into s Ga and s Tex; n into se Mo, s Ill, and e Ky. Apr-July.

Heal-all   *Prunella vulgaris* L.

Perennial to 80 cm tall, with short branches anywhere below the central flower cluster. Leaves variable. Flowers in dense almost globose spikes, or later cylindrical, the spikes over 1 cm wide excluding corollas. Corolla white to pink and purple. Pollen bearing stamens 4. Common. Natzd. in a variety of habitats; Fla to Cal and northward into s Canada and Alas. Apr-frost.

P. laciniata L. is smaller, the margins of the upper leaves usually with projections, the flower clusters under 1 cm wide excluding the corollas. Rare. Natzd. in moist habitats; n Ga into NY. June-Sept.

Scutellaria integrifolia × 1/2

Scutellaria montana × 2/3

Physostegia virginiana × 1/3

Prunella vulgaris × 3/5

Macbridea   *Macbridea caroliniana* (Walt.) Blake

Perennial to 90 cm tall, the stem simple or branched near the tip. Leaves in 7–11 pairs, to 13 cm long, the blades elliptic to linear-elliptic. Flowers in 1 to 3 tight, bracted, separated clusters. Calyx 2-lipped. Pollen bearing stamens 4. Occasional. Moist to wet places in open or thin woods; Fla into se NC, lower C.P. of Ga, and s Ala. July-frost. *M. pulchra* Ell.

M. alba Chapm. is shorter, has a white corolla, and the leaf blades are blunt at the apex instead of pointed. Rare. Low places in thin pinelands or in open. N Fla. June-Aug.

Henbit   *Lamium amplexicaule* L.

Annual or winter-annual to 35 cm tall, branching from the base, most branches arched and ascending. Leaves beneath the flower clusters sessile, the blades horizontal or ascending. Corolla 12–18 mm long. Pollen bearing stamens 4. A troublesome weed, especially in yards and gardens. Has been used as a cooked green when young, but is possibly poisonous if used in large quantities. Common. Natzd. in a variety of open habitats; Fla into Cal and northward into Canada. Throughout freeze-free winter-May.

In *L. purpureum* L. the leaves beneath the flower clusters are stalked and are horizontal to drooping. The leaves are also deeper green or purplish. Corolla 10–16 mm long. Occasional. Natzd. in open places; n SC into Tex and c Cal, and northward into s Canada. Feb-May.

Hairy Stachys   *Stachys riddellii* House

Our members of this genus are perennials, the calyx with 5 nearly equal lobes, and the nutlets nearly terete and rounded at their tips.

Plants of this species grow to 1.2 m tall. Sides of the stem are finely hairy. Leaves broader than in *S. tenuifolia* and having petioles 1 cm or longer on the largest leaves. Occasional. Mtn woods; n Ga into e Tenn, w NC, WVa, s Ill, and Md. May-Aug.

S. nuttallii Schuttlw. is similar but the leaves are sessile or almost so. Occasional. Rich woods; n Ga into e Tenn, Ky, WVa, and Md. June-Aug.

Stachys   *Stachys tenuifolia* Willd.

Plants to 1 m tall. Upper part of the stem glabrous although the corners may have hairs. Leaves acuminate. Calyx teeth two-thirds to as long as the tube. Variable and perhaps not separable from the next species below. Common. Rich woods and open places; Pied. of Ga into Tex, Minn, s Que, and NH. May-Aug.

S. hyssopifolia Michx. has narrowly linear to narrowly oblong leaves with acute to obtuse tips. The underground tubers are crisp and nutty and good to eat from fall into early spring. Occasional. Moist places; C.P. of SC into C.P. of Va, mts of Va, and se Mass; also sw Mich and nw Ind. *S. latidens* Small is separated by some on the basis of its having calyx teeth about half as long as the tube. Occasional. Mts of Ga into e Tenn, WVa, and DC. June-Aug.

Macbridea caroliniana × 3/5

Lamium amplexicaule × 1¼

Stachys riddellii × 3/5

Stachys tenuifolia × 2/3

Blue Sage *Salvia azurea* Lam.

In our members of this genus the flowers are in terminal spike-like clusters, the calyx without a cap or protuberance on the tube, and the corolla 2-lipped.

Perennial to 1.5 m tall. Stems one to several from the base, simple or with a few branches above. Leaves above the base, linear to elliptic-lanceolate, at the base, cuneate. Calyx 2-lipped. Corolla blue to almost white, rarely purplish. Pollen-bearing stamens 2. Occasional. Dry places in thin woods or open; se NC into Fla, Pied. of Ga, Tex, e Colo, Neb, Minn, and e Tenn. Aug-Oct.

Nettle-leaved Sage *Salvia urticifolia* L.

This perennial vegetatively resembles some nettles and verbenas. Stems to 80 cm tall, simple or little branched near top. Leaves in 4 to 7 separated pairs, the blades tapering onto the petiole. Flowers in 3–9 separated whorls. Occasional. In deciduous woods, sometimes with pine or cedar; sw Ga into Miss, Ky, Va, se Pa; also s O. Apr-July.

The leaves of our other species of *Salvia* are unlike those of *S. urticifolia*.

Lyre-leaved Sage *Salvia lyrata* L.

The leaves of this perennial are all basal or nearly so. They are often lyrate in shape, prompting the common and scientific name. There may be several stems from the base although there is usually one. The main stem may have two leafless branches from the upper part. Pollen-bearing stamens 2. Common. Various habitats in thin woods or open, sometimes weedy; Fla into Tex, s Ill, s Pa, and Conn. Feb-May, sometimes in Fall.

Bee-balm *Monarda didyma* L.

Our members of this genus have flowers in dense head-like clusters or whorls, the calyx lobes are nearly equal, and there are 2 pollen-bearing stamens.

This species is a perennial to 1.8 m tall. Leaves petioled, the blades ovate-lanceolate, 6–15 cm long. Flowers in one tight head, or rarely a second above the first, those on the inside opening last, as seen in the picture. Corolla scarlet. The leaves have been used as a mint flavoring in cooking and in making tea. Occasional. Moist woods or in open; mts of Ga into mts of Va and WVa, Mich, Me, and NJ. July-Sept.

Individual flowers of *Salvia coccinea* L. are of similar color and shape but are arranged loosely in 3 to 9 whorls. Occasional. Sandy soils in open, or thin woods; Fla into e and s Tex, and coastal Ga and SC. May-frost.

Salvia azurea × 2/5

Salvia urticifolia × 2/3

Salvia lyrata × 1/4

Monarda didyma × 1¼

Horse Mint　　　　　　　　　　　　　　　　　　*Monarda punctata* L.

Perennial to 1 m tall. Flowers in 2 or more tight clusters on the end of each flowering stem, each cluster with several wholly or partially pink to lavender leaf-like bracts beneath. Calyx teeth acute to acuminate, to 2 mm long. Corolla yellow, spotted with purple. Common. Dry places in open or in thin woods. Fla into Tex, Minn, e Vt, and Miss. July-Sept.

　　M. citriodora Cerv. is similar, but is an annual with aristate calyx teeth 3 mm or more long and a white to pink corolla. Common. Open areas; La into Tex, Kan, and Mo; adventive east to Mich, Tenn, e SC, and n Fla. May-July.

Wild Bergamot　　　　　　　　　　　　　　　　*Monarda fistulosa* L.

Perennial to 1.2 m tall. Flowers in dense heads, one at the tip of each main stem or branch. Corolla white to pink and purple, the tip of the upper lip with a tuft of hairs. Stamens 2. Used similarly to *M. didyma* as a flavoring and in tea. Common. Dry places in open, or in thin woods; ne NC into n Ga, e Tex, Sask, and se Me; w into BC. May-Sept.

　　In *M. clinopodia* L. the corolla is white to pink and the tip of the upper lip without a tuft of hairs. Occasional. Moist areas in woods or open; n SC into n Ala, se Mo, c Ill, s Ont, and Conn. May-Sept.

Blephilia　　　　　　　　　　　　　　　　*Blephilia ciliata* (L.) Benth.

Perennial resembling some species of *Monarda* but the calyx is two-lipped and has many hairs. In this species the petioles of the leaves beneath the lowest cluster of flowers are less than 10 mm long. The corolla may be almost white. Stamens 2. Occasional. Dry places in woods or open; c Ga into ne Tex, e Ia, Wisc, s Vt, and c SC. Mostly absent from the southern Appalachian Mts. Apr-July.

　　In *B. hirsuta* (Pursh) Benth. the petioles of the leaves beneath the lowest flower cluster are 10 mm or more long. The corolla is pale with purple dots. Occasional. Moist woods; mts of w NC and Ga into Tenn, ne Tex, Minn, w Que, Vt, and cn NC. June-Aug.

Rose Dicerandra　　　　　　　　　　　*Dicerandra odoratissima* Harper

Annual to 45 cm tall. Lower calyx teeth subulate, over 2.5 mm long. Corolla pink to rose-purple, longer than the stamens. Stamens 4, the anther sacs tipped with blunt to acute horns. Rare. Sandy soils in open, or thin scrub or live oak woods; cs Ga into s tip of SC. Sept-Oct.

　　In the similar *D. densiflora* Benth. the stamens are longer than the corolla and the lower calyx teeth are 2.0–2.6 mm long. Rare. Northern pen of Fla into Long Co., Ga. Sept.-Oct.

Monarda punctata × 2/5

Monarda fistulosa × 1/3

Blephilia ciliata × 1/5

Dicerandra odoratissima × 1/6

White Dicerandra   *Dicerandra linearifolia* (Ell.) Benth.

Annual to 50 cm tall. Lower calyx teeth triangular, 1.0–1.7 mm long. Corolla white to light lavender, the upper lip lined and spotted with purplish red on the inside. Stamens longer than the corolla. Anther horns acuminate. Plant quite aromatic. Abundant locally, often forming spectacular colonies. Occasional. Sandy soil in open or thin pine, scrub oak, or live oak woods. Fla into sw Ala and C.P. of Ga. Sept-Nov.

White Horse-mint   *Pycnanthemum incanum* (L.) Michx.

A perennial to 2 m tall. The calyx teeth are distinctly unequal in length, the longest ones are less than half as long as the calyx tube and bear long hairs at their tips. Corolla white to pink-tinged and spotted with purple. Occasional. Dry habitats in open or in thin woods; Pied. of Ga into n Ala, s Ill, s NH, and Pied. of NC. June-Sept.

In *P. pycnanthemoides* (Leavenw.) Fern. the corollas are deeper colored and the longest calyx lobes more than half as long as the calyx tube. Pied. of Ga into s Ill, s Ind, WVa, and SC. June-Sept. *P. albescens* T. & G. lacks long hairs on the tips of the calyx teeth. Dry habitats; c Fla into s Ala, e Tex, s Mo, and e Tenn. June-Sept. *P. montanum* Michx. differs by having glabrous but ciliate bracts below the flowers. Rare. Woods or in open in mts; nw SC into n Ga, e Tenn, and c WVa. June-Sept.

Common Horse-mint   *Pycnanthemum tenuifolium* Schrad.

A perennial to 1.2 m tall. Stems glabrous. Leaves sessile, 1.5–5.5 mm wide. Calyx teeth sharp, nearly equal, 1–2 mm long. Corolla white to pink, dotted with purple. Stamens 4. Common. Dry to wet places in open or in thin woods; c SC into sw Ga, e Tex, Minn, s Ont, and Me. May-Aug.

Other similar species are: *P. flexuosum* (Walt.) B.S.P. with hairy stems. Calyx teeth 2.3–5 mm long, awned. Fla into s Ala, C.P. Ga, and DC. June-Sept. *P. virginianum* (L.) Durand & Jackson with hairs on angles of stem only and deltoid calyx teeth 0.7–1 mm long. Rare. Pied. of NC into nw Ga, n Ark, ne Kan, se ND, and c Me. July-Sept. *P. verticillatum* (Michx.) Pers. with leaves 10–15 mm wide, minutely hairy stems, and calyx teeth 1.3–1.7 mm long. Occasional. Various places; nw SC into w NC, Va, Ky, nw Tenn, Mich, sw Que, and Mass. July-Sept.

Dittany; Stone Mint   *Cunila origanoides* (L.) Britt.

Perennial to 45 cm tall, usually with several branches from the upper half of the main stem. Leaves ovate or nearly so. Calyx lobes nearly equal. Corolla rose purple to nearly white. Stamens 2. Indians and early settlers used this plant for treating colds and fevers. Occasional. Dry habitats in open or in woods; Pied. of Ga into cn Tex, c Mo, c Pa, and se NY. Aug-Sept. *Mappia origanoides* (L.) House.

Dicerandra linearifolia × 2/5

Pycnanthemum incanum × 1½

Pycnanthemum tenuifolium × 1/2

Cunila origanoides × 1/2

Horse-balm   *Collinsonia canadensis* L.

Perennial to 1.5 m tall. Leaves at flowering time 6 or more in separated pairs, the largest with 15–40 teeth on each side. Lower teeth of the calyx with subulate tips. Corolla yellow, the lower lip fringed. Stamens 2. Common; rare in C.P. Moist rich woods; nw Fla into se Mo, Wisc, and s NH. Aug-frost. *C. punctata* Ell.

C. *tuberosa* Michx. has 5–15 teeth on each leaf margin. Rare. Pied. of Ga into se La and sw Tenn; also into SC and c NC. Aug-Oct. In *C. serotina* Walt. the lower calyx teeth are subacute to acuminate. Stamens 4. Occasional. Rich woods, n Fla into se La, Pied. of Ga, and c NC. July-Oct. *C. anisata* Sims. In *C. verticellata* Ell. there are usually 4 closely crowded leaves. Flowers are in close set groups of 3–6. Stamens 4. Occasional. Rich woods; c Ga into ne Ala, e Tenn, sw NC, and nw SC. Apr-May.

Hyptis   *Hyptis alata* (Raf.) Shinners

Perennial to 3 m tall. Stem single or sparsely branched in the upper portion. Flowers in dense heads, one head on each peduncle. The peduncles are up to 8 cm long and arise from the upper leaf axils. Calyx nearly regular. Corolla almost white, spotted with purple, the lower lip with a sac-shaped lobe. Stamens 4 protruding from the corolla tube, 2 longer than the others. Common. Moist situations in open or in thin pine or cypress woods; Fla into se Tex, C.P. of Ga, and ce NC. June-Oct. *H. radiata* Willd.

In *H. mutabilis* (A. Rich) Briq. there are as many as 18 tight clusters of flowers on each of usually several spikes, the spikes terminal and on axillary peduncles. Occasional. Various habitats; Fla into sw Ala and s Ga. July-Oct.

SOLANACEAE: Nightshade Family

Ground-cherry; Husk-tomato   *Physalis heterophylla* Nees

Members of this genus are annuals or perennials and the fruit is enclosed in a considerably larger papery sac with only a small opening at the tip. The sepals, united and enlarged, form the sac. Fruits are berries. Ripe fruits of all our native species are probably edible; those of some of the exotic species, several of which have become naturalized, may be poisonous, especially if green.

This species is a perennial with simple spreading sticky hairs. Leaves cordate to broadly rounded at the base. Anthers 3.5–4.5 mm long, on wedge-shaped filaments. Common. Thin woods, fields, waste places, dry situations; Fla into e Tex, se ND, s Que, and sw Me. Apr-Oct.

P. *viscosa* L. is also a perennial but has very small branched hairs. Common. Sandy soil of coastal dune areas, thin woods; Fla into e NM, cs Kan, and s Ala; coast of Ga into se Va. Apr-Sept.

Horse-nettle; Bull-nettle   *Solanum carolinense* L.

Erect, simple to branching perennial to 80 cm tall from deep vigorous horizontal rhizomes. Stems and undersides of leaves with straw-colored prickles. Leaf blades generally ovate in outline with 2–5 large teeth or shallow lobes on each side. Stem and leaves also loosely covered with small 4–8–rayed hairs. Corolla light purple to white. The fruits, green at first and later yellow, are much like little tomatoes but are poisonous when eaten. Common. Bad weed in gardens, pastures, fields, and other places. Fla into e Tex, e Neb, Minn, s Ont, and Vt. Apr-Sept.

Two other species are similar vegetatively, but are annuals, larger, the spines stouter, and the fruits (berries) partially or wholly covered by the enlarged prickly calyx. *S. rostratum* Dunal has yellow petals. *S. sisymbriifolium* Lam. has red berries. Both are rare, weedy, and about the same range as *S. carolinense*. May-Oct.

Collinsonia canadensis × 1/3

Hyptis alata × 1/4

Physalis heterophylla × 3/5

Solanum carolinense × 4/5

Thornapple; Jimson-weed   *Datura stramonium* L.

Coarse glabrous annual to 1.5 m tall, bushy-branched in the upper part, with a foul odor. Leaves alternate. Corolla long funnel-shaped, white and usually tinged with lavender. Fruit an erect ovoid spiny many-seeded capsule. Seeds black, roughened, and finely pitted. *Datura* contains several alkaloids and the entire plant is extremely poisonous when eaten. Fortunately, the plant is distasteful. Children have been poisoned by sucking nectar from the base of the corolla tube and from eating seeds. Poisoning of many kinds of animals has been traced to *Datura*. Once used in several ways medicinally but this is dangerous. Common. Fields, pastures, animal lots, waste places; throughout the United States and s Canada. July-Oct.

SCROPHULARIACEAE: Figwort Family

Woolly Mullein; Flannel-plant   *Verbascum thapsus* L.

Members of this family have weakly to strongly irregular corollas and superior 2-carpelled ovularies with a terminal style.

This species is a densely woolly biennial to 2 m tall. Stem upright, stout, unbranched. Leaves having feel of thick flannel, in a basal rosette only during the first year; those of the second year as much as 40 cm long, bases of upper leaves extending down sides of the stem. Flowers and fruits in a very dense elongated cylindrical spike. Corollas yellow, or rarely white. Filaments with yellow hairs. Seeds many and long-lived. Common. Fields, pastures, roadsides, and other open places; Fla into Cal, BC, and NS. June-Nov.

V. phlomoides L. is similar but the upper leaves merely clasp the stem, and some of the flower and fruit clusters are separated by distinct spaces. Rare. Open places; se SC into WVa, Minn, and Me; Ia.

Moth Mullein   *Verbascum blattaria* L.

Erect annual or biennial to 1.2 m tall, with small scattered glandular hairs. Stems sometimes branched in upper part. Leaves coarsely toothed, those of the first season in a basal rosette. Flowers and fruits in elongated racemes, on pedicels 10-17 mm long. Petals yellow or rarely white. Filaments bearing prominent purple hairs. Common. Fields, roadsides, other open places; Fla into e Tex, ne Mo, s Ont, and Me. May-July.

V. virgatum Stokes is similar but the pedicels are only 3-5 mm long. Rare. Roadsides, weedy places; s SC; c NC; e Tex; scattered localities in the ne United States. Apr-May.

Toadflax   *Linaria canadensis* (L.) Dum.

Slender glabrous biennial or winter annual to 75 cm tall, with a rosette of prostrate stems to 10 cm long. Upper leaves alternate, linear; those on the prostrate stems opposite or nearly so, and wider. Flowers in one to several racemes. Corolla blue to purple or rarely white, with a spur at base, the spurs 5-9 mm long. Plants with corollas over 1 cm long excluding the spur are separated by some as *L. texana* Scheele. Others treat these as a variety. Common. In fields especially, roadsides, waste places; Fla into e Tex, e SD, se Minn, sw Que, and NS; Cal to BC and scattered localities. Mar-May.

L. floridana Chapm. has smaller flowers, the spur is under 1 mm long; and plants are only to 40 cm tall. Occasional. Dry sandy places in open or thin woods; Fla into s Miss; se Ga. Mar-Apr.

Verbascum thapsus × 2/5

Datura stramonium × 1/3

Verbascum blattaria × 1/2

Linaria canadensis × 1½

Turtlehead; Snakehead   *Chelone glabra* L.

Members of this genus are perennials with opposite leaves, flowers in spike-like racemes, calyx lobes longer than the tube, a tubular corolla, and densely hairy anthers.

   This species is a perennial to 1.6 m tall. Leaves mostly widest at or near the middle, acuminate, serrate, and with an acute base. Petioles 2–10 mm long, or less. Flowers in a dense cluster. Petals white or pink to rose-purple toward the tip. Pollen-bearing stamens 4, the sterile filament green. Common. Stream banks, wet woods, moist pastures, other moist habitats; sw Ga into nw Mo, Minn, s Ont, Nfld, and c coast of SC. Aug-Oct. *C. montana* (Raf.) Penn. & Wherry; *C. chlorantha* Penn. & Wherry.

Turtlehead; Snakehead   *Chelone obliqua* L.

Perennial to 1 m tall. Leaves widest mostly at or near the middle, serrate, and with an acute base. Petioles slender, 5–15 mm long. Flowers in a dense cluster. Corolla purple. Sterile filament white. Occasional. Stream banks, wet woods, swampy meadows, margin of springs; sw Ga into n Miss, e Mo, s Minn, c Ind, and e Tenn; e SC and sw NC; se NC into c and e Md. Sept-Oct.

   C. cuthbertii Small is similar but the leaves are sessile and widest toward the base. Sterile filament purple. Occasional. Swampy woods, bogs, wet meadows; mts of NC; se Va. In *C. lyonii* Pursh the leaves are ovate, rounded at their bases and the petioles 1.5–6 cm long. Rare. Rich woods in mts; nw SC into w NC, e Tenn, and sw Va; Conn into Mass. July-Sept.

Beard-tongue   *Penstemon australis* Small

Members of this genus are opposite-leaved perennials with 4 fertile stamens and a prominent bearded one (staminode). Basal leaves in a rosette and shaped differently from the cauline ones. A genus of about 300 species, perhaps 20 being found in the Southeast. Identification to species is often difficult.

   In this species the axis of the inflorescence, midculm blades, and stems are finely hairy. Staminode golden and projecting beyond the corolla tube. Corolla 20–24 mm long and to 6 mm wide. Common. Dry pinelands, thin upland woods, sandhills, dry fallow fields; Fla into s and ce Ala, SC, and se Va. Apr-July.

   In *P. smallii* Heller the axis of the inflorescence is also hairy but the leaves just below the inflorescence are broader and bigger, at least two-thirds as large as the midcauline leaves. Occasional. Woods, cliffs, roadbanks, usually shaded; nw SC into ce and ne Tenn; nw Ga. Apr-June.

Beard-tongue   *Penstemon canescens* Britt.

Plants erect, to 80 cm tall. The axis of the inflorescence, midculm blades, and stems of this species are also finely hairy, but the staminode is yellow and does not project outside the corolla tube. Corolla violet purple to pinkish, 25–32 mm long, and over 6 mm wide at the widest section. Common. Thin woods, rocky places, dry sandy soils, fallow fields, roadsides; nw SC into ne Ala, ne Tenn, se Ind, s WVa, c Pa, and cn Va. Apr-July. *P. brittonorum* Penn.

   P. dissectus Ell. is unique in having finely dissected cauline leaves. The basal ones are entire or merely few-toothed. Rare. Gravelly soil and thin soil on rocks; c and ne C.P. of Ga. Apr-May. *P. multiflorus* Chapm. is unique among southeastern species in having each anther sac opening by a short slit in the end attached to the filament. Fla into c C.P. of Ga. May-July.

Chelone glabra × 1

Chelone obliqua × 1/3

Penstemon australis × 1/3

Penstemon canescens × 1/2

Beard-tongue   *Penstemon laevigatus* Ait.

Plants erect, to 1 m tall. Leaves entire. Axis of inflorescence glabrous or with glandular hairs that are separated by more than their lengths. Sepals 3–6 mm long, ovate-lanceolate. Corolla 15–22 mm long, at first nearly white, later purplish. Anthers brown, staminode yellow. Common. Thin woods or in open, usually moist places, meadows, along streams, cedar barrens; ne Fla into ce Miss, ne Tenn, s Pa, s NJ, and SC. May-June. *P. pentstemon* (L.) MacM.

P. *calycosus* Small is similar but the leaves are serrated. Sepals are 5–12 mm long and linear-attenuate. Occasional. Thin woods, meadows, thin soil on limestone, stream banks; nw SC into n Ala, e Tenn, cw and ne Ill, sw O, c Ky, and w edge NC; scattered localities from se Pa into se and w NY, ne O, s Mich, and Me. *P. tubaeflorus* Nutt. is peculiar in having microscopic glandular hairs over the inner surface of the corolla tube. Occasional. Open woods, fallow fields, prairies; ce Miss into e Tex, ce Neb, and s Ont; e Pa into Me and Mass.

Monkey-flower   *Mimulus ringens* L.

Erect glabrous perennial to 1.3 m tall. Stems 4-angled. Leaves opposite, serrate, and sessile or clasping, the blades lanceolate to ovate lanceolate. Flowers solitary from leaf axils, calyx lobes 5, 3–5 mm long, shorter than the tube. Corolla strongly irregular. Stamens 4. Common. Marshes, edge of ponds and slow-moving streams, and other wet places in partial shade or open; c Ala into c Okla, sw Man, James Bay in Ont, NB, NS, and ce NC. June-Sept.

M. *alatus* Ait. is similar but the leaves petioled, calyx lobes under 2 mm long, and fruiting pedicels under 2 cm long. Common. Similar habitats; cn Fla into e Tex, ce Kan, cn NY, Conn, and SC. July-Oct.

Creeping Gratiola   *Gratiola ramosa* Walt.

Members of this genus have opposite leaves, 5 nearly equal sepals with usually 2 small bracts below, and 2 pollen-bearing stamens, the 2 sterile stamens absent or minute.

This species is a slender perennial to 35 cm tall from branching rootstocks, often forming conspicuous colonies. Leaves glabrous or minutely glandular, linear-lanceolate, 1–2 mm wide. Flowers solitary in leaf axils. Sepals 5, 3–8 mm long, sometimes with 1 or 2 bracts just below. Pollen-bearing stamens 2, small, on inside of the corolla tube. Common. Moist to wet places, pinelands, swamps, edge of quiet water, ditches; Fla into e Tex, se Okla, c C.P. of Ga, se SC, and se NC. Apr-Aug.

All plants with sepals 5–7 mm long and 1–2 sepal-like bracts just below are considered by some to be a separate species, *G. brevifolia* Raf. Mostly west part of range east to n Fla and s Ga; nw Ga into ne Ala and adj Tenn. Apr-Aug.

Florida Gratiola   *Gratiola floridana* Nutt.

A perennial to 40 cm tall from slender whitish rhizomes. All flowers axillary and solitary, on pedicels 20–45 mm long. Easily recognized because of its relatively large flowers. Corolla 15–20 mm long, later ones sometimes smaller, lobes white or the lower one yellowish. Corollas of other species are 6–15 mm long. Rare. Wet places in open or in woods, edges of streams, depressions, swamps; nw Fla into nw Ala, se Tenn, and c Ga. Mar-July.

G. *aurea* Pursh is also easy to recognize. The corollas are golden yellow and 10–15 mm long. Leaves are intermediate in width between those of G. *ramosa* and G. *neglecta*. Rare; n Fla into se NC; w to s Ala; also Nfld s to ne Va and scattered w into ne Ill and e Wisc. May-Sept.

Penstemon laevigatus × 3/4

Mimulus ringens × 3/4

Gratiola ramosa × 1⅓

Gratiola floridana × 3/5

Gratiola

Gratiola neglecta Torr.

Annual to 40 cm tall. Stems minutely glandular hairy. Leaves linear to elliptic, 2–12 mm wide. Flowers solitary in leaf axils, the pedicels slender, 10–30 mm long. Corolla 8–10 mm long, lobes white, the tube yellowish and with fine dark lines. Occasional. Moist to wet places in open or woods, depressions, edges of ponds and lakes; n Ga into e Tex, e Kan, ND, BC, se Que, c Me, and NC. Apr-May.

G. *virginiana* L. is similar but the pedicels are stout and usually 1–5 mm long, single pedicels rarely to 10 mm long; stem usually glabrous. Common. Fla into e Tex, c Kan, nw Ind, c WVa, se into c Va, and NJ. Mar-May. In *G. viscidula* Penn. the mature fruits are 2–2.5 mm in diameter and the plants are perennial. Occasional. NC into Pied. of Ga and w of Appalachian Mts. to s O, and e of them to Del. June-frost.

Blue Water-hyssop

Bacopa caroliniana (Walt.) Robins.

Creeping or floating perennial to 30 cm tall. Lemon-scented when crushed. Young stems hairy. Leaves opposite, ovate to broadly elliptic, with 3–7 palmate veins. Flowers solitary from leaf axils, on short pedicels bearing 2 small bracts below the sepals. Corolla bell-shaped, 9–11 mm long, the lobes slightly different in shape and size. Stamens 4. Common. Shallow water and moist edges of ponds, streams, and marshes; ditches; Fla into se Tex, C.P. of Ga, and se Va. Apr-Oct. *Hydrotrida caroliniana* (Walt.) Small.

B. *rotundifolia* (Michx.) Wettst. is similar vegetatively but not lemon-scented, the pedicels bractless and 2–3 times longer than the calyx, the corolla white and only 6–8 mm long. Occasional. Shallow water of ponds and pools; sw Miss into se and c Tex, c Mont, se ND, and s Ind. May-Nov. *Macuillamia rotundifolia* (Michx.) Raf.

Smooth Water-hyssop

Bacopa monnieri (L.) Penn.

Glabrous and not lemon-scented. Stems prostrate, decumbent, or ascending to 30 cm; often forming mats. Leaves opposite, spatulate to cuneate-obovate, with one vein. Pedicels, at least in fruit, exceeding leaves. Sepals unequal. Corolla bell-shaped, white to light purple, the lobes slightly unequal. Stamens 4, small. Occasional. Margins of streams, ponds, ditches, and fresh or brackish marshes; often on sandy soils; Fla into s Miss, e and s Tex; also s Ga and along the coast into se Va. Apr-Nov. *Bramia monnieri* (L.) Penn.

B. *cyclophylla* Fern. has a similar growth form but the stems are finely hairy, pedicels shorter than the leaves, petals white, and there are only 2 stamens. Rare. Drainage ditches, muddy banks, marshes; cn Fla and southward, northeast along the coast into se NC. June-Nov. *Herpestis rotundifolia* C. F. Gaertn.

Amphianthus

Amphianthus pusillus Torr.

This diminutive annual is an amazing plant, being restricted to shallow flat-bottomed pools in granitic rocks. In November or December rooted seedlings can be seen under the water, forming small rosettes of leaves. In late winter when the water warms slightly a slender scape arises to the water surface, supported by two floating leaves. The first flowers, 6–8 mm long, are borne above the water between these two leaves. Soon flowers which do not open but bear seeds form at the rosette. The seeds from both types of flowers rest in the dry thin soil, withstanding summer temperatures often unbearable to the bare skin. Sometimes a wet fall season combined with a delayed freeze may allow plants to complete a life cycle before winter. Rare. Shallow pools on granitic rocks; Pied. of Ga; cn SC; cw Ala. Jan-May.

Gratiola neglecta × 1

Bacopa caroliniana × 1½

Amphianthus pusillus × 1

Bacopa monnieri × 1¼

False Pimpernel *Lindernia monticola* Nutt.

Members of this genus have opposite leaves, single flowers in upper leaf axils, no bracts below the 5-lobed calyx, 4 stamens of which 2 are sterile, and 2 separate stigmas.

This species is a perennial to 30 cm tall; with a basal rosette of leaves, cauline leaves usually small, the upper ones bract-size. Stem strongly angled and glabrous. Fruits 3–5 mm long. Seeds as wide as long. Occasional, common locally. Shallow soil at margins of granitic and sandstone outcroppings, moist pinelands, swamp margins; ne Fla into ce and ne Ala, Pied. of Ga, and se SC; nw SC into nw NC; c NC. Mar-June, sporadically until freezing. *Ilysanthes monticola* (Nutt.) Benth.

L. saxicola M. A. Curtis is rarely over 10 cm tall, upper leaves slightly smaller than those of the rosette, and fruits only 1–2 mm long. Rare. On rocks in Hiawassee and Tallulah Rivers; ne Ga and sw NC. July-Sept.

False Pimpernel *Lindernia anagallidea* (Michx.) Penn.

An annual to 35 cm tall, much branched near the base. Stems slender, 4-angled. Leaves generally widest near the base. Flowers on peduncles longer than the leaves. Corolla white to pale purple, 6–9 mm long, the lobes expanding. Fruits 25–35 mm long. Seeds distinctly longer than wide. Occasional. Margins of ponds, lakes, and slow-moving streams; depressions; marshes; usually in open; Fla into c Tex, cn SD, se ND, Ind, Md, and s NH but absent from Appalachian Mts; Cal into Wash. June-Oct. *Ilysanthes inequalis* (Walt.) Penn.

L. dubia (L.) Penn. has conspicuously larger leaves, the stems are thicker, pedicels mostly shorter than the leaves, flowers often not opening, fruits 4–6 mm long. Common. Swamps; marshes; ditches; margins of ponds, lakes, and streams; in woods or open; nw Fla into se Tex, se Neb, ce ND, s Que, and NS. May-frost. *Ilysanthes dubia* (L.) Barnh.

Bird's-eye Speedwell *Veronica persica* Poir.

In members of this genus the flowers are solitary in the axils of alternate leaves or bracts, the other leaves being opposite. Sepals 4. Corollas small, being 2 to 12 mm broad, the lobes nearly alike. Stamens 2.

This species is a decumbent annual; the stems bear scattered glandless hairs. Leaves wider than long. Flowers in the axils of leaves which are the same size as those without flowers. Corolla 7–12 mm broad. Fruits hairy, strongly flattened, and on pedicels longer than the leaves. Occasional. Fencerows, fields, lawns, waste places; Fla into Cal, s Alas, Man, and Nfld. Feb-Aug.

V. hederaefolia L. is similar vegetatively but the leaves are longer than wide, the corolla only 2–2.5 mm broad, and the fruit is glabrous. Rare. Similar habitats; c SC into e Tenn, e WVa, e O, s NY, and ne NC. Mar-May.

Gerardia; False-foxglove *Agalinis fasciculata* (Ell.) Raf.

About 30 species of this genus occur in the Southeast. They have opposite filiform to linear leaves, often with leaf clusters in the axils; 5 sepals, the lobes alike and shorter than the tube; a pink to purple, or rarely white, corolla with a bell-shaped tube and nearly equal lobes, the lower lobe being on the outside when in bud; and 4 stamens in 2 unequal pairs. Identification of most species is difficult. About half are entirely or essentially confined to the C.P.

This species is an annual to 120 cm tall, has prominent clusters of leaves in axils of the main leaves, stems finely rough to touch, and pedicels shorter than the calyx. Corollas are 20–35 cm long. Plants usually blacken in drying. Common. Fields, thin pinelands, savannahs, usually in sandy soils; Fla into c Tex, sw Mo, c Ala, C.P. of SC, and ce NC. Aug-Oct. *Gerardia fasciculata* Ell.

Lindernia monticola × 3/5

Lindernia anagallidea × 1/2

Veronica persica × 1½

Agalinis fasciculata × 1

Gerardia; False-foxglove   *Agalinis tenuifolia* (Vahl.) Raf.

Annual to 80 cm tall. Stems slender and smooth. Upper leaves narrow, to 1 mm wide. Pedicels longer than the calyx, usually longer than entire flower. Corolla tube at inner base of two upper lobes glabrous, upper lobe arching forward over the stamens and sometimes nearly closing the throat. Capsule globose, 3–5 mm long. Seeds dark. Common. Thin woods or in open, slopes, sandhills, fallow fields, prairies; nw Fla into e Tex, c Wyo, se Man, c Mich, s Que, and s Me. Aug-Oct. *Gerardia tenuifolia* Vahl.

    A. setacea (Walt.) Raf. is similar but averaging smaller; upper leaves quite narrow, about ⅓ mm wide; and all corolla lobes spreading, with long hairs at the inner base of the two upper lobes. Occasional. Dry sandy pinelands, poor upland soils, thin woods, or in open; ce Ala into ne Fla, SC, and se NY. Sept-Oct. *Gerardia setacea* (Walt.) J. F. Gmelin.

Gerardia; False-foxglove   *Agalinis purpurea* (L.) Penn.

This annual is the most abundant species of the genus in the Southeast. It is abundantly branched in the upper part, the branches spreading widely. Stems are glabrous or faintly roughened, the main leaves linear, leaf clusters in the axils inconspicuous or absent, pedicels shorter than the calyx, corolla hairy within and 15–23 mm long, fruit globose to globose-ovoid, and seeds dark brown to blackish. Common. Thin woods, low open areas, upland sands, fallow fields; Fla into e Tex, Ark, ce Minn, s Pa, and e Mass. Aug-frost. *Gerardia purpurea* L.

    A. maritima (Raf.) Raf. is peculiar among all species of the genus in that it grows in salt marshes. Plants slightly succulent and glabrous, pedicels shorter than the flowers, and leaf tips and calyx lobes obtuse. Rare. Sea coasts Tex into Fla and NS. June-Sept. *Gerardia maritima* Raf.

Hairy False-foxglove   *Aureolaria pectinata* (Nutt.) Penn.

Members of this genus have opposite leaves; 5 calyx lobes; yellow corollas 3 cm or more long, the lobes spreading and nearly equal; and 4 fertile stamens, the anthers hairy and awned at the base.

    This species is a much branched densely glandular hairy annual to 1 m tall, leaves deeply dissected, and the calyx lobes toothed. Common. Dry places, thin woods, sandhills, open places; Fla into se Tex, La, s Mo, s Ky, Ga, cs Va, and ce NC. May-Oct. *Gerardia pectinata* (Nutt.) Benth.

    A. pedicularia (L.) Raf. is similar but the upper parts of the plant are almost glabrous, the lower part of the stem being glandular hairy. Occasional. Similar habitats; ne Ga into se Ky, NY, ne Ill, ce Minn, Mass, and s Me. July-Oct. *Gerardia pedicularia* L.

Downy False-foxglove   *Aureolaria virginica* (L.) Penn.

Perennial to 1.5 m tall; stems finely hairy, little branched. Lower leaves with one or two pairs of large lobes near base of blade, upper leaves smaller and less lobed, the uppermost often entire. Fruits finely but densely hairy. Common. Thin woods, usually in dry places; ne Fla into se Ala, Ind, c Mich, s NH, and Mass. May-Sept. *Gerardia virginica* (L.) B.S.P.

    A. laevigata (Raf.) Raf. is similar but the fruits glabrous, stems usually glabrous, and leaves lanceolate and rarely lobed. Occasional. Thin to rich woods; n Ga into s O, c Pa, and c Md. July-Sept. *Gerardia laevigata* Raf. In *A. flava* (L.) Farw. the fruits are also glabrous but the leaves are elliptic-ovate, the lower ones being deeply lobed or cut along their entire margins. Common. Open woods, dry pinelands; Fla into se Tex, cs Mo, se Wisc, and sw Me. Aug-Sept. *Gerardia flava* L.

Agalinis tenuifolia × 3/5

Agalinis purpurea × 1/2

Aureolaria pectinata × 3/5

Aureolaria virginica × 3/5

Blue-hearts   *Buchnera floridana* Gand.

Perennial to 80 cm tall, rarely branched, from a small rootstock, probably root-parasitic, and turning very dark in drying. Leaves 3-veined and opposite, or the uppermost alternate. Corolla purple or white, the lobes less than 5 mm long. Flowers in gradually elongating spikes up to 15 cm long. Fruits many-seeded. Some verbenas are similar but their fruits consist of 4 readily separable nutlets. Common. Open areas, or thin woods, usually moist places; Fla into e NC, s Ga, and s Tex. Apr-Oct.

   B. americana L. is similar except the lower leaves are not 3-veined and the flowers usually larger. Occasional. Dry to wet places in open, or thin woods; Fla into e Tex, c Mo, s Mich, s Ont, w NY, and NJ. May to frost.

Indian Paint-brush   *Castilleja coccinea* (L.) Spreng.

Hairy, usually biennial, rarely an annual, to 70 cm tall, with one unbranched stem from a basal rosette of leaves. Stem leaves varied, from entire to more commonly 3–5 cleft. Flowers in the axils of scarlet, or rarely yellow, leaf-like bracts. Corollas yellow to greenish-yellow. Occasional. In thin woods, around rock ledges and cliffs, meadows; nw Fla into n La, e Okla, Mo, se Man, and s NH. Apr-July.

   There are perhaps 200 species of Castilleja but this is the only one occurring in the southeastern United States.

Cow-wheat   *Melampyrum lineare* Desr.

An erect annual to 50 cm tall, usually branched in the upper half, the stems finely hairy. Leaves opposite. Flowers 1 per leaf axil. Calyx with 4 lobes. Corolla 2-lipped. Stamens 4. Seeds 1–4. Fruit an asymmetrical capsule. Occasional. Woods, bogs, open places, peaty soils; nw SC into cn Ga, e edge of Tenn, w NC, Pa, ne O, ne Ill, Man, BC, Lab, and NS. May-July.

Lousewort; Fernleaf   *Pedicularis canadensis* L.

Members of this genus are perennials with pinnately-lobed leaves. Sepals are strongly unequal and united. The corolla is extremely irregular, the lower lobes outermost in the bud. Stamens 4, anthers glabrous, the two pollen sacs equal and parallel. Fruit an asymmetrical flattened capsule. Seeds numerous.

   This species has hairy stems with alternate leaves. Corollas of various combinations of yellow, red, rusty red, and purplish. Common. Rich woods and soils, in open, usually well drained; Fla into e Tex, cs Man, Wisc, s Ont, c Que, and c Me. Mar-May.

   P. lanceolata Michx. has a similar inflorescence and leaves, but the stem is glabrous and the stem leaves are opposite. Occasional. Moist open places, often in calcareous areas; sw NC into ce WVa, ce Va, Pa, cs Mo, Ill, se Man, Wisc, s Ont, and Mass; e half of Neb. Aug-Oct.

Castilleja coccinea × 1/2

Buchnera floridana × 1

Melampyrum lineare × 1

Pedicularis canadensis × 3/5

Squaw-root   *Conopholis americana* (L.) Wallr.

Parasitic on the roots of several kinds of trees, mostly oaks and beeches. Usually several stems in a tight cluster. As the plants grow older they become darker and often blend with the surrounding leaves. Occasional. In various types of woods; Fla into n Ala, Wisc, and NS. Mar-June.

A related species, *Epifagus virginiana* (L.) Bart., Beech-drops, is parasitic on beech trees. The stems are slim and usually branched. The flowers are mostly separated from each other, often by 1 cm or more. Occasional. Fla into e Tex, Wisc, and NS. Sept-Nov.

Cancer-root   *Orobanche uniflora* L.

These nongreen plants are parasitic on roots of various kinds of plants. Stems are underground or nearly so with a few overlapping scales and 1 to few erect finely hairy bractless pedicels to 16 cm tall. There is, therefore, 1 flower per stalk. Corollas are 12–20 mm long, white to yellowish, sometimes tinged with light purple. They wither with age but persist, capping the capsule. Rare. Rich woods; c Fla into Cal, BC, Yukon, and Nfld. Apr-May.

In *O. minor* Smith the flowers are sessile and several on a prominent spike. Corollas shorter, 10–15 mm long. Very rare. Parasite on clover, tobacco, and other crops; c NC; Va into NS.

LENTIBULARIACEAE: Bladderwort Family

Yellow Butterwort   *Pinguicula lutea* Walt.

Perennial to 50 cm tall. Leaves broad, 1–6 cm long, succulent, in a basal rosette. Flowering stems 1 to 8. Corolla, including spur, 20–35 mm long. All species of *Pinguicula* bear short glandular hairs, their leaves are clammy and sticky, trapping small insects, and thus are carnivorous. Common. Moist places, thin pinelands, savannahs; se La into Fla, C.P. of Ga, and se NC. Feb-May.

Violet Butterwort   *Pinguicula caerulea* Walt.

Perennial to 30 cm tall. Leaves mostly ovate, 1–6 cm long, succulent, in a basal rosette. Flowering stems 1–6, with long nonglandular hairs, at least in lower parts. Corolla, including spur, 25–40 mm long, light violet-blue with darker veining. Common. Moist places, sandy and peaty soils, pinelands, savannahs; cn and s Fla into sw Ga, and se NC. Feb-May.

In *P. primuliflora* Wood & Godfrey the flowering stems are glabrous, leaves oblong, to 9 cm long; the flowers 20–26 mm long, violet to almost white with a yellow and sometimes brown-veined spur. Rare. Under woody vegetation in wet situations, often at edge of running water; nw Fla into se Miss, se Ala, and sw Ga. Feb-Apr.

Conopholis
americana × 1/3

Orobanche uniflora × 3/5

Pinguicula caerulea × 1

Pinguicula lutea × 3/4

Dwarf Butterwort   *Pinguicula pumila* Michx.

Perennial to 18 cm tall. Leaves broad, 1–2 cm long, succulent, in a basal rosette. Flowering stems 1 to 10. Corolla, including spur, less than 20 mm long, almost white to lavender, pink, or light yellow. Occasional. Moist places, sandy soil, pinelands and savannahs; se NC into cs Ga, Fla, and se Tex; c La. Feb-May.

   P. planifolia Chapm. differs from other species by having narrow and deeply cleft corolla lobes. Corolla violet, 10–20 cm long including the spur. Rare. Pond margins, ditches, other moist places; cn Fla into coastal Miss. Mar-Apr.

Horned Bladderwort   *Utricularia juncea* Vahl.

Flowers of this genus are on erect leafless stems. Leaves dissected or forked into filiform segments and on stems underwater, or at the surface of wet soil or muck, in which case they may be small and even simple. They bear bladders, or traps (see picture), that catch small aquatic life which provides food. Petals united, irregular, and usually yellow. There are two pairs of stamens.

   Plants to 45 cm tall. Leaves quite small, little dissected or simple, with only a few small bladders, and at the surface of the soil or muck in which the plant grows. Bracts at the base of pedicels attached at their bases. Lower flower not reaching basal end of the pedicel of the one above. Corolla, including the spur, 6–15 mm long. Occasional. Wet sand, peat, or mud; Fla into se Tex, se Ark, C.P. of Ga, and se NY. July-Sept. *Stomoisia juncea* (Vahl.) Barnh.

   U. cornuta Michx. is quite similar but the lower flower reaches above the base of the one above and the corolla including spur is over 15 mm long. Occasional. Similar habitats; Fla into s Tex, cn SC, e WVa, ne Ill, e Minn, and e Nfld. Apr-Sept. *Stomoisia cornuta* (Michx.) Raf.

Floating Bladderwort   *Utricularia inflata* Walt.

Besides finely dissected leaves, this species has some partially swollen floating, radiating leaves over 5 cm long. Corolla about 2 cm broad. Occasional. Ponds, lakes, pools, sluggish waters; Fla into e Tex, C.P. of Ga into NC, and s NJ. Feb-Nov.

   U. radiata Small is quite similar but the radiating leaves are under 5 cm long and the corolla about 15 mm broad. Occasional. Similar habitats; Fla into e Tex, C.P. of Ga into NC, and NS; nw Ind. Feb-Nov. *U. inflata* var. *minor* (L.) Chapm.

Pinguicula pumila × 1

Utricularia juncea × 1

Utricularia inflata × 1/3

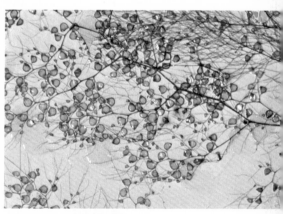

Utricularia inflata × 2

Purple Bladderwort   *Utricularia purpurea* Walt.

Flowering stems to 15 cm tall from long immersed stems with whorled finely dissected leaves, some with bladders at the tips. Corolla purple to deep pink, 10–13 mm broad. Rare. Ponds, lakes, pools; Fla into se Tex, s Ga, e NC, Mass, n Ind, s Mich, e Minn, and NS. Apr-Sept. *Vesiculina purpurea* (Walt.) Raf.

The Dwarf Bladderwort, *U. olivacea* Griseb. is delicate, the flowering stem under 1 cm tall and bearing one flower about 2 mm long. Petals yellowish but almost white. Leaves alternate, usually of only one segment, and one bladder. Fruit reported to have only one seed. Plants are easily overlooked and may be more common than records indicate. Very rare. In mats floating on water, frequently among the leaves of other Bladderwort species; Fla into s Ga and se NC. Sept-Oct; Mar. *Biovularia olivacea* (Wright) Kam.

Two-flowered Bladderwort   *Utricularia biflora* Lam.

Flowering stems to 15 cm tall from leafy stems creeping on the surface of wet soil or in mats on water. Bracts at base of pedicel fastened at their bases. Leaves alternate, with 3 or more segments bearing bladders. Corolla lip 8–10 mm long, spur about as long. Capsule 3.5–4 mm wide. Occasional. Shallow water, wet margins; Fla into se Tex, La, se Okla, nw Ga, C.P. of SC, and se Mass. Apr-Oct.

Similar species are: *U. gibba* L. with spur stubby and much shorter than the lower lip. Capsule only 2–3 mm wide. Rare. Fla into Tex, Minn, and NS; also Pacific states. Mar-Oct. In *U. subulata* L. the bract at base of pedicel is peltate. Common. Fla into e Tex, Tenn, sw NC, se Va, and w NS. Mar-Oct. In *U. fibrosa* Walt. the plants are larger, to 35 cm tall, and flowers to 25 mm long. Occasional. Fla into e Tex, se Okla, C.P. of Ga, NJ, and se Mass. Mar-Nov.

ACANTHACEAE: Acanthus Family

Dyschoriste   *Dyschoriste oblongifolia* (Michx.) O. Ktze.

A dull-green perennial to 50 cm tall. Leaves opposite. Calyx lobes slender, alike, less than half as long as the corolla. Petals united, slightly irregular, narrow part of the tube shorter than the wider part. Stamens 4, anther sacs sharp pointed at the base. Ovulary superior, carpels 2, seeds 1 per carpel and borne on a hooked projection. Occasional. Sandhills, dry pinelands, occasionally in pine flatwoods; Fla into C.P. of Ga and adj SC. Apr-Aug.

D. humistrata (Michx.) O. Ktze. is the only other species of this genus in our area. The corolla is shorter, under 12 mm long and about as long as the calyx. Rare. Woods in low places; c and cn Fla into ne C.P. of Ga, and vic Charleston, SC. Apr-June.

Ruellia   *Ruellia caroliniensis* (Walt.) Steud.

A perennial to 80 cm tall with petioled opposite entire leaves. Flowers in sessile axillary clusters, usually only 1 or 2 being open on any given day. Calyx lobes linear, alike, less than 2 mm wide. Corolla light purple, 25–50 cm long, the lobes as a unit not quite at right angles to the slender corolla tube. Seeds borne on hooked projections. Quite variable and several varieties have been named. Common. Open woods, usually in dry upland soils; Fla into e Tex, s Ill, c WVa, and NS. Apr-Sept.

R. ciliosa Pursh is similar but dwarf, only to 15 cm tall and often forming a rosette. Rare. Sandy soils, open woods; Fla into se La, c Ala, C.P. of Ga, and cn SC. Apr-Sept. *R. humilis* is also similar but leaves are sessile or nearly so, and stems are often branched. Occasional. Dry woods; c NC into WVa, nw Ga, e Tex, e Neb, s Mich, and cs Pa. June-Sept.

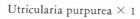
Utricularia purpurea × 1

Utricularia biflora × 2/5

Dyschoriste oblongifolia × 2/3

Ruellia caroliniensis × 1/2

Water-willow   *Justicia americana* (L.) Vahl.

Perennial to 1 m tall from a coarse rhizome. Leaves opposite, shaped like those of the black willow tree. Flowers in dense axillary long-peduncled spikes. Corolla united, 2-lipped, upper lip 2-notched, lower one 3-lobed and about as long as the tube. Stamens 2, anther sacs of each separated. Fruit a club-shaped capsule, smooth, mostly 4-seeded, 15–20 mm long. Occasional. In and edge of streams and occasionally lakes, often in rocky or sandy places; Pied. of Ga into e Tex, ce Kan, Wisc, sw Que, nw Vt, and ne NC. June-Oct. *Dianthera americana* L.

J. ovata (Walt.) Lindau is slender, to 50 cm tall, from slender rhizomes. Leaves in 5–8 pairs, ovate to elliptic or oblanceolate. Flowers in loose axillary spikes. Corolla similar to that of the above species but thinner. Capsule about 1 cm long. Occasional. Wooded bottomlands and swamps, pond and stream margins, occasionally in marshes; Fla into La, se Mo, s Ill, w Tenn, s Miss, C.P. of Ga, and se Va. May-July.

RUBIACEAE: Madder Family

Bluets   *Hedyotis crassifolia* Raf.

Members of this family have opposite or whorled entire leaves with stipules between them on the stem. Flowers regular, petals united, ovulary wholly or partly inferior.

Erect annual to 10 cm tall. Leaves mostly near the base. Corolla violet to deep purple with a reddish eye, the tube 2–5 mm long. Capsule 4–5 mm wide. Common. Open woods, fields, pastures, usually in dry places; Fla into e Tex, cs Mo, s Ill, Pied. of Ga, and se Va. Feb-Apr. *Houstonia pusilla* Schoepf; *H. patens* Ell.

Hedyotis caerulea (L.) T. & G. is a perennial, to 20 cm tall. Corolla light blue to light purple and with a yellow eye, the tube 5–10 mm long. Capsule 2.0–3.5 mm broad. Common. Open deciduous woods, fields, pastures, wet or dry places. Mar-May. *Houstonia caerulea* L. In *Hedyotis michauxii* Fosb. stems are creeping, the tips and some branches erect and each bearing a flower. Occasional. Margins of streams, wet slopes, other moist places; nw SC into ne Ala, sw Pa, and mts of Va. Mar-June. *Houstonia serpyllifolia* Michx.

Summer Bluet   *Hedyotis purpurea* (L.) T. & G.

Erect perennial to 40 cm tall. Stems 1 to many from a common base. Stem leaves ovate to ovate-lanceolate. Flowers several to many in terminal clusters or from upper leaf axils. Petals white to light or reddish purple. Common. Deciduous woods, rocky places, roadsides; sw Ga into se Tex, La, e Okla, s Ill, sw Pa, s NJ, and cs SC. Apr-July. *Houstonia purpurea* L.

Other species with similar flowers but narrower leaves include: *He. canadensis* (R. & S.) Fosb., the only species with basal leaves ciliate and present at flowering time. Rare. Rocky woods on slopes; nw Ga into n Ala, c Ky, e O, s Ont, and NY. Apr-May. *He. nigricans* (Lam.) Fosb. (*Ho. angustifolia* Michx.) with the middle and upper stipules finely tipped. Common. Dry, usually open places; s and cn Fla into Ariz, e Neb, and s Mich. May-July. In *He. longifolia* (Jackson) Hook. (*Ho. tenuifolia* Nutt.) the stipules are rounded or deltoid. Common. Dry, usually open places; n Fla into e Okla, n Ill, se Sask, and Me. May-July.

Hedyotis crassifolia × 4/5

Hedyotis purpurea × 1

Buttonweed
Diodia virginiana L.

Prostrate, ascending, or erect branching perennial. Stems nearly glabrous to quite hairy. Leaves opposite, blades at base narrowed to nearly cordate, stipules membranous at base, the tip consisting of 3–5 linear projections. Flowers 1, or rarely 2, per leaf axil, sessile. Sepals 2, persistent. Ovulary inferior. Stigmas 2, filiform. Carpels 2, each 1-seeded. Common. Moist places, usually in open; Fla into e Tex, s Mo, WVa, and s NJ. June-frost. *D. tetragona* Walt.

Plants with quite hairy stems are considered by some to be a separate species, *D. hirsuta* Pursh. Rare. Moist places; Fla into se Ala, s Ga, and se NC. *D. teres* Walt. is an erect to spreading hairy annual. Leaves linear- to elliptic-lanceolate. Stipules with about 5 filiform projections. Sepals 4, persistent. Stigma shallowly 2-lobed. Dry open areas, fields, waste places, especially in sandy soils; Fla into cs Tex, c Kan, s Mich, se Pa, and Conn. June-frost.

Mexican-clover
Richardia scabra L.

Weedy annual with branching and spreading often decumbent stems. Leaves opposite, nearly glabrous but outer parts and lower midrib rough to the touch, with bristle-bearing stipules between the petiole bases. Flowers and fruits sessile in dense terminal clusters. Corolla tubular, with 6 lobes, white, 5–6 mm long. Ovulary inferior. Fruit covered with small tubercles, separating into 4 indehiscent 1-seeded units. Common. Open places, fields, roadsides, waste places; Fla into e half of Tex, s Ark, c Ga, and se Va; rarely in Pied. of Ga into NC. June-frost.

R. brasiliensis (Moq.) Gomes is similar but the leaves are appressed hairy on both surfaces and the fruits hairy. The roots are used in South America as an emetic. Occasional. Similar places. Fla into coastal Tex, C.P. of Ga, and se Va. Apr-frost.

Field Madder
Sherardia arvensis L.

Much branched annual, often forming dense masses. Leaves 5–15 mm long, in whorls of 4–6. Flowers in terminal heads surrounded by a whorl of leaves fused near their bases. Corolla with a tube about 3 mm long. Occasional. Fields, lawns, waste places; Ga into e Tex, sw Mo, Tenn, ne O, sw Que, and NS. Mar-Aug.

Some species of *Galium* are similar to Field Madder, but there are no fused leaves surrounding the flower clusters. Similar species include: *G. virgatum* Nutt. which has solitary flowers and bristly fruits. Occasional. Dry places; La into Tex, s Mo, sw Ill, and c Tenn. *G. tinctorium* L. which has smooth fruits, glabrous pedicels, and greenish white petals. Common. Wet places; Ga into c Tex, Neb, Minn, and Nfld.

CAMPANULACEAE: Bellflower Family

Bellflower
Campanula divaricata Michx.

Glabrous perennial with 1 to many spreading to drooping or erect stems from a root-stock. Leaves elliptic to lanceolate, serrate, tips usually acuminate, and bases acute. Flowers in a terminal, mostly drooping, open panicle. Corolla nearly white to blue or light purple, 6–9 mm long. Stamens 5, separate. Stigmas 3. Ovulary inferior. Fruit many-seeded, opening by basal pores. Common. Rocky woods, cliffs, unstable soil on steep slopes, ce Ga into c Ala, s and e WVa, w Md, and c NC, but not common in Pied. Aug-frost. *C. flexuosa* Michx.

C. americana L. is a biennial and otherwise quite different. Corolla 2–3 cm wide, the lobes wide-spreading. Style curved abruptly upward near the tip. The ovulary is inferior, but the fruit opens by pores near the top. Common. Rich deciduous woods; cn Fla into e Okla, se SD, s Ont, w NY, c C.P. of Va, and c NC. July-frost. *Campanulastrum americanum* (L.) Small.

Diodia virginiana × 1¼   Richardia scabra × 2/3

Sherardia arvensis × 1¼

Campanula divaricata × 1½

Venus' Looking-glass   *Triodanis perfoliata* (L.) Nieuw.

Erect annual to 1 m tall, but most often half that tall or less, simple or with a few branches, with fibrous roots. Stem leaves strongly clasping. Flowers sessile in leaf axils, those on the lower half of the stem not opening. Petals united, deep purple to pale lavender. Stamens 5, separate. Stigmas 3. Ovulary inferior. Fruit many-seeded, opening by 3 small elongate pores at or just below the middle. Common. Fields, waste places, gardens; Fla into s Tex, Mont, BC, s Minn, s Que, and s Me. Apr-July. *Specularia perfoliata* (L.) DC.

T. biflora (R. & P.) Greene is similar but the stem leaves are sessile to barely clasping and the opening in the fruit is near the top. Occasional. Similar habitats; cn Fla into Ariz, s Ill, se Tenn, nw Ga, Pied. of Ga, and se Va; also places in the western United States. Mar-June. *Specularia biflora* (R. & P.) Fisch. & Mey.

Purple Lobelia   *Lobelia elongata* Small

Glabrous perennial to 1.6 m tall, from horizontal basal shoots. Leaves narrowly lanceolate, tapering to both ends. Flowers 20–25 mm long. Calyx lobes entire. Corolla tube 8–14 mm long, with openings in the side. Inner base of lower corolla lip glabrous. Occasional. Marshes, bogs, swamp woods; se Ga into c and e NC and Del. July-frost.

L. glandulosa Walt. is similar but the inner base of the lower corolla lip is hairy. Common. Damp pinelands, savannahs, swamp forests, marshes; c and cn Fla into C.P. of Ga, nw NC, and se Va. Aug-Oct. *L. puberula* Michx., the most abundant of our large-flowered species, is also similar but has finely hairy stems, at least near the base. Fla into e Tex, e Okla, se Mo, s Ill, WVa, and s NJ. July-Oct.

Cardinal-flower   *Lobelia cardinalis* L.

The brilliant flowers allow this species to be recognized at considerable distances. As is true of all our species of *Lobelia*, the corolla is 2-lipped, the upper lip generally erect and the lower spreading and 3-cleft. The 5 anthers are united. This and other *Lobelia* species have been used medicinally but probably are best considered as poisonous. Overdoses of plants or extracts produce adverse symptoms and may cause death. Common. Moist to wet places; Fla into e Tex, se Kan, Minn, and NB. July-Oct.

Our other species have purple or lavender to blue or white corollas. Most are difficult to name. One species, *L. inflata* L., is easy to recognize when the fruits are fully grown. They are ovoid to subglobose, and on thin pedicels. Common. Open woods, fields, waste places; n Ga into e Okla, Minn, se Sask, Lab, and cn SC. July-frost.

Triodanis perfoliata × 1

Lobelia elongata × 1/3

Lobelia cardinalis × 2/3

Ironweed   *Vernonia flaccidifolia* Small

Members of this genus are erect perennials with prominent stem leaves, all flowers perfect, and with deep reddish-purple corollas, but no rays or receptacular bracts. The
pappus consists of an inner circle of long capillary bristles and outer circle of short
ones.

Plant 1–2.5 m tall, leaves narrowly to broadly lanceolate, only 16–26 flowers per head,
and pappus straw-colored. Rare. Upland deciduous woods, pastures, roadsides; ce and
ne Ala into nw Ga and adj. Tenn. June-Aug.

Other tall species with 30 or fewer flowers per head are: *V. gigantea* (Walt.) Trel.
(*V. altissima* Nutt.) which has a tan-brown and sometimes purple-tinged pappus. Common. Usually in low places, pastures, thin woods, roadsides; Fla into La, e Okla, se Neb,
sw Mich, e Pa, cw Va, sw NC, and sw SC. June-Oct. *V. angustifolia* Michx. which has
linear to broadly linear leaves and tawny-purplish pappus. Common. Sandy, well-
drained pinelands, sandy ridges and scrub; Fla into se Miss, c Ala, ce Ga, and se NC.
July-Aug. *V. pulchella* Small which grows only to 70 cm tall, has 20–36 flowers per
head. Rare. Sandy scrub and pinelands; se Ga into sw SC. July-Aug.

Ironweed   *Vernonia glauca* (L.) Willd.

This species grows to 1 m tall, has stem leaves only, 32–48 flowers per head, and a
straw colored pappus. Occasional. Well-drained soil of deciduous woods; ne Ga, cs Va,
e WVa, se Pa, and sw NJ; cw Ala. July-Aug.

Other species with 30–50 flowers per head are: *V. acaulis* (Walt.) Gl. which has
basal as well as cauline leaves. Occasional. Well-drained soils of thin woods or open,
roadsides; sw Ga into e Pied. of Ga, c and se NC, and se Ga. July. *V. noveboracensis*
(L.) Michx. which is 1–2 m tall and has a brownish-purple pappus. Common. Moist
places in open, fields, pastures, along streams; cn Fla into e Ala, se Ky, Pa, and e Mass
July-Sept.

Elephant's-foot   *Elephantopus tomentosus* L.

Perennial to 60 cm tall. Leaves basal, soft hairy beneath, over 7 cm wide. Flowers in
heads surrounded by 3 conspicuous bracts 10 mm or more long. Petals pink to purple,
rarely white. Common. Dry places, evergreen or deciduous woods; Fla into e Tex, se
Okla, se Ky, Ga, and cs and se Va. July-Oct.

Two other species are similar but leaves are narrower and bracts are 8 mm or less
long. In *E. nudatus* Gray the glandular hairs on the bracts are easily seen because other
hairs are scanty. Occasional. Thin woods or in open; Fla into se Tex, se Ark, C.P. of
Ga, and Del. In *E. elatus* Bert. the glands are mostly hidden by long and dense hairs.
Occasional. Dry pinelands; Fla into s Miss, s Ga, and se SC. *E. carolinianus* Raeusch.
has similar flower clusters but at flowering time the basal leaves are usually absent, large
leaves being on the stem. Occasional. Fla into se and cn Tex, cw Mo, and s NJ.

Vernonia flaccidifolia × 2/5

Vernonia glauca × 1/5

Elephantopus tomentosus × 1/4

Dog-fennel   *Eupatorium compositifolium* Walt.

Our species of this genus are mostly perennials, the leaves are opposite or whorled or rarely alternate, the flowers bisexual, achenes 5-angled, and pappus of capillary bristles bearing small barbs which are turned toward the tip. Plants are often difficult to name to species.

This species is a perennial to 1.8 mm tall, the upper stem leaves alternate and deeply and finely dissected, the divisions over 0.5 mm wide, and the heads with 3–6 flowers. Common. Thin woods, fields, pastures, Fla into e Tex, C.P. of Ga, and ce NC. Aug-frost.

E. capillifolium (Lam.) Small is similar but is an annual, the leaf segments are under 0.5 mm wide. Common. Similar places; and the heads evenly placed around branches of inflorescence. Common. Similar habitats; Fla into e Tex, s Tenn, SC, and s NJ. In *E. leptophyllum* DC. the flower heads hang on one side of the branches. Rare. Similar habitats; Fla into s Miss, s Ga, and se NC.

False-hoarhound   *Eupatorium rotundifolium* L.

Perennial to 1.2 m tall, finely and densely hairy. Leaves sessile or with petioles up to 3 mm long, blades not more than twice as long as broad and with 2 prominent lateral veins. Branches of inflorescence opposite. Heads 5-flowered, bracts around them obtuse to acute. Corollas white. Common. Rare in the mts, and occasional in the Pied. Thin woods, pine barrens, savannahs; Fla into e and cn Tex, s O, and se NY. July-Sept.

E. album L. has leaves 3 times or more as long as wide, the blades 15–35 mm wide. The bracts are long acuminate, the tips and margins white. Corollas white. Common, rare in higher mts. Dry thin woods, especially in sandy pinelands; Fla into se La, se Ark, s O, and se NY. July-Sept.

White Snakeroot   *Eupatorium rugosum* Houtt.

Perennial to 1.5 m tall. Leaves opposite, with petioles over 2 cm long. Blades narrowly to broadly ovate, rather thin, acuminate, 6–18 cm long. Flowers 15–30 in each head. Bracts glabrous or lightly hairy, acute to acuminate at the tips, their margins not overlapping. Corollas white. The plant contains a poison which can kill an animal eating it. The poison is also readily transmitted from a grazing animal to suckling young or to people using milk or butter from that animal. Many deaths from snakeroot have been recorded for human beings and grazing animals. Common. Rich woods and openings, pastures; n Fla into c Tex, se ND, Minn, s Sask, and NS. July-Oct. *E. urticaefolium* Reich.

E. aromaticum L. is similar but the petioles are under 2 cm long and the leaf blades acute to obtuse. Common. Drier woods; Fla into se La, s O, and Mass.

Pink Eupatorium   *Eupatorium incarnatum* Walt.

Petioled leaves, pink to purplish corollas, and 13–24 flowers per head with a flat receptacle to which they are attached serve as identifying characters for this species. Plants have an odor resembling vanilla. Rare. Rich woods, swampy places; Fla into cs and cn Tex, cs Ind, s O, w WVa, nw Ga, and se Va. Aug-Oct.

E. coelestinum L. is similar but there are 35–70 flowers per head, the receptacle is conic, and the corollas are blue to reddish purple. Often used as a perennial in flower beds although it sometimes becomes overplentiful because of creeping underground stems and abundant seeding. Occasional. Moist woods and meadows, stream borders; Fla into se and cn Tex, cw Ind, Va, and se Pa. July-Oct. *Conoclinium coelestinum* (L.) DC.

Eupatorium
compositifolium × 1/20

Eupatorium
rotundifolium × 2/5

Eupatorium rugosum × 1/5

Eupatorium incarnatum × 2/5

Joe-pye-weed   *Eupatorium fistulosum* Barr.

Perennial to 2 m tall. Stems purplish throughout, strongly glaucous and hollow. Mid-stem leaves mostly in whorls of 4 to 7, the blades not resin-dotted beneath or only with a few scattered ones. Inflorescence strongly rounded. Flowers 5–8 per head, bracts around the heads and corollas generally bright pink-purple. Common. Moist places in thin woods and open; Fla into e Tex, se Ia, sw Que, and s Me. July-Oct.

    E. purpureum L. is similar but the stem is usually greenish and not hollow. The bruised fresh plant is strongly vanilla-scented. Corollas generally very pale pinkish or purplish. Common. Thin woods, usually in drier places than the above species; cw SC into e Okla, e Kan, s Wisc, and s NH. July-Oct. In *E. maculatum* L. the stems are not hollow and there are 9–22 flowers per head. Occasional. Moist places in woods or open; high mts of w NC and e Tenn into WVa, n Ind, BC, and Nfld. July-Oct.

Climbing Hempweed   *Mikania scandens* (L.) Willd.

Twining perennial, often forming extensive masses over other low vegetation. Leaves opposite. Flowers in each head 4, none with ligules, bracts around the head narrowly acute, the corollas nearly white to lilac or light pink. The genus contains about 250 species. They are common in the tropics, especially in South America. Common. Moist to wet places in open; Fla into e Tex, se Mo, w Tenn, Ala, se Tenn, nw and Pied. of Ga, and sw Me. June-frost.

    M. cordifolia (L.) Willd. is quite similar but the bracts are obtuse or broadly acute. It is also more vigorous. Rare. Low places and hammocks; pen Fla and s La; abundant in subtropical and tropical localities. Flowers during frost-free periods.

Blazing-star   *Liatris graminifolia* Willd.

Members of this genus are erect perennials from a tuberous underground base, with alternate entire leaves, the inflorescence a spike or raceme, flowers all bisexual, without rays or receptacular bracts, the surrounding bracts much overlapped, achenes about 10-ribbed, and a pappus of 1 of 2 rings or fine bristles. Most plants are difficult to name to species.

    In this species the flower heads are longer than broad, sessile or on peduncles to 1 cm long, and the bracts obtuse. The basal rosette of leaves is absent, the lower stem leaves linear and to 20 cm long, corolla lobes under 3 mm long and the tube hairy inside. Common. Dry places, uncultivated fields, thin woods, especially among pines; Fla into se Miss, nw and Pied. of Ga, SC, and NJ. Aug-Oct.

    L. gracilis Pursh is similar but the peduncles are over 1 cm long. Rare. Similar places; Fla into cs Ala and sw SC. Aug-Oct.

Blazing-star   *Liatris asper* Michx.

Plant stiffly erect, to 2 m tall. Leaves 25–90, the lower ones narrowly elliptic, the upper ones nearly linear. Flowers 16–35 per head. Bracts around the head with obtuse to rounded, thin, pink to white margins and tip. Occasional. Thin woods or open places, usually dry and sandy or rocky; cw SC into e Tex, e ND, and s Ont. July-Sept.

    L. elegans (Walt.) Michx. also has pink to white bracts, these acute to acuminate and broadest above the middle. There are usually 5 flowers per head. Occasional. Similar places; Fla into e and cn Tex, se Okla, C.P. of Ga, and cs SC. Aug-Oct. *L. squarrosa* (L.) Michx., which grows to 1 m tall, can be recognized by its green to purple bracts, the tips of which are pointed away from the flowers. Common. Dry open places, thin woods; Fla into e and cn Tex, se SD, s Ind, sw WVa, Ky, NC, and Del; but mostly absent from Appalachian Mts. June-Aug.

Eupatorium fistulosum × 1/4

Mikania scandens × 1/2

Liatris asper × 2/5

Liatris graminifolia × 1/3

Deer-tongue; Vanilla-plant　　　*Carphephorus odoratissimus* (J. F. Gmel.) Hebert

Glabrous perennial to 2 m tall, with a distinct odor of vanilla which can sometimes be detected in the wild from a distance. Leaves alternate, the basal ones to 35 m long and 7 cm wide. Flowers, all bisexual, rays absent, bracts in several overlapping series, achenes 10-ribbed, the pappus of tawny to purplish finely barbed bristles 3–4 mm long, entire heads well under 1 cm long. Tons of leaves are collected from the wild each year and sold for flavoring smoking tobacco. Common. Pinelands, savannahs, thin mixed woods, usually in poorly drained places. Fla into se La, c Ala, C.P. of Ga, and se NC. July-Oct. *Trilisa odoratissima* (J. F. Gmel.) Cass.

C. paniculatus (J. F. Gmel.) Hebert is closely related. Stems have a dense coat of fine hairs and flower heads are usually in a cylindrical rather than spreading inflorescence. Common. Similar habitats; Fla into s half of NC C.P. Aug-Oct. *Trilisa paniculata* (Walt.) Cass.

Carphephorus　　　　　　　*Carphephorus corymbosus* (Nutt.) T. & G.

Perennial to about 1 m tall with a single finely and densely hairy stem, and spatulate to elliptic-spatulate basal leaves. Inflorescence flat-topped or rounded. Larger heads over 1 cm long. Flowers are bisexual, with no rays. Involucral bracts obtuse, in several overlapping series. Achenes 10-ribbed, the pappus of finely barbed bristles. Occasional. Thin, dry pinewoods, scrub oak sandhills; cs and se Ga and southward into Fla. June-Oct.

In *C. tomentosus* (Michx.) T. & G. the involucral bracts are acute and the corollas have small resin droplets on the outside surface. Occasional. Similar habitats; se Ga into se Va. Aug-Oct. *C. bellidifolius* (Michx.) T. & G. is also similar but the stem is usually glabrous below the inflorescence and the inflorescence is usually more open and more slenderly branched. Occasional. Sandhill scrub oaks, thin pine woods of uplands, sandy fields; ce Ga into C.P. of SC and se Va. July-Oct.

Golden-aster　　　　　　　*Heterotheca mariana* (L.) Shinners

In members of this genus the cauline leaves, and often the basal ones, are alternate. Outer flowers of the head have yellow ligules, disc flowers with yellow corollas. Receptacular bracts absent. Involucral bracts much overlapping. Pappus of capillary bristles in two rings, the outer much shorter than the inner.

This species is an erect perennial to 80 cm tall, loosely woolly-hairy when young. Lower leaves pinnately veined, elliptic to oblanceolate, to 12 cm long, serrate. Upper stem leaves much smaller. Involucral bracts with stalked glands and not woolly-hairy. Common. Thin woods, pine barrens, uncultivated fields; Fla into e Tex, s O, and se NY. July-Oct. *Chrysopsis mariana* (L.) Ell.

In *H. gossypina* (Michx.) Shinners the involucral bracts are conspicuously woolly-hairy. Occasional. Sandy pinelands, scrub oak; Fla into s Ala, C.P. of Ga, and se Va. Aug-Oct. *Chrysopsis pilosa* (Walt.) Britt.

Carphephorus corymbosus × 1/3

Carphephorus
odoratissimus × 1/6

Heterotheca mariana × 1/2

Grass-leaved Golden-aster   *Heterotheca pinifolia* (Ell.) Ahles

Glabrous perennial with grass-like leaves, to 50 cm. tall. Rare. Sandy soils, scrub oak, thin pinelands, uncultivated fields; n C.P. of Ga, and along the Fall Line to halfway across NC. Aug-Sept. *Chrysopsis pinifolia* (Ell.) Nutt.

Other species with grass-like leaves but with silvery-silky hairs on stems and leaves include: *H. graminifolia* (Michx.) Shinners with no glands on peduncles and bracts, and no stolons. Common. Usually dry places in thin woods or open; Fla into e Tex, s O, and Del. June-Nov. *H. microcephala* (Small) Shinners has small stalked glands on the bracts and none on the pedicels. Common. Similar places; Fla into e Ark, C.P. of Ga, and sw SC. July-Nov. *H. adenolepsis* (Fern.) Ahles with glands on peduncles as well as the bracts. Common. Thin woods, usually sandy soils; Fla into s Miss, Pied. of Ga, and se Va. July-Oct.

Camphorweed   *Heterotheca subaxillaris* (Lam.) Britt. & Rusby

Plants annual or biennial, glandular and sticky, with a camphor-like odor when crushed. Stems to 2 m tall, erect, ascending, or decumbent, the former type usually inland and w of the Mississippi River, and the latter along the coasts. The tall western form of this species became introduced around Athens, Ga, and Spartanburg, SC, before 1950. It is aggressive, occupying abandoned farmlands, thin woods, and other open areas, and is spreading rapidly. It is often abundant in fields the first year after crops. Whereas it occupied only about 1500 square miles around Athens in 1954, it now occurs in much of the Pied. of Ga. Heads of flowers numerous. Ray flowers essentially without a pappus. Common. Open areas; Del into Fla, Ga, and Tex, on w into Ariz and n into Kan and Ill. Flowering in frost-free periods but most abundantly July-Oct. Includes *H. latifolia* Buckl.

Slim Goldenrod   *Solidago stricta* Ait.

Placing plants into this genus with certainty is difficult because distinguishing characteristics are troublesome and differences between the 50 or more species in the Southeast are hard to interpret. Species hybridize, adding to the confusion. Goldenrods are perennials with fibrous roots, alternate simple and entire or variously toothed leaves, and yellow petals (white in one species). There are no receptacular bracts. The style has flattened branches which are glabrous inside and finely hairy outside. The pappus is one ring of capillary bristles. The few species included here show some of the variability in the genus.

This species grows to 2 m tall, is glabrous, the flowers in narrow panicles, and the upper stem leaves small and pressed against the stem. Common. Usually in moist places, open pinelands, savannahs; Fla into e Tex, C.P. of Ga and pine barrens of NJ. Aug-frost.

Field Goldenrod   *Solidago altissima* L.

Plants to 2.5 m tall. Stems with appressed fine hairs. Lower leaves narrowly lanceolate, acuminate at tip, with two prominent lateral veins, and short petioles. May be only a variety of the northern *S. canadensis* L. Common. Old fields, thin woods; Fla into Tex, e ND, sw Que, and sw Me. Aug-frost.

S. odora Ait. usually may be recognized by having an odor of anise when crushed. It has a 1-sided panicle. The leaves numerous, spreading, linear-lanceolate, entire, sessile, and glabrous except for the roughened margin. Dried leaves of this species have been used to make a tea. Fungal infected plants of this and other species are suspected of causing poisoning. Common. Thin woods or open places, usually in dry poor soils; Fla into e Tex, se Mo, c NY, and s NH. July-Oct.

Heterotheca subaxillaris × 1/7

Heterotheca pinifolia × 2/5

Solidago altissima × 1/6

Solidago stricta × 1/5

Wreath Goldenrod   *Solidago caesia* L.

One of a few species with flowers in axillary clusters. Sometimes the upper clusters are
not in leaf axils. The stems are round and glaucous. Stem leaves are 3–10 times as long
as wide and pinnately veined from a single large vein. Achenes persistently hairy.
Common. Rich deciduous woods, ravines, slopes; Fla into e Tex, Wisc, and NS. Aug-
Oct.

In *S. curtisii* T. & G. the stems are angled by fine lines running from the petiole
bases, and the larger leaves are elliptic-lanceolate to oblanceolate. Occasional. Similar
places; n half of Ga Pied. into n Miss, c WVa, c Va, and nw SC.

Broad-leaved Solidago   *Solidago flexicaulis* L.

Plants to 1.2 m tall. Stem below the flowers glabrous, and angled similarly to those of
S. curtisii. Leaves with 1 main vein, elliptic-ovate to ovate, not more than 2.5 times as
long as wide, those at the top usually larger than in any other species. Achenes persistently hairy. Occasional. Rich woods, cool slopes, cn Ga into e Tenn, Ky, n Ark, ne Kan,
se ND, NB, NS, and cw NC. Sept-frost.

S. buckleyi T. & G. is similar but the upper leaves are thin, not as wide, and are
sharply serrate. The stems are finely hairy. The mature achenes are glabrous. Rare. Rich
woods, in and around bluffs; n Ga into n Ala, n Ark, s Mo, s Ill, se Ind, and w NC.
S. albopilosa Braun is quite similar but the stems are conspicuously hairy. Rare. Under
cliffs; between c and ne Ky only.

Rayless-goldenrod   *Bigelowia nudata* (Michx.) DC.

A perennial to 60 cm tall with a basal cluster of spatulate to linear-spatulate leaves,
the stem leaves much shorter, those of midstem and upward under 2 cm long and 3 mm
wide. Similar to some goldenrods but with no ray flowers. Involucral bracts greenish
yellow and overlapping. Petals yellow. Receptacular bracts absent. Achene hairy. Pappus of one circle of capillary bristles. Common. Open pinelands, savannahs, usually
moist places; Fla into s La and C.P. of Ga and NC. Aug-Oct. *Chondrophora nudata*
(Michx.) Britt.

B. nuttallii L. C. Anderson is similar but the basal and stem leaves are filiform. Occasional. Shallow soil of granitic and sandstone rocks, gravelly or sandy soils; cw Fla
into e Tex, s Miss, ne Ala, and ce Ga. *Chondrophora virgata* (Nutt.) Greene.

White-topped Aster   *Aster paternus* Cronq.

Asters are difficult to name. There may be 100 species of them in the Southeast and
hybrids are abundant. They have many characteristics in common with *Erigeron* and
Solidago species. Species of the latter genus, except for *S. bicolor* L., may be recognized
by their yellow rays; those of *Aster* and *Erigeron* are blue to purple, red, pink, or
white. The time of flowering is helpful in separating the latter two, most species of
Erigeron usually blooming in the spring or summer and those of *Aster* usually in late
summer or fall.

In this species the basal and lower stem leaves are broadly oblanceolate to obovate or
elliptic and taper to petioled bases. The flower heads are in corymb-like clusters. The
rays are white. Common. Dry woods, clearings, roadbanks; n Fla into cw Ala, s O, and
s Me. June-July. *Sericocarpus asteroides* (L.) B.S.P.

Solidago caesia × 1/3

Solidago flexicaulis × 1/4

Aster paternus × 1

Bigelowia nudata × 1/2

White-topped Aster   *Aster reticulatus* Pursh

Conspicuous perennial with 1 to several stems from a rootstock. Leaves and at least the upper part of the stem are glandular and hairy. Rays over 10 mm long. Pappus of two distinct series, the outer of short bristles and the inner of elongate capillary bristles. Common. Low pinelands; Fla into se Ga and s tip SC. Apr-Aug. *Doellingeria reticulata* (Pursh) Greene.

    A. umbellatus Mill., which is closely related, is taller (to 2.5 m), has rays under 10 mm long, short-hairy achenes, and a stoloniferous base. Occasional. Wet places in open or thin woods; mts of Ga into s Miss, Ky, Minn, s Ont, and Nfld. Aug-Oct. *A. infirmus* Michx. is without stolons. Occasional. Dry deciduous woods; n Ga into n Miss, Ky, Ohio, and Mass.

Bushy Aster   *Aster dumosus* L.

Perennial, usually with creeping rhizomes; stems slender and much branched, spreading or ascending to 1.5 m tall. Stem leaves scabrous above, not auriculate-clasping. Middle and upper stem leaves sessile, soft and flexible, linear to lance-linear or narrowly elliptic, and entire or nearly so. Flowering heads abundant and panicled. Involucral bracts collectively 4–6 mm long, each acute but not sharp pointed. Rays white to blue or lavender. A very common plant in old fields, pastures, and meadows; less abundant in thin woods and marshes; Fla into e Tex, cs Mo, Va, e WVa, e Pa, n O, s Mich, s Ont, and sw Me. Aug-Oct.

    A. pilosus Willd. is similar but the leaves are often not scabrous above and the involucral bracts are sharp pointed. Common. Similar habitats; SC into Ark, ne Okla, se Kan, Wisc, se Ont, and NS. July-Oct.

Swamp Aster   *Aster puniceus* L.

This is one of several species with auriculate-clasping leaves. A perennial with a stout stem to 2.5 meters tall from a short stout rhizome. Stem with spreading hairs, at least beneath the heads, and no glands. Leaves widely serrated, acute, gradually narrowed to the base, 7–16 cm long. Involucral bracts, at least the inner ones, long-acuminate to long-tapering. Common. Moist, thin woods, swamps, wet meadows, and other open places; Pied. of Ga into ne Ark, Ill, s Man, Nfld, and Pied. of SC. Sept-Oct.

    A. prenanthoides Muhl. is similar but has long rhizomes and grows only to 1 m tall. The leaves are usually abruptly contracted into the base and the involucral bracts are acute to barely obtuse. Occasional. Similar places; nw and cw NC into e Ia, se Minn, Del, and e Mass. Aug-Oct.

Robins-plantain   *Erigeron vernus* (L.) T. & G.

Members of this genus have many narrow pink, violet, purple, or white ligules and yellow or yellowish disc corollas. The pappus is a single circle of capillary bristles.

    This species is a perennial to 60 cm tall with prominent basal leaves, but only a few nonclasping stem leaves. Rays 25–40, white or rarely lavender. Common. Moist places, savannahs, open pinelands, bogs; Fla into s La, c C.P. of Ga, and se Va. Feb-June.

    E. pulchellus Michx. also has prominent basal leaves, but the stem leaves are wider and clasp the stem. Plants have stolons and the flower heads, which are solitary or few, are much larger. Rays 50–100, blue-purple or sometimes pink or white. Common. Wooded slopes, meadows, roadside banks; Ga into e Tex, ce Minn, and s Me; uncommon in Pied., rare in C.P. Apr-June.

Aster reticulatus × 1/8

Aster dumosus × 1/4

Aster puniceus × 2/5

Erigeron vernus × 1/5

Daisy Fleabane   *Erigeron philadelphicus* L.

Biennial or short-lived perennial to 1 m tall with a few basal leaves. Stem leaves several and clasping. Involucral bracts over 4 mm long. Rays 150 or more, 5–10 mm long, pink or light rose to whitish. Occasional. Fields, rich open woods, rich waste places; Fla into se and cn Tex, e Kan, e ND, BC, and Nfld. Mar-June.

 E. quercifolius Lam. is similar but usually shorter. Involucral bracts under 4 mm long. Rays 100–150, only 3–5 mm long, violet to blue. Occasional. Moist open pinelands or savannahs, fields, roadsides; Fla into s La, s Ga, and se Va. Mar-June, rarely in Fall.

Camphorweed; Stinkweed   *Pluchea camphorata* (L.) DC.

Foul-smelling annual or perennial to 1.6 m tall. Basal leaves absent at flowering. Flowering heads about as long as broad. Involucral bracts several, overlapping, not spine-tipped, glabrous or glandular but not hairy. Flowers bisexual, ray flowers absent. Common. Pastures, thin woods, ditches, moist to wet places. Fla into e and cn Tex, s Mo, s Ind, se WVa, Va, and Del but absent from higher mt areas. Aug-Oct.

 P. purpurescens (Sw.) DC. is similar but the bracts are both glandular and short pubescent. Occasional. Brackish or occasionally fresh marshes along the coast; Tex into Fla and s Me. In *P. foetida* (L.) DC. the leaves are sessile and clasping and the corollas creamy white. Common. Marshes, ditches, shallow water; Fla into e Tex, se Mo, s Miss, sw and se Ga, and s NJ. The corollas are pink in *P. rosea* Godfrey but otherwise much like the latter species. Occasional. Similar places; Fla into se Tex, se Ga, and e NC.

Black-root   *Pterocaulon pycnostachyum* (Michx.) Ell.

Perennial from large dark roots. Leaf undersides and stem with the feel of kid leather because of short, densely felted, and light-colored hairs. Flowers very small, these in tight heads which in turn are in tight elongate terminal clusters. Three clusters are shown in the photograph. Common. Sandy pinelands and open sandy areas; C.P.—se NC into sw Ga and Fla. May-June. *P. undulatum* (Walt.) Mohr.

 Individual leaves of some species of the related *Antennaria* and *Gnaphalium* are similar. In *G. purpureum* L. plants look like small forms of *Pterocaulon* but with the flower heads less densely arranged. Common. Thin woods, various open habitats such as yards and fields; Fla into Cal, BC, c Ill, and Me. Mar-June.

Pussy-toes   *Antennaria plantaginifolia* (L.) Richards.

Male plants are shown in the picture, the female plants usually being taller. The stolons, mats of hairs on the stems and underside of the 3–5-nerved leaves, and the several heads of flowers identify this species. Common. Dry situations, in thin woods or open; n Fla into La, e Okla, Minn, and se Me. Mar-May.

 A. neglecta Greene is similar but the leaves are narrower and have only 1 vein, or rarely an additional 2 obscure veins. Occasional. Similar places; Va into e Tenn, Ky, Kan, Ariz, Cal, Yukon, and Nfld. Mar-May. *A. solitaria* Rydb. is usually smaller and has only 1 head of flowers at tip of stem. Occasional. Woods, occasionally thin and sometimes alluvial. Ga into La, s Ind, se Pa, and Md. Mar-May.

Erigeron philadelphicus × 1/4

Pluchea camphorata × 1/3

Pterocaulon pycnostachyum × 2/5

Antennaria plantaginifolia × 1/4

Rabbit-tobacco; Everlasting   *Gnaphalium obtusifolium* L.

Biennial, leaves the first year in rosettes, oblanceolate to spatulate, very hairy. Second year stem leaves, alternate, many, sessile, green and glabrous above, hairy below, narrowly lanceolate to narrowly oblanceolate. Stems with a mat of long whitish hairs. Flowers perfect. Ray flowers none. Involucral bracts imbricate. Pappus capillary. Plants have a fragrant balsamic odor. Leaves are eaten by wild turkeys. Deer eat the plants in the winter. Common. Fallow fields, pastures, roadsides, thin woods; Fla into cs Tex, c Kan, se Man, and NS. Aug-Oct.

G. helleri Britt. is similar but has glandular hairs on the stem making it sticky to touch. Occasional. More likely in thin woods; n Pied. Ga into ne Ark, se Mo, s Me, and ne Va. Sept-Oct.

Green-eyes   *Berlandiera pumila* (Michx.) Nutt.

Perennial to 1 m tall from a large root. Leaves alternate, coarsely crenate or only slightly lobed at the base, hairy on both surfaces. Ray flowers bearing fruits, the disc flowers with stamens and pistils but sterile. When in bud the disc flowers are green, thus the common name. Involucral bracts 4 mm or more wide. Pappus absent. Occasional. Sandy soils in thin woods or open; Fla into se Tex, C.P. of Ga, and upper C.P. of SC. Mar-frost.

B. subacaulis Nutt. has very similar flower heads but with almost leafless stems and the lower leaves pinnately lobed. Occasional. Dry pinelands; ne and cn Fla and southward. Flowers in frost-free periods.

Rosin-weed   *Silphium compositum* Michx.

Members of this genus are coarse erect perennials and have yellow corollas, winged achenes, no receptacular bracts, sterile disc flowers, and a pappus of 2 two small awns or absent.

In this species the blades of the basal leaves are to 30 cm long and wide, and merely dentate to deeply pinnately lobed, the ones above much smaller. Plants to 4 m tall. Flower heads exclusive of the rays are 8–12 mm wide. Common. Dry places, thin woods, uncultivated open places; SC into ce Ala, se Tenn, and se Va. June-Sept.

S. terebinthinaceum Jacq. is similar but the flower heads usually 20 mm or more broad and the leaf blades distinctly longer than broad. Occasional. Open woods, glades, prairies, nw Ga into n La, s Minn, s Ont, and O; cs and cn NC. July-Sept. *S. ovatifolium* (T. & G.) Small also has large heads but the basal leaves have petioles as long as the blades and the plants smaller. Rare. Sandy woods; pen and cn Fla into se Ga. May-Sept.

Starry Rosin-weed   *Silphium dentatum* Ell.

Plants to 2.5 m tall with well-developed alternate or opposite leaves to high on the stem, basal leaves usually absent. Receptacular bracts with small stalked glands on the back near the tip. Common. Dry thin woods, uncultivated fields; Fla into ce Miss, Pied. and adj R.V. of Ga, cn NC, and SC. May-Sept.

Other species with well-developed stem leaves but lacking glands on the chaff include: *S. asteriscus* L. with the upper stem having coarse spreading hairs or being very rough to touch. Common. Dry woods and open places; cn and nw Fla into nw and c Ga; Pied. of NC into ne Tenn and cs Va. May-Sept. *S. trifoliatum* L. with the upper stem glabrous or nearly so, leaves rough and usually whorled. Occasional. Similar places; cn Ga into sw and ne Ind, Pa, and ne NC. June-Sept. *S. laevigatum* Pursh with essentially glabrous leaves and stems. Rare. SC into n Ala, s Ind, and s O. June-Sept.

Berlandiera pumila × 1/3

Gnaphalium obtusifolium × 1/6

Silphium dentatum × 1/3

Silphium compositum × 1/11

Yellow Leafcup; Bears-foot   *Polymnia uvedalia* L.

Perennial to 3 m tall. Leaves opposite, palmately lobed or cut, the blades about as long as wide, their shape promoting the name "Bears-foot." Receptacular bracts absent, disc flowers sterile and with an undivided style, ray flowers fertile and producing rounded and faintly grooved achenes, and pappus absent. Common, but only scattered in the C.P. Usually in rich soil of low places, deciduous woods, pastures; Fla into c Tex, se Kan, ce O, s NY, and NJ. June-Oct. *Smallanthus uvedalia* (L.) Mack.

In *P. canadensis* L. the leaves are pinnately lobed, stems with small stalked glands, and rays white to pale yellow. Occasional. Rich woods, usually calcareous places; nw Ga into nw Ark, c Ia, c Minn, s Vt, Conn, and nw NC. July-Oct. In *P. laevigata* Beadle the leaves are usually smaller and pinnately lobed, stems glabrous, flower heads smaller, rays white, and achenes 5-angled. Rare. Rich woods; in nw Fla, nw Ga, c Ala, se Tenn, and se Mo.

Chrysogonum; Green-and-gold   *Chrysogonum virginianum* L.

Perennial, at first stemless as shown in the picture, or very short-stemmed, later elongating to 5–40 cm, often trailing and rooting in open situations; in the shade becoming mostly erect. Leaves opposite, hairy, with winged petioles. Ray flowers bearing fruits, the disc flowers opening but sterile. Involucral bracts overlapping. An excellent ornamental for open, sunny borders. Common. Well-drained soils in woods; SC into nw Fla, se La, se O, cs Pa, and Va. Mar-June; occasionally Nov. *C. australe* Alex.

Tetragonotheca   *Tetragonotheca helianthoides* L.

The generic name is from Greek words meaning "four-angled case" which alludes to the 4 large involucral bracts which enclose the unexposed flower buds in the head. Two such heads are seen in the picture. A perennial with 1 to several erect to ascending stems, to 90 cm tall. Occasional. Dry soil, usually sandy; Fla into s Miss, Ga, and se Va; ce Tenn. Apr-July.

Heliopsis helianthoides (L.) B.S.P., Ox-eye, is similar but often taller, to 1.5 m, without the 4 large involucral bracts, and with no hairs on the stems and leaves. Occasional. Open places and thin woods; Fla into NM, s Sask, and se Me. June-Sept. Incl. *H. scabra* Dunal.

Wild-quinine; American Feverfew   *Parthenium integrifolium* L.

Coarse perennial to 1.1 m tall from a tuberous-thickened root. Stem single or branched near the top, glabrous to minutely hairy. Leaves alternate, firm, coarsely toothed. Rays 5, white, inconspicuous, 1–2 mm long. Receptacular bracts present. Ray flowers fertile, the disc flowers sterile. Achenes conspicuously flattened. Pappus of 2–3 scales or awns. Common. Dry open woods, prairies; Pied. of Ga into e Okla, se Minn, Pa, se NY, and ce NC. May-Sept.

In *P. auriculatum* Britt. the stems have coarse, spreading hairs. Rare. Dry woods, old fields; cn NC into cn Va. May-Aug.

Polymnia uvedalia × 1/6

Chrysogonum virginianum × 2/3

Tetragonotheca helianthoides × 1/2

Parthenium integrifolium × 1/3

Black-eyed-Susan   *Rudbeckia hirta* L.

Members of this genus have alternate leaves, rays are yellow to orange or marked with purple or reddish-brown at the base. Disc flowers are fertile and accompanied by receptacular bracts, but the ray flowers are not. The receptacle is strongly conic or columnar. Identification to species may be difficult. There are reports of livestock being poisoned from eating plants of some species.

This species is a biennial or short-lived perennial with unlobed leaves and dark-purple disc corollas and no pappus. The receptacular bracts are acute to sharp-pointed but not spine-tipped. Common. Old fields, pastures, roadsides, thin woods; Fla into cs Tex, BC, and Nfld. May-frost.

In *R. mollis* Ell. stems are densely covered with spreading hairs, leaves are clasping, and receptacular bracts are obtuse. Dry places in thin woods or open; Fla into se Ala, s Ga, and sw SC. June-Oct.

Purple Coneflower   *Echinacea pallida* (Nutt.) Nutt.

Perennial to 1.2 m tall. Leaves alternate, hairy above and below, lanceolate to linear-lanceolate, tapered at base, never serrate. Receptacular bracts with spine tips and longer than the disc flowers. Rays 4–9 cm long, deep pink to purplish pink, fading with age. Pappus a toothed crown. Rare e of Mississippi River. Thin woods, rocky glades, prairies; c Ga into e Tex, e Kan, n Mich, and cn NY. May-July.

In *E. purpurea* (L.) Moench the leaves are broadly to narrowly ovate, rounded at base, often serrate, and rough above. Rare e of Mississippi River. Similar places; sw Ga into ne Tex, e Okla, se Ia, s Mich, and cs NC. June-Sept. In *E. laevigata* (Boynt. & Beadle) Blake the upper surface of the leaves is smooth. Rare. Fields, thin woods; ne Ga into se Pa and cw SC. June-July.

Coneflower   *Ratibida pinnata* (Vent.) Barnh.

Perennial to 1.3 m tall from a strong rootstock. Leaves alternate, pinnately-compound, with 3–9 mostly lanceolate leaflets, the upper ones small and sometimes simple. Rays 5–10, spreading or drooping, 3–5 cm long. Receptacular bracts not spine-tipped. Ray flowers sterile. The receptacle is columnar. Achenes flattened and smooth. Pappus none. The crushed fresh receptacle has an anise-like odor. Occasional. Dry places, thin woods, in open, roadsides, fencerows, prairies; nw Ga into c Ala, e Okla, e SD, s Ont, and c O. May-Sept.

In *R. columnifera* (Nutt.) Woot. & Standl. the leaves are mostly linear and the rays less than 3 cm long. Achenes usually slightly winged. Rare. Prairies, roadsides, along railroads, usually calcareous soils; c Ala into NM, Mont, s Man, and Ill. June-Sept.

Viguiera   *Viguiera porteri* (Gray) Blake

An annual to 1 m tall, often occurring in spectacular flowering colonies. Leaves narrow, entire, and at least those of the main stem opposite. All corollas yellow. Anthers dark brown. Flower heads to 4 cm wide from tip to tip of the ligules, the involucral bracts overlapping. Common. On or about granitic outcrops. Pied. of Ga and Ala. July-Oct.

Another yellow-petaled member of the Asteraceae, *Coreopsis grandiflora* Hogg, is sometimes abundant on granitic outcrops and superficially resembles *Viguiera*, but it has two distinctly separate series of bracts around the head of flowers. This species of *Coreopsis* is distinguished from others by its opposite petioled deeply lobed leaves, the end lobe of its basal leaves more than 4 times as long as wide, and peduncles usually under 15 cm long. Occasional. Drier places in thin woods or open; Pied. of Ga into se and cn Tex, se Kan, and se Tenn; with scattered introductions to the north and east. May-Sept.

Rudbeckia hirta × 1/6

Echinacea pallida × 1/6

Ratibida pinnata × 1/3

Viguiera porteri × 1

Narrow-leaved Sunflower   *Helianthus angustifolius* L.

Members of this genus are mostly coarse erect plants with undissected leaves, flower heads 1 cm or more broad, light to dark yellow to reddish purple corollas, sterile ray flowers, fertile disc flowers, receptacular bracts, nonwinged achenes, and a pappus of 2 awnless scales. Most species are difficult to name.

This species is a perennial to 2 m tall with a single stem that is often much branched in upper half. Leaves occur all along the stem, to 18 cm long, usually less than 1/10 as wide, the few basal leaves (if any) much wider. Lobes of disc corollas usually purple. Common. Moist shady places or open depressions; Fla into s Tex, se Okla, Tenn, NC, se Va, and se NY; Ohio River valley into O. July-frost.

In *H. longifolius* L. the basal as well as upper leaves are narrow and lobes of the disc corollas are yellow. Rare. Dry rocky soil; cw and nw Ga into ce and ne Ala; sw NC. Aug-Oct.

Purple-disc Sunflower   *Helianthus atrorubens* L.

Perennial to 2 m tall, without rhizomes. Basal leaves large with petioles often as long as the blade, lower stem leaves only slightly smaller, the upper one much reduced. Lobes of disc flower corollas red. Common. Thin woods in dry situations, uncultivated open places; SC into nw Ga, se La, Tenn, se Ky, and Va. July-Oct.

Other similar species include: *H. silphioides* Nutt. with leaves gradually smaller upward and the petioles much shorter than the blades. Occasional. Thin woods or open; se Tenn into n Ala, c La, Ark, and s Ill. *H. occidentalis* Ridd. with disc flower corollas yellow and much reduced stem leaves. Rare in the Southeast. Dry often sandy soils, thin woods or open; nw Fla into cn La, sw Mo, Wisc, Mich, and s WVa; ce NS and near DC. *H. radula* (Pursh) T. & G. with rays lacking or only 1-2 mm long. Rare. Low open pine barrens; Fla into se La and sw SC.

Rough Sunflower   *Helianthus hirsutus* Raf.

Perennial to 2 m tall, with long rhizomes and stems rough to touch. Stem leaves well developed, opposite or rarely a few upper ones alternate, with petioles 5-20 mm long, and base of main lateral veins 5-20 mm from base of blade. Disc corollas and ligules yellow. Common. Dry open places or thin woods; SC into e Tex, se Neb, Wisc, sw Pa, and c Ky. July-Oct.

H. divaricatus L. is similar but usually has sessile leaves and the bases of the main lateral veins are at base of blade. Common. Similar habitats; nw Fla into e Ala, Tenn, e Okla, se Mo, e Ill, Mich, Vt, Mass, and NC. In *H. strumosus* L. the stems are essentially glabrous and petioles are 10-30 mm long and slender. Common. Rich woods to open places; n Fla into ne Tex, Ia, Wisc, and s Me. In *H. mollis* Lam. the stem and lower leaf surfaces are soft and white hairy. Occasional. Dry places; n Ga into e Tex, s Ia, Wisc, O, and e Me.

Crown-beard; Wingstem   *Verbesina occidentalis* (L.) Walt.

Single-stemmed perennial to 2.5 m tall. Stems 4-winged. Involucral bracts overlapping, less than 3 mm wide. Rays 2-5, more than 5 mm long, unevenly spaced around the head. Fruit flattened, not winged, with two strong awns. Common. Woods, fields, pastures; less common in the C.P.; Fla into ne Miss, se Pa, and se Va. July-Oct.

V. alternifolia (L.) Britt. has similar individual flowers but the heads are globose, the bracts reflexed, the rays 2-10, and the fruits 2-winged. Common, but rare in C.P. Moist places, woods, swamps, marshes, pastures; C.P. of Ga into c La, Mo, c Kan, Ill, s Ont, se NY and Pied. of SC. July-Oct. *Actinomeris alternifolia* (L.) DC.

Helianthus atrorubens × 1/6

Helianthus angustifolius × 1/2

Helianthus hirsutus × 1/2

Verbesina occidentalis × 2/5

Tickweed

Verbesina virginica L.

Perennial to 2.5 m tall, with a single, densely fine-hairy, winged stem, Leaves alternate, ovate to lance-ovate, to light green beneath, to 25 cm long, with winged petioles. Ray and disc corollas white; rays 1–5 and 5–10 mm long. Fruits flattened, hairy, usually winged, with 2 short awns. Common. Fla into e and cn Tex, se Kan, e and nc Ky, nw Ga, Pied. of Ga and c NC; ce Va. Aug-Oct. *Phaethusa virginica* (L.) Small.

Tall Coreopsis

Coreopsis tripteris L.

Members of this genus have opposite or rarely alternate leaves, ray flowers around the margin of the head, the rays usually yellow or rarely pink-purple or white. The disc flowers are fertile, the involucral bracts are in 2 series and of 2 sizes, about 8 of each, the outer narrower and somewhat spreading, the inner broader and appressed. Narrow receptacular bracts are present. The achenes are flattened and usually winged. The pappus consists of 2 short rows of teeth.

This species is a perennial to 2.5 m tall. Leaves are distinctly petioled and have 3, rarely 5, linear to lanceolate or narrowly elliptic blades. Common. Thin woods, open places; Ga into se La, ne Tex, e Kan, Wisc, Mass, and NC. July-Sept.

Narrow-leaf Coreopsis

Coreopsis angustifolia Ait.

Perennial to 1 m tall. Leaves alternate or opposite, simple, not lobed, entire, lowermost ones less than 15 mm wide and 7 cm long, the upper ones much reduced. Rays yellow. Occasional. Moist or wet places in thin woods or open; C.P.—Fla into se Va and s Miss. June-Oct.

Similar species are: *C. linifolia* Nutt. which has alternate stem leaves, the lowermost leaves longer than 7 cm. Rare. Moist pinelands and savannahs, open sandy places; Fla into lower C.P. of Ga and se NC. July-Nov. *C. gladiata* Walt. with alternate stem leaves more than 15 mm wide and usually longer than 7 cm. Occasional. Swamps, bogs, wet open pinelands; Fla into SC, e NC, and s Miss. Aug-Oct.

Whorled-leaf Coreopsis

Coreopsis major Walt.

Perennial to 1 m tall. Although there appear to be 6 whorled leaves at each of the middle and upper nodes, the leaves are really opposite and deeply palmately divided into 3 segments. Rays yellow. In var. *major* the leaves and stems are pubescent and the leaf segments 10–30 mm wide. In var. *rigida* (Nutt.) Boynt. the leaves and stems are glabrous or nearly so and the leaf segments only 5–11 mm wide. Common. Thin woods, usually dry places; Fla into Miss, s Ohio, c Va, and SC. May-Aug.

C. verticellata L. also has sessile and dissected leaves which often appear whorled, but the leaf divisions are under 2 mm wide. Rays yellow. Occasional. Dry thin woods and pinelands; n Fla into e Ark, e Tenn, e WVa, and Md. May-Aug.

Verbesina virginica × 1/6

Coreopsis tripteris × 1/4

Coreopsis angustifolia × 1/2

Coreopsis major × 1/4

Swamp Coreopsis   *Coreopsis nudata* Nutt.

Perennnial to 1.2 m tall from an elongate rootstock about 6 mm in diameter. Leaves few, terete except toward base, 3 mm or less in diameter. This is unlike our other *Coreopsis* species in having purplish-pink to reddish-purple rays. Occasional. Swamps, ditches, and other depressions. Lower C.P. of Ga into Fla and s Miss. Apr-May.

C. *auriculata* L. is unusual in having stolons and usually having only the lower half of the stem with leaves, or the leaves basal only. Rays yellow. Occasional. Rich woods or openings; se SC into ne La, ne Miss, s WVa, and se NC. Apr-June.

Calliopsis   *Coreopsis basalis* (Dietr.) Blake

Winter annual to 70 cm tall. Leaves dissected, the segments elliptic to ovate. Rays yellow with red bases. Outer involucral bracts 4 mm long or longer, about as long as the inner. Fruits about as broad as long, wingless. Occasional. Open, usually sandy areas; La to Minn and westward; escaped eastward especially in C.P. May-July.

Two other species have ligules with red bases. In C. *tinctoria* Nutt. the fruits are also wingless but the leaf segments are narrower, the outer involucral bracts 3 mm or less long and shorter than the inner ones, and the fruits about twice as long as broad. Occasional. Also western and escaped eastward, but more frequently inland than in C.P. May-Oct. In C. *cardaminaefolia* (DC.) Nutt. fruits are winged. Occasional. Low places; La into Tex, s Neb, and n Miss; escaped eastward. May-July.

Shepherd's-needle   *Bidens pilosa* L.

Members of this genus are annuals or perennials with opposite simple or compound leaves, have disc flowers only or both ray and disc flowers. The head is surrounded by two well separated circles of bracts. The achenes are flattened and without a neck or wings, in two species spindle-shaped and quadrangular. A pappus of 2-6 usually retrorsely barbed awns enable the achenes to cling to clothing, hence the name "Beggar's-ticks" which is applied to several species.

This species is an annual or short-lived perennial, the rays are white or nearly so, the leaves compound, and the achenes quadrangular and spindle-shaped. Occasional. Waste places, old fields, roadsides; Fla into se Tex, s Ga, and se NC. Mar-frost.

B. *bipinnata* L. also has spindle-shaped achenes but the ligules are yellow and smaller. Common. Fields, pastures, waste places; Fla into e Tex, se Neb, and Mass. July-Oct.

Tickseed-sunflower   *Bidens aristosa* (Michx.) Britt.

Annual or biennial to 1.5 m tall. Leaves once or twice pinnately compound, the segments lanceolate or lance-linear, acuminate and sharply serrate. Rays 10-25 mm long. Achenes flat, the margins ciliate, mostly obovate to elliptic-obovate, 5-7 mm long. Often forms dense colonies which are spectacular when in flower. Common. Marshes, meadows, ditches, open low ground; n SC into e Tex, s Minn, Me, and NC; mostly absent from the Appalachian Mts. Aug-frost.

B. *mitis* (Michx.) Sherff is similar but the leaves are often more finely divided. The achenes are not ciliate on the margins or only slightly so and only 2.5-5 mm long. Occasional. Fresh or brackish marshes or swamps; Fla into se Tex, s Ga, and e Md. In B. *coronata* (L.) Britt. the leaves are usually more finely divided. Achenes ciliate, narrowly cuneate-oblong to cuneate-linear, 5-9 mm long. Occasional. Swamps, rich bottoms, brackish marshes; Fla into Mass, nw Pa, Ind, e Neb, Wisc, and s Ont.

Coreopsis nudata × 3/5

Coreopsis basalis × 1/3

Bidens pilosa × 1/2

Bidens aristosa × 1/4

Wild-goldenglow; Bur-marigold   *Bidens laevis* (L.) B.S.P.

A glabrous perennial to 1 m tall, stems ascending or reclining and rooting at the nodes, often forming dense colonies. Leaves serrate and unlobed. Rays about 8, yellow, 15–30 mm long. Bracts between the flowers reddish at the tip. Occasional. Marshes, margins of pools and streams, either fresh or brackish; Fla into Tex, C.P. of Ga, s NH; Cal; locally inland to s Ind and e WVa. Sept-frost.

B. cernua L. also has simple leaves, which often clasp the stem and even may have opposite leaf bases united. Stems glabrous or rough-hairy. Rays seldom over 15 mm long. Involucral bracts yellowish-tipped. Occasional. Low wet places, marshes, bogs; nw Ga into Colo, Wash, BC, PEI, and cw NC. July-frost.

Annual Balduina   *Balduina angustifolia* (Pursh) Robins.

Members of this genus are easily recognized by having yellow ray corollas and the receptacle surface to which the flowers are attached being honeycombed.

In this species the stem has 0–20 branches. It resembles Bitterweed, *Helenium amarum*, but has narrow rays and fewer leaves and is less branched above. Both species are annuals and have linear leaves and yellow disc and ray corollas. Occasional. Deep, well-drained sandy soils of pinelands, sandhills, and scrub oak; Fla into s Miss; lower C.P. of Ga. Sept-Nov. *Actinospermum angustifolium* (Pursh) T. & G.

There are two other species in the genus, *B. uniflora* Nutt. which resembles *Helenium vernale* (see under this for characteristics) and *B. atropurpurea* Harper which has 0–4 stem branches, longer rays, and reddish purple disc corollas. Rare. Bogs, moist pine barrens and savannahs; ne Fla into lower C.P. of Ga; se SC. Aug-Oct.

Barbara's-buttons   *Marshallia trinerva* (Walt.) Trel.

Members of this genus are glandular-dotted perennials with alternate leaves, peduncles over 5 cm long, no ray flowers, entire involucral bracts, receptacular bracts present, achenes with 5 finely hairy angles, and a pappus of 5–6 short thin scales.

This species has no remnant fibers of old basal leaves, the middle and upper leaves of an ovate to lanceolate type and about the same size, white corollas, acute involucral and receptacular bracts. Rare. Rocky stream banks and cliffs, damp deciduous woods; sw Ala, into se La, cn Tenn, and sw NC; cs SC. May-July.

Other species with ovate to lanceolate types of stem leaves include: *M. obovata* (Walt.) Beadle & Boynt. with obtuse bracts and chaff. Common. Old fields, meadows, thin deciduous or pine woods; nw Fla into e Ala, cs Va, and se NC. Apr-June.

Barbara's-buttons   *Marshallia tenuifolia* Raf.

This species has linear to linear-lanceolate stem leaves, gradually reduced to mere bracts at top. Basal leaves are horizontal spreading, spatulate to oblong-ovate, and leave no old wiry fibrous bases. Stem usually branched about midway, each branch with one head of flowers surrounded by strongly acuminate to subulate-tipped bracts. Common. Thin longleaf pine areas, moist pinelands, bogs, swamps; Fla into se and ce Tex and se Ga. July-Sept.

M. graminifolia (Walt.) Small is similar but the basal and lower stem leaves are ascending and leave old wiry fibrous bases. Occasional. Low pinelands, bogs, swamps, wet roadsides; se Ga into s half of C.P. of NC. May-Sept. In *M. ramosa* Beadle & Boynt. involucral bracts are acute to barely obtuse and 4–6 mm long. The stem is branched above the middle and bears 4–20 heads. Rare. Places dry except during rainy seasons; rocky outcrops, pine barrens; c C.P. of Ga. May-June.

Bidens laevis × 3/5

Balduina angustifolia × 1/4

Marshallia trinerva × 1/4

Marshallia tenuifolia × 2/5

Bitterweed   *Helenium amarum* (Raf.) Rock

Members of this genus have alternate stem leaves, usually yellow rays, no receptacular bracts, a pappus of papery scales, and truncate style tips.

An annual to 1 m tall, much branched above, the leaves linear, to 7 cm long, 1–4 mm wide, often with smaller axillary clusters of leaves. It is a serious pest in pastures. Although bitter and usually avoided by animals, it is often eaten when forage is scarce. The milk of cows that have grazed on the plant contains a bitter flavor and horses and mules have been reported poisoned by it. Common. Pastures, fields, roadsides, waste places; Fla into cs Tex, e Kan, s Ind, and Mass, being rare in the mts and the northern parts of its range. May-frost. *H. tenuifolium* Nutt.

Balduina angustifolia, which see, is similar but is less branched above and has narrower rays.

Sneezeweed   *Helenium flexuoṣum* Raf.

Perennial with 1 to several finely hairy stems from a rootstock. Leaves alternate, base of the blades extending down the stems making them winged. Flower heads usually many and short peduncled. Pappus of scales. This and the species below are poisonous when eaten. Animals usually avoid eating the plants, which are bitter, but may do so when other forage is scarce. Common. Moist to wet meadows, pastures, waste places; n Fla into e Tex, se Kan, s Mich, O, sw Pa, and sw Me. May-Aug. *H. nudiflorum* Nutt.

H. brevifolium (Nutt.) Wood is similar but has only 1–4 heads and blooms in the late spring. Rare. Bogs, swamps, depressions; cw Ga into nw Fla, se La, and ne Ala; NC into se Va. May-June. In *H. autumnale* L. the disc corollas are yellow but otherwise it is much like *H. flexuosum*. Common. Similar habitats; n Fla into se and cn Tex, e ND, s Que, and Mass. Aug-Oct.

Spring Helenium   *Helenium vernale* Walt.

Perennial to 70 cm tall with 0–3 long glabrous branches, each with a head of flowers. Sometimes with more than one stem from the basal cluster of spatulate to linear leaves. Leaves opposite. Achenes glabrous. Common. Wet pinelands, pond margins, open swamps, ditches; n Fla into se La, s Ga, and se NC. Mar-May.

H. pinnatifidum (Nutt.) Rydb. is similar but the lower leaves are often lobed or cleft and the achenes are finely hairy on the ribs. Occasional. Similar habitats; pen, cn, and ne Fla into s Ga and se NC. *Balduina uniflora* Nutt. is also similar but flowers July-Sept, has a honeycombed receptacle surface and thick- instead of thin-margined involucral bracts. Common. Moist to wet savannahs and pinelands, ditches; n Fla into se La, C.P. of Ga, and sw SC; se SC into se NC. July-Sept. *Endorina uniflora* (Nutt.) Barnh.

Gaillardia; Fire-wheel   *Gaillardia pulchella* Foug.

Annual, or biennial in the warmer parts of our area, to 70 cm tall, decumbent to erect, branches few to many but the plant not compact. Leaves alternate, entire to serrate or pinnately cut. Flower heads long-peduncled, bracts around flowers overlapping. Rays 15–25 mm long, red to purplish-red, or the tip yellow, or all yellow. Disc corollas the same color as the rays. Achenes 4-angled. Pappus a crown of 5–7 long tapering scales. Occasional. Fields, roadsides, dunes, prairies, usually sandy soils; Fla into Ariz, s Neb, La, C.P. of Ga, and se Va. Apr-frost. *G. picta* Sweet.

In *G. aestivalis* (Walt.) Rock the rays are 10–20 mm long, yellow and tinged with red, sometimes absent. Disc corollas purplish red or nearly maroon. Pappus of 7–10 scales. Occasional. Sandy soils in thin woods or open; Fla into e Tex, s Ill, La, nw Ga, C.P. of Ga, into sw C.P. of NC. May-frost. *G. lanceolata* Michx.

Helenium flexuosum × 2/3

Helenium amarum × 1/6

Gaillardia pulchella × 1/2

Helenium vernale × 1

Ox-eye Daisy   *Chrysanthemum leucanthemum* L.

Perennial to 1 m tall with short rhizomes. Leaves alternate, the numerous basal ones usually pinnately lobed or cleft. Flower heads 1 or few, with no receptacular bracts. Rays 15–30, white, 10–25 mm long. Disc flowers producing achenes, the corollas yellow. Pappus absent. It is useful as an ornamental, either in clusters or colonies, or as cut flowers, but can be a bad weed. Common. Fields, pastures, lawns, waste places; nearly throughout the United States and from BC into Lab. Apr-July; sometimes in the fall. *Leucanthemum leucanthemum* (L.) Rydb.

Indian-plantain   *Cacalia lanceolata* Nutt.

Members of the genus are erect glabrous perennials with alternate leaves. Involucral bracts in one circle or with a few small bracts at their bases. Receptacular bracts absent. Flowers all perfect and without rays. Corollas white.

In this species the lower leaves are lanceolate to lance-ovate and entire to serrate or dentate. Involucral bracts smooth on the back. The entire inflorescence is whitish. Occasional. Open pinelands or savannahs, usually wet places; Fla into se Tex, c C.P. of Ga, and se NC. June-Oct. *Mesadenia lanceolata* (Nutt.) Raf.

C. ovata Walt. is similar but has ovate to broadly ovate leaves. Occasional. Wet pinelands, swamps; Fla into se La, s Miss, and s Ga. Aug-Oct. *Mesadenia elliottii* Harper. In *C. atriplicifolia* L. the lower leaves are palmately-veined, triangular-reniform and glaucous beneath. Common but only scattered in Pied. and C.P.; thin woods, pastures; Fla into ne Okla, s Miss, and s NY. June-Oct.

Butterweed   *Senecio glabellus* Poir.

Erect glabrous succulent annual to 1 m tall, often forming dense stands. Stems mostly one and unbranched to the inflorescence. Leaves deeply pinnately lobed. Individual flowers in the heads not accompanied by chaff. Pappus of capillary bristles. Suspected of being poisonous when eaten. Common. Wet places in open or in woods, especially in stream bottoms; Fla into e Tex, e Kan, sw O, nw and ce Ga, and se NC. Mar-May.

S. obovatus Willd., a perennial, has a similar inflorescence, but not as tight and the nearest leaves not so large. Recognized by obovate basal leaves and well-developed stolons. Occasional. Rich woods, usually on slopes; n Fla into Tex, e Kan, s Ont, s NH, and cw SC. Mar-June. In *S. aureus* L., another perennial, the basal leaf blades are nearly orbicular, being less than 1.5 times as long as wide. Common. Moist woods and swamps; cn SC into cn Ga, se Ky, Ill, n Ark, e ND, s Ont, and Lab. Apr-June.

Southern Ragwort   *Senecio smallii* Britt.

Perennial to 70 cm tall, the stem densely woolly at base. Basal leaves cuneate, lanceolate, and crenate to serrate or once pinnately dissected. Common. Fields, pastures, open woods, savannahs, roadsides; Fla into Ala, cs Ky, se Pa, and s NS. Apr-June.

S. millefolium T. & G. is similar but the leaves are twice pinnately divided or are divided into finer divisions, less than 3 mm wide. Rare. On or near rock outcrops in mts; ne Ga into sw NC and nw SC. In *S. tomentosus* Michx. the lower leaves are not dissected and are persistently hairy, at least on the stem and lower surfaces of the leaves which are usually densely felted. Occasional. Sandy or rocky places, often on granitic outcrops, but in moist places, at least temporarily so; Fla into e Tex, s Ark, Pied. of Ga, e Va, and s NJ.

Chrysanthemum leucanthemum × 2/5

Senecio glabellus × 1/2

Senecio smallii × 1/4

Yellow Thistle   *Cirsium horridulum* Michx.

Members of the genus have no ray flowers, the leaves are spiny, and the pappus of capillary plumose bristles.

This species is usually a biennial to 1 m tall. The involucral bracts are spiny tipped and these are closely surrounded by a series of narrow, spiny-toothed leaves. The terminal head may be 5 cm broad. Corollas may be yellow, purple, or rarely white. Plants at first are dense and unbranched, later often becoming branched and to 1.2 m tall. Common. Roadsides, fields, and other open places; se Tex into Ga, Fla, and SC; then into s Me. Mar-June. *Carduus spinosissimus* Walt.

C. smallii Britt. is similar but usually less robust and the leafy bracts around the involucral bracts are densely ciliate. Occasional. Open places; Fla into C.P. of Ga and e NC. May-July.

Purple Thistle   *Cirsium carolinianum* (Walt.) Fern. & Schub.

Biennial to 2.5 m tall and the flower heads on naked peduncles, no leafy bracts being present beneath the heads. Heads usually less than 2.5 cm broad, the middle involucral bracts tipped with spines about 3 mm long. Stem leaves around 10–30. Corollas bright red-purple. Achenes 3–4 mm long. Young stems of this and other species can be eaten after peeling off the rind, cutting into pieces, and boiling in salted water. Occasional. Thin woods, dry, often sandy or rocky soils; cw SC into e Tex, se Mo, s O, Ky, and c NC. May-July. *Carduus carolinianus* Walt.

C. virginicum (L.) Michx. is similar but the spines on the middle involucral bracts are only 2 mm long or less and the stem leaves more abundant, around 35–70. Occasional. Moist to wet places, pine barrens, savannahs, roadside ditches; ne Fla into s NJ. Aug-frost. *Carduus virginianum* L.

Common Chicory; Blue-sailors   *Cichorium intybus* L.

Milky-juiced perennial to 1.7 m tall from a long taproot. Basal leaves numerous, the stem usually much branched. Flower heads sessile or short-peduncled, 1–3 of them in axils of the much smaller upper leaves. All flowers with rays, these usually bright blue, sometimes pink or white. Achenes angled. Pappus of 2–3 rows of very short scales. Young leaves are used by some as a potherb. The water is usually poured off twice to remove the bitter taste. The ground roots are roasted and used as a substitute for or to flavor coffee. Occasional. Fields, roadsides, wasteplaces; nearly throughout the United States but less common in C.P. May-frost.

Potato-dandelion   *Krigia dandelion* (L.) Nutt.

Members of this genus have milky juice, all corollas yellow and with ligules, one circle of equal sized (or nearly so) involucral bracts, and achenes which are not beaked.

This species is a perennial with basal leaves, has leafless and unbranched stems and a slim rhizome, a false taproot which bears a globose or ovoid tuber a few cm underground. The involucral bracts are 7–15 mm long. Occasional. Thin woods or open places, chiefly in sandy soil; Fla into se and cn Tex, se Kan, s Ind, se Tenn, cw Ga, Pied. of SC, and s NS. Mar-May. *Cynthia dandelion* (L.) DC.

K. virginica (L.) Willd. also has leafless stems but is an annual, lacks the tubers, and the involucral bracts are only 4.0–6.5 mm long when in flower, up to 9 mm when achenes are mature. Common. Open places, usually sandy soils; Fla into se and cn Tex, Wisc, and s Me. Mar-June.

Cirsium horridulum × 1/8

Cirsium carolinianum × 4/5

Cichorium intybus × 3/5

Krigia dandelion × 1/4

Dwarf-dandelion   *Krigia montana* (Michx.) Nutt.

Perennial with leafy stems. The leaves are much alike and may be crowded near the base when the plant first flowers. Peduncles single, arising from axils of ordinary foliage leaves. Involucral bracts 4–8 times as long as wide. Occasional. Moist places on exposed rocks, stream margins; nw SC into cn Ga and e NC. May-Oct. *Cynthia montana* (Michx.) Standl.

    K. biflora (Walt.) Blake is similar but the peduncles are 1 to several arising from the axils of the upper smaller sized leaves. Common. Rich woods, sometimes in fields and pastures; cw Ga into ne Okla, se Kan, Ill, se Man, Mass, and sw NC. Mar-July. *K. oppositifolia* Raf. is also similar, but an annual with the involucral bracts 1.5–3 times as long as wide. Common. Fields, pastures, disturbed ground; nw Fla into se and cn Tex, c Kan, sw Ind, nw and Pied. of Ga, and se Va. Mar-June. *Serinia oppositifolia* (Raf.) O. Ktze.

Dandelion; Blowballs   *Taraxicum officinale* Wiggers

Perennial from a deep taproot to 1 cm thick. Leaves all basal, barely lobed to sharply pinnately cut or divided. Flowers with rays only, many in each head, and surrounded by more than 1 set of bracts. Heads single, 2–5 cm broad, on hollow naked stems to 50 cm tall. Fruits olive green to greenish brown, with a long neck and "parachute" at the top. Leaves are much used as a salad and potherb and are best gathered young and tender. For a potherb the leaves are boiled in water for a short time, the water being changed once or twice if the bitter taste is undesirable. Common. Lawns, pastures, other open places; nearly throughout the United States and s Canada. Mar-Sept, occasionally in winter.

    T. laevigatum (Willd.) DC. (*T. erythrospermum* Andrz.) is recognized by some as a species; the fruits are reddish brown. Occasional. Similar places and distribution.

Wild Lettuce   *Lactuca floridana* (L.) Gaertn.

Members of this genus have milky juice and all flowers have rays. Heads have 5–56 flowers; rays yellow, orange, blue, or purple; achenes flattened; and the pappus is one circle of capillary bristles.

    This species is an annual: The leaves do not clasp the stem. Rays are blue to violet. Achenes have 3 equal ribs on each side and a short stout neck, or not any. Pappus pure white. Common. Rich woods, roadsides, open and usually moist places; Fla into e and cn Tex, se Neb, O, and se Mass. July-frost. *L. villosa* Jacq.

    L. biennis (Moench) Fern. has similar fruits but the leaves clasp the stem, the rays are blue to white or sometimes yellow, the pappus is light brown. Usually in open moist places; c and w NC into Ind, BC, and Nfld; Colo, Ore, Wash. Aug-frost.

Wild Lettuce   *Lactuca canadensis* L.

Annual or biennial to 3 m tall with green to reddish stems. Leaves oblanceolate to lanceolate, entire or toothed to pinnately lobed or sagittate. Heads with 13–22 flowers, rays yellow. Involucral bracts collectively 10–15 mm long when achenes are mature. Achenes 5–6 mm long including a narrow neck 2–2.5 mm long, each side of the body with one main rib and sometimes a pair of indistinct ones. Pappus bristles 4.5–6 mm long. Common. Fields, pastures, waste places, thin woods; Fla into e Tex, Sask, and PEI. June-frost.

    L. graminifolia Michx. has similar fruits but with mostly basal linear to oblanceolate rarely toothed leaves, blue to violet rays, and pappus bristles 7–8 mm long. Occasional. Fla into Ariz, Pied. of Ga, and s NJ. Apr-Sept. *L. serriola* L. has prickly margined leaves and 5 or more ribs on each side of the achenes. Throughout most of the United States. Common in the Southeast. June-frost.

Krigia montana × 1/5

Taraxicum officinale × 2/5

Lactuca floridana × 1/4

Lactuca canadensis × 1/3

False-dandelion   *Pyrrhopappus carolinianus* (Walt.) DC.

Milky-juiced annual or biennial to 1.2 m tall from a taproot. Stem leaves 3–12, upper ones gradually smaller, basal ones oblanceolate to narrowly elliptic, pinnately lobed or dissected to merely toothed. All flowers with rays, these yellow or pale cream-colored. The longest involucral bracts are 2-lobed or widest at the tip. Achenes not flattened, finely 5-groved. Pappus a ring of very light tan capillary bristles. Common. Fields, pastures, roadsides; Fla into e and cn Tex, se Neb, sw Ind, Va, and Del. Mar-June.

P. georgianus Shinners is similar but often perennial, 12–50 cm tall, with 0–4 stem leaves and 1–5 abruptly smaller leafy bracts below the inflorescence. Some people treat this as a variety of the above species with which it hybridizes. Rare. Similar places; Fla into s Ala, s Ga, and se NC. Feb-June.

TYPHACEAE: Cattail Family

Common Cattail   *Typha latifolia* L.

The dense cylinders of tiny flowers identify Cattails. Male flowers, which drop soon, are in a cylinder above the larger mass of female flowers. In this species male and female flower clusters are usually adjacent and the stigmas are lanceolate to ovate. Rootstocks can be eaten raw or cooked, and a flour obtained from them. Pollen can be collected and used as a flour. Young stems and young flowers can be cooked and eaten. Leaves are used to make chair seats. Common. Shallow water, sometimes brackish, in open; all of the United States and into s Canada. Apr-July.

T. domingensis Pers. is the only other species common in the Southeast. The masses of male and female flowers are usually separated and the stigmas are linear. Similar habitats; Fla into coastal Ga, e Va, and Del; along the Gulf coast into Tex, inland into cs Kan, and w into Cal and sw Ore.

SPARGANIACEAE: Bur-reed Family

Bur-reed   *Sparganium americanum* Nutt.

Leaves elongate, sometimes 2 cm wide, and with rounded tips. Flowers and fruits in dense globose heads, the staminate flowers being on the upper and outer parts of the inflorescence. The pistillate flower heads mature into "burs" which are usually in leaf axils. Individual sections (fruits) of the "burs" are dull and finely pitted. Its underground tubers have been boiled or roasted for food. Occasional. In mud at edge of or in water; Fla into e Tex, e ND, and Nfld. May-July.

S. androcladum (Engelm.) Morong is similar but has smooth shiny fruits. Rare. Similar places; Va into Mo, e Tex, Minn, s Que, and s Me. *S. chlorocarpum* Rydb. is another species with lustrous fruits, but one or more of the "burs" is out of the leaf axil. Rare. Similar places; nw NC into w Pa, c O, Ia, s Que, and Nfld.

Pyrrhopappus carolinianus × 2/5

Typha latifolia × 1/4

Sparganium americanum × 2/5

Arrowhead *Sagittaria latifolia* Willd.

The generic name comes from the arrow-shaped leaves of some species. Others have no such leaves. Sagittarias have many small "seeds" (carpels) in dense rounded heads. Lower flowers female, or all flowers female, or all male; flowers never perfect.

In this variable species the fruit-bearing pedicels are not curved downward. The bracts at pedicel bases are thin and obtuse at apex. Beaks on the "seeds" are at right angles to the body. Common. Various wet places; Fla into Me and to the w, except for a few states. June-Nov.

Other acquatic species with arrow-shaped leaves are: *S. engelmanniana* J. G. Sm., with erect beak and thick pedicels. Rare. Ark into s Ind, Mass, and n SC. *S. longirosta* (Micheli) J. G. Sm., with erect beak and thin pedicels. Occasional. Fla into Ark, Ky, and NJ. *S. montevidensis* Cham. & Schlect., with mature pedicels curved downward. Rare. Fla into Cal, ND, Mich, O, Del, and se NC.

Narrow-leaved Sagittaria *Sagittaria graminea* Michx.

Perennial to 60 cm tall. Above-water leaves linear to ovate, to 30 cm long. Submersed leaves narrow, to 50 cm long and 2.5 cm wide. Male flowers with many stamens, the filaments finely hairy and widened at the base, equal to or shorter than the anthers. Common. At edge of or in water, especially in swamps; Fla into cs and e Tex, e Kan, s Minn, and s Lab. Apr-Oct.

S. subulata (L.) Buch. also has narrow leaves, occasionally with some ovate or lanceolate blades on the floating ends of the leaves, but the filaments are glabrous. Occasional. Shallow water and mud, in open; C.P. of Fla into s Miss, s Ga, and Mass.

POACEAE: Grass Family

Sugarcane Plumegrass *Erianthus giganteus* (Walt.) Muhl.

This is one of our largest native grasses, growing to 3 m tall. As in all grasses the flowers are quite small and consist mostly of a few stamens and a pistil with two fuzzy stigmas, all borne between two stiff scale-like structures, the lemma and palea, the whole group being called a floret. A grain, part of which is the seed, develops between the lemma and palea. Identification of grasses is based largely on characteristics of the florets and the various ways they are assembled into clusters, including whole inflorescences. In this species the lemmas have long copious hairs fastened to their bases and a terete awn on the tip. Common. Moist open places; Fla into e Tex, se Okla, Ky, Va, and se NY. Mostly absent from the Appalachian Mts. Sept-Oct.

Five other species of *Erianthus* occur in the Southeast, the most common species being *E. alopecuroides* (L.) Ell. It also has copious hairs on the spikelet but the awn is flat and spirally coiled. Common. Various open places and thin woods, n Fla into e Tex, s Mo, s Ind, e Ky, Va, and se NJ. Aug-Nov.

Coastal Broomsedge *Andropogon capillipes* Nash

Tufted perennial to 85 cm tall. Florets hairy, some of them clasped by sheathing leaves. Most Broomsedges look much alike and identification to species is usually difficult. This species is no exception so characters for positive identification will not be given. Broomsedges are generally poor for forage. They can be controlled by mowing and proper management of fields in which they may happen to grow. Rare. Sandy places in open or thin woods; se NC into e Fla; s Ala. Sept.

Over 20 species occur in some part of our area, the most conspicuous species being *A. glomeratus* (Walt.) B.S.P. It is easily recognized by the large dense mass of hairy florets at the top of the stems. Common. Moist open areas; Fla into s Cal, Tenn, Ky, Va, and e Mass. Sept-Oct.

Sagittaria latifolia × 1/4

Sagittaria graminea × 1/6

Erianthus giganteus × 1/18

Andropogon capillipes × 1/6

Pink Muhlenbergia   *Muhlenbergia filipes* M. A. Curtis

Tufted perennial to 80 cm tall. The inflorescence is a loose panicle, pinkish when mature. When these panicles are in full color and bending with the wind they are outstandingly attractive, especially when there are many clumps over a large area. The florets are borne singly on thin pedicels at ends of the panicle branches. The stems are collected by natives along the SC coast and used as one of the components in the weaving of attractive and serviceable baskets, table mats, and the like. Occasional. Along or near the coast in moist open places, between dunes, in pinelands; NC into Fla and e Tex. Sept-Oct. *M. capillaris* var. *filipes* (M. A. Curtis) Beal.

At least ten species of this large genus occur in the Southeast. Identification of most species is difficult.

Dune Sandbur; Sandspur   *Cenchrus tribuloides* L.

Stems decumbent or spreading, sometimes rooting. The small flowers are almost completely inclosed in a "bur" which bears many short fine hairs and several very sharp and minutely barbed spines 5–9 mm long. The burs of this species are the largest in the genus, the body and spines together sometimes 15 mm wide. Common. Dunes and other loose sands, in open; along the coast, La into Fla and NY. July-Nov.

Seven species occur in the Southeast, the most widespread one being *C. longispinus* (Hack.) Fern., an annual which has been found in all of our states except 5 northern ones. The spines are under 5 mm long and the body of the bur over 5 mm in diameter. Common. Mostly in sandy open places. *C. pauciflorus* Benth.

CYPERACEAE: Sedge Family

Saltmarsh Bulrush   *Scirpus robustus* Pursh

Most members of this family appear much like grasses, but have leaves in three rows, whereas in grasses there are two rows of leaves. Also each flower is in the axile of a single "scale" while in the grasses the flowers are between two scales. The flowers, which are very small, consist of 2–3 stamens, a pistil with 2–3 stigmas, and a perianth represented by bristles or scale-like structures, or absent. In the genus *Scirpus* the flowers and their subtending scales are spirally arranged in tight, cone-shaped clusters called spikelets.

In this species plants may be 140 cm tall with 3–4 leaves at the inflorescence and several longer ones from lower parts of the plant. The spikelets are 15–45 mm long and in a cluster of 3–25 near the top of the plant. Common. Brackish marshes and ditches; se Tex into Fla and Mass; Cal. July-Sept.

Marsh Bulrush   *Scirpus cyperinus* (L.) Kunth

Perennial to 1.5 m tall, often in conspicuous colonies. A very variable species. Leaves many and curving. The spikelets are 4–6 mm long, many in large terminal clusters, brownish at maturity, and forming a conspicuous top layer on the colony as seen in the picture. The bristles on the flowers are reddish, strongly curled, and project beyond the subtending scales. Common. Marshes, swamps, shallow margins of ponds and lakes, other open wet places; Fla into e Tex, s Minn, and Nfld. July-Sept.

S. polyphyllus Vahl. is another tall, to 1 m, leafy species. The stem bears 12 or more leaves. The spikelets are only 3–4 mm long and the bristles mostly shorter than the scale. Common. Wet habitats, usually in open; nw SC into se Mo and s Vt. There are over 20 species of *Scirpus* in our area, and their identification is usually difficult.

Cenchrus tribuloides × 1½

Muhlenbergia filipes × 1/10

Scirpus cyperinus × 1/40

Scirpus robustus × 2/3

Whitetop Sedge   *Dichromena latifolia* Baldw.

The 7–10 conspicuous white leaves (bracts) at the top of this grass-like plant enable it to be seen from considerable distances. The bases of the bracts surround the inconspicuous flowers. The plants arise from a rhizome 2–4 mm in diameter. Occasional. Moist to wet situations in open, often in depressions, in savannahs or thin woods; C.P.—NC into Fla, and se Tex. Apr-Sept.

The similar but generally smaller *D. colorata* (L.) Hitchc., Star-rush, usually has less than 7 bracts and the rhizome is less than 1.8 mm in diam. Common. Similar habitats; C.P.—se Va into Fla and c Tex; c Ala.

Sedge; Carex   *Carex lupuliformis* Dewey

The male and female flowers of species of this genus are in different parts of the same spike, as seen in the picture, or in separate spikes of the same plant, or rarely on different plants. The female flowers are quite odd in being enclosed in a sac-like structure, the perigynium. The apex of the perigynium has a small opening through which the stigmas protrude. There are many species of *Carex* in the Southeast, probably over 125. Most occur in wet habitats, although some grow in very dry places such as rock crevices. They vary from small fine-leaved species to conspicuous plants well over 1 m tall. Very few persons can identify more than a few species with confidence. The species in the photograph is one of the largest flowered species of the genus. Rare. Moist to wet places; n Ga into e Tex, Minn, and s Vt.

ARACEAE: Arum Family

Golden-club; Never-wet   *Orontium aquaticum* L.

The common name "Never-wet" alludes to the leaves which, when submerged, will come out of the water dry. Water drops will run across the leaf surface. If a drop remains on the surface it often appears as a jewel when reflecting light. The flowers are many at the surface of the golden club (the spadix). Fruits blue-green, thin-walled, one-seeded. Although the raw fruits usually cause an unbearable burning sensation the Indians used the fruits abundantly for food, boiling them extensively in water or drying them thoroughly before eating. Roots were sliced and dried, or boiled or roasted and eaten or used for flour. Occasional. Swamps, bogs, and shallow streams; Fla into La, se Ky, c NY, and Mass. Feb-June.

Dichromena latifolia × 3/5

Carex lupuliformis × 4/5

Orontium aquaticum × 1/5

Jack-in-the-pulpit; Indian-turnip   *Arisaema triphyllum* (L.) Schott

A variable herbaceous perennial from a corm up to 5 cm thick. Plants sometimes over 1 m tall. Leaves 1 or 2, palmately divided into 3–5 leaflets, the outer leaflets sometimes with a lobe near the base. Flowers unisexual, sessile on the fleshy axis (the spadix or "Jack"), the male flowers above and female below, or all one sex. The spadix is sometimes curved. The spathe (the "pulpit") with a tube and a hood which arches over the spadix. The upper part of the spadix may be green to deep maroon, and the spathe green to partly maroon (sometimes completely so on the inner side). Fruits fleshy, 1–few-seeded, scarlet when mature. The plant contains small needlelike crystals of calcium oxalate, particularly in the corm, which, if taken into the mouth, become imbedded in tissues and provoke intense irritation and a burning sensation. The corms usually are not edible even after cooking. Thin slices thoroughly dried for several months are reported to be palatable. Common in rich woods, often moist to wet; Fla into e Tex, Minn, and PEI. Mar-June.

In *A. dracontium* (L.) Schott, the Green-dragon, the flowers are arranged similarly to those of Jack-in-the-pulpit. The spadix tapers to a long slender tip beyond the much shorter sheathing spathe. Fruits in a tight cluster, orange-red when ripe. The one leaf is divided into 7–15 leaflets arranged somewhat in a band parallel to the ground. The corms are similar to those of Jack-in-the-pulpit in respect to being eaten. Common. Usually moist places, rich soil of dense deciduous woods; Fla into c Tex, se Minn, s Que, and se NH. May-June. *Muricanda dracontium* (L.) Small.

White Arum   *Peltandra sagittaefolia* (Michx.) Morong

Perennial with arrow-shaped leaves. A large white sheath (spathe) surrounds the fleshy axis (spadix) which bears the flowers. The flowers are of 2 sexes, the male flowers being on the upper part of the spadix and female flowers on the lower part. The mature fruits are red. Apparently all parts of the plant contain calcium oxalate which may cause severe burning when eaten. Thorough and prolonged drying of the rootstocks has been reported to render them edible. Rare. Swamps; C.P. of NC into Fla and Miss. July-Aug. *P. glauca* (Ell.) Feay.

The vegetatively similar *P. virginica* (L.) Kunth has a green spathe which is tighter around the spadix, and has greenish to amber fruits. Common. The fruits are an important food of the wood duck. Wet habitats; Fla into Tex, se Okla, e Mo, s Ont, and Me.

LEMNACEAE: Duckweed Family

Duckweed   *Lemna perpusilla* Torr.

Plants small, floating on water, lacking any distinct stem or leaves, consisting of one to several fleshy masses of cells called fronds. Each frond has a single descending root from the underside. Flowers are minute, occurring in small pouches on the sides of the fronds, and consisting of a single pistil or a single stamen. This species is difficult to separate from others of similar shape and usually requires examination under a microscope. Duckweeds are important food for wildfowl, muskrats, and small animals. Common. Water surfaces in open or shade; Fla into Cal, BC, and Lab. Sept-Nov. *L. minor* L. of many authors.

Spirodela polyrhiza (L.) Schleid. fronds are similar but are larger, about 5 mm long, and bear 2 or more roots. The fronds are usually conspicuously 5–18–nerved. Common. Similar habitats and distribution.

Arisaema triphyllum × 1/3

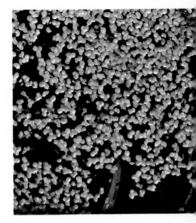

Lemna perpusilla × 3/5

Peltandra sagittaefolia × 1/7

Pipewort; Buttonrods; Hatpins   *Eriocaulon decangulare* L.

Members of this genus are conspicuous when in flower because of the dense white heads of flowers, "buttons," on the tip of leafless stems. The buttons provide a strong contrast in a sea of other generally less conspicuous plants, such as grasses and sedges. They are perennials with basal linear leaves and are separated from related genera by having in the leaves air spaces visible to the naked eye, jointed essentially unbranched roots, and a jet-black gland on each petal lobe.

In this species the scape is finely 8–12 ridged, the leaves are longer than the sheath around the base of the scape, and the mature heads are 10–20 mm broad. Common. Sandy or peaty soils of pine flatwoods, cypress swamps, ditches, and lakeshores; Fla into se La, se Miss, s Ala, C.P. of SC, and c and ce NJ; se and ce Tex and adj La; nw SC into sw and c NC; w Pied. of Ga.

XYRIDACEAE: Yellow-eyed-grass Family

Yellow-eyed-grass   *Xyris ambigua* Kunth

Species of this genus are annuals or perennials with inconspicuous flowers and basal linear to terete-filiform leaves which often resemble in shape and arrangement those of Irises. Individual plants can be fairly easily located by looking for small yellow spots, the bright yellow corollas. These protrude from behind woody scales which are in a compact terminal spike on a leafless stem. Identification to species is often dependent on minute characters of the seeds and the peculiar sepals as well as on characters of the leaves and scape. About 18 species occur entirely or mostly in the Southeast.

In this species the sheaths around the base of the scape are shorter than the larger foliage leaves, the spikes 1–3 cm long and lance-ovate to ellipsoidal, and the lateral sepals shorter than the subtending scales and with margins rough to the touch. Common. Moist sands or sandy peats of pine flatwoods, savannahs, bog margins, lakeshores, and roadside ditches; Fla into e Tex, lower C.P. of Ga, and se Va; also scattered localities inland from e Ala into c NC. Apr-Aug.

BROMELIACEAE: Pineapple Family

Spanish-moss   *Tillandsia usneoides* L.

This relative of the pineapple hangs from trees and sometimes from other objects such as telephone lines and fences. The stems are slender and wiry, the leaves filiform. Both bear numerous small silver-gray scales that are important in trapping water and nutrient-providing dust particles necessary for life. The plants superficially resemble mosses, but are flowering plants. A flower is shown in the picture. Plants have been used as forage, and in upholstery and mattresses. Campers should be careful about using Spanish-moss as bedding because of the danger of Red-bugs or Chiggers. Common. Pendant on trees from swamp to upland; Fla into s and c Tex, se Pied. of Ga, and e Va. Apr-July.

Eriocaulon decangulare × 1/10

Eriocaulon decangulare × 1⅓

Xyris ambigua × 1¼

Tillandsia usneoides × 3

Dayflower   *Commelina erecta* L.

A variable perennial from thickened roots. Two petals blue, the third whitish and
much smaller than the other 2. All 3 are ephemeral, sometimes withering before noon.
Flowers appear singly each day or so from within the fold of greenish bracts called
spathes. The spathes are terminal or axillary and the margins not fused. Young stems
and leaves of some species of Dayflowers have been used as a potherb in foreign
countries. The seeds are eaten by Mourning Doves, Quail, and several kinds of song-
birds. Common. Dry, usually sandy soils, usually in open; Fla into Ariz, cn Neb,
Tenn, and se NY. May-frost.

    C. communis L. also has 1 pale petal. The species is a weedy annual with fibrous
roots. The spathes are fused at the base. Common. Moist places, in woods or open,
gardens, ditches; n Ga into ne Tex, e SD, Mich, and Mass.

Woods Dayflower   *Commelina virginiana* L.

Erect perennial to 1.2 m tall from a creeping and branching rhizome. Flowers from
within greenish spathes which are usually in a terminal cluster. The spathes are fused
at their bases. All petals blue, ephemeral, one slightly smaller than the others. Occasional. Moist to wet places, in woods or rarely in open; n Fla into e and c Tex, Ill,
Ky, s Pa, and s NJ. June-Oct.

    C. diffusa Burm. f. also has 3 blue ephemeral petals but is smaller, an annual, the
spathe bases are not fused, and the much-branched stems are decumbent and rooting
at the nodes. Common. Moist to drier places, in woods or open; Fla into s and e Tex,
e Kan, s O, and Md; mostly absent from mts.

Spiderwort   *Tradescantia virginiana* L.

Members of the genus are perennials, have ephemeral petals and 5 or 6 fertile stamens,
each with the filaments bearded.

    This species has blades of the upper leaves narrower than to about as broad as the
basal sheath, which is unfused. Pedicels and sepals hairy their entire length. Petals
blue to purple or purplish-pink, or rarely white. Occasional. Usually in well-drained
areas in the open; n Ga into ne Ark, Wisc, Pa, and Me. Mar-July.

    T. ohiensis Raf. is similar but the pedicels and sepals, except perhaps the tips, are
not hairy and the leaves are glaucous. Common. In a variety of open better-drained
places; Fla into Tex, Neb, Minn, and Mass. *T. hirsuticaulis* Small is densely hairy and
has glandular as well as nonglandular hairs on the sepals. Occasional. Dry woods and
rocky places; Ga into Pied. and mts of NC, and Ala.

Roseling   *Tradescantia rosea* Vent.

Perennial, glabrous or nearly so, to 50 cm tall with a tuft of narrow basal leaves. The
flowers are subtended by bracts no more than 1 cm long in contrast to the prominent bracts of other species. In var. *rosea* the leaves are more than 3 mm wide. Common. Sandy soil, usually thin woods or in open; c Fla into c C.P. of Ga, cn and coastal
SC. May-Aug. *Cuthbertia rosea* (Vent.) Small.

    In var. *graminea* (Small) Anderson & Woodson the leaves are less than 3 mm
wide. Common. Dry sandy areas, scrub oak or pine barrens; pen Fla into c C.P. of
Ga, and s C.P. of NC; se Va. *Cuthbertea graminea* Small.

Commelina erecta × 2/5

Commelina virginiana × 1

Tradescantia virginiana × 1

Tradescantia rosea × 1

Water-hyacinth   *Eichhornia crassipes* (Mart.) Solms

Often seen floating on water in such a dense mass of deep-green foliage that the water and the distinctive inflated petioles are not easily seen. Largest leaves on any one plant may be only a few centimeters long, or reach a meter. The flower clusters are on erect peduncles and are a striking contrast to the deep-green foliage. The plant masses are a serious problem in drainage ditches, canals, lakes, ponds, etc. Its abundance diminishes greatly in the cooler parts of its range. Young leaves and flower clusters have been steamed or boiled and eaten in foreign countries. Abundant as Water-hyacinth is in some areas, it might well be tried as a food. Southern C.P. of NC into Fla and Tex; introduced and sometimes persisting in Pied. localities, such as in nearly constant temperature water of springs. May-Sept.

Pickerel-weed   *Pontederia cordata* L.

A soft-stemmed perennial to 1 m tall. One leaf not far below the flowers, the others basal. Leaves cordate to lanceolate or rarely linear, the largest 1–14 cm wide. Perianth purplish-blue or rarely white, the upper segment with a yellow area. The mature fruits are reported by some to be a pleasant food. The stems and leaves may be edible. The roots are inedible, producing a severe burning sensation. Common. Usually open places, at margin of, or in, water; Fla into Tex, se Kan, ce Minn, and NS; rare to absent inland to the Great Lakes area. Mar-Oct.

   P. lanceolata Nutt. has been separated as a species and a variety, but intergradation of characters seems too great for taxonomic recognition at either level.

JUNCACEAE: Rush Family

Black Rush   *Juncus roemerianus* Scheele

A perennial forming prominent dense stands or occasionally small dense clumps. Some of the basal leaves are terete, to over a meter tall, and with stiff sharp points, the others being mere basal sheaths. Stem resembling the leaves, at its top, as shown in the picture, bearing a repeatedly forked inflorescence and a terminal sharply pointed leaf. The inflorescence thus appears lateral. The flowers are in clusters at the tips of the branches. Common. Salt marshes and brackish ditches along the coast; Fla into se Tex and Md. Mar-Oct.

   J. effusus L. is similar but the flowers are borne singly at tips of the branches and the terminal leaf is soft pointed. Common. Moist depressions, edges of ponds and lakes, freshwater marshes; Fla into e Tex, se Kan, ce Wisc, and Nfld. Apr-Sept.

Eichhornia crassipes × 1/30

Pontederia cordata × 1/3

Juncus roemerianus × 4/5

False-asphodel   *Tofieldia racemosa* (Walt.) B.S.P.

Slender perennial to 70 cm tall from a short rhizome; leaves mostly basal, linear, to 40 cm long. Flowers in a terminal raceme, usually 2–6 from each node, the upper ones opening first. Scape roughened with minute projections. Perianth persisting and becoming rigid against the fruit. Mature fruit about equaling the perianth. Common. Wet sandy soils of pinelands and savannahs; Fla into se Tex, sw SC, and NJ; w Pied. of Ga. June-Sept. *Triantha racemosa* (Walt.) Small.

   T. glutinosa (Michx.) Pers. is similar except the perianth does not become rigid and the mature fruit is about twice as long as the perianth. Rare. Bogs, marshes; ne Ga into ne Tenn, e WVa, ne O, ne Ill, Alas, and Nfld. June-Aug. *Triantha glutinosa* (Michx.) Baker. *T. glabra* Nutt. is also similar but the scapes are glabrous and smooth to touch. Rare. Wet savannahs and pinelands; n C.P. of SC into ce and se NC.

Swamp-pink   *Helonias bullata* L.

The beauty of the tight cluster of many small pink lily-like flowers on the leafless stalk is enhanced by the elongate evergreen leaves at the base. After flowering, the stalk elongates to as high as 1 m. Rare. Swamps and bogs; nw SC, nw Ga, sw NC, nw and e Va into mts of Pa and se NY. Apr-May.

Crow-poison; Black-snakeroot   *Zigadenus densus* (Desr.) Fern.

Perennial to 1 m tall from a bulb, with 1–3 basal leaves, 2–7 mm wide, those above reduced to widely separated bracts. Flowers in a raceme. Bracts at base of each flower stalk yellowish and nearly straight at the tip. Tepals 6, nearly white to pink, each with 2 small glands at their base. Stamens 6. Probably not poisonous. Common. Wet places in thin pinelands or open; C.P.—e Tex into Fla and se Va. Mar-May.

   The above species is often confused with *Amianthium muscaetoxicum* (Walt.) Gray, Fly-poison, but the basal leaves of the latter are more abundant and usually wider, 4–23 mm; the bracts at base of flower stalks are brownish and slightly cupped at the tip; and glands are absent. Leaves and bulbs are quite poisonous. Occasional. In various situations, wooded or open, usually moist. Fla into Okla, s Mo, Ky, and s NY. Apr-July.

Blazing-star; Devil's-bit   *Chamaelirium luteum* (L.) Gray

Glabrous perennial with male flowers on one plant and female on another. Female plants are the taller, to 120 cm. Basal leaves large, the upper much smaller. Male inflorescence yellow at first, erect or nearly so, as shown. When all flowers have opened the inflorescence is drooping. Female inflorescence less conspicuous, the small flowers greenish and white. Occasional. Rich woods; Fla into se Ark, Tenn, s Ill, s Ind, s Ont, and w Mass. Mar-June.

Helonias bullata × 1¼

Tofieldia racemosa × 1

Chamaelirium luteum

Zigadenus densus × 1/2   × 2/5

Bellwort   *Uvularia perfoliata* L.

Glabrous perennial to 40 cm tall. Most leaves perfoliate, the blade-bearing leaves below lowest branch usually 3–4. The 6 tepals conspicuously granular-papillate within. Capsule lobes deeply 2-lobed or 2-horned. Occasional. Usually in deciduous woods on well-drained areas; occasionally elsewhere; nw Fla into La, s Ont, and Mass. Feb-May.

Another species, *U. grandiflora* J. E. Sm., also has perfoliate leaves. There is usually only one leaf below the lowest branch, the tepals are smooth within, and the main capsule lobes are neither 2-lobed nor 2-horned. SC into e Okla, ND, Que, and Me.

Bellwort   *Uvularia pudica* (Walt.) Fern.

Perennial to 45 cm tall. The upper stems 3-angled and usually finely hairy. Leaves sessile. Tepals and stamens 6 each. Capsule pointed. Occasional. Usually in rich well-drained woods; SC into Ga, e Tenn, s Pa, and se NY. Mar-May.

Two other species have sessile leaves. Both have glabrous stems. One, *U. floridana* Chapm., may be recognized by a sessile capsule and a bract 1–3 cm long near the tip of the short flowering branchlet. Rare. Bottomland and floodplain woods; n Fla into e Ala, and SC. Mar-Apr. The other, *U. sessilifolia* L., has no bract and the capsule has a short stipe. Common. Hardwood forested slopes; nw Fla into La, ND, Que, and NS. Mar-May.

Day-lily   *Hemerocallis fulva* L.

Perennial to 1 m tall. The basal tube of the flower tightly encloses the ovulary but is not fused with it. Fully grown flower buds and flowers have been used for food. These may be cooked in oil and butter in a batter of eggs, flour, and milk. They may be added for flavor in final stages of cooking of soups, meats, and other foods. Occasional. Widely domesticated, and escapes occur along roadsides, abandoned homesites, and borders of fields; Fla into e Tex, e Neb, Minn, and NB. May-July.

H. flava L., which has yellow flowers and is smaller, is naturalized locally as are a few of the many other horticultural types that have been introduced more recently than the two above species.

Wild Onion; Canada-garlic   *Allium canadense* L.

The odor identifies this species as one of the onions. Smooth flat mostly basal leaves 2–6 mm wide, netted fiber bulb-coats, and bulblets usually replacing some or all flowers characterize this species. The bulbs and young leaves are boiled and eaten, the liquid sometimes being used to make soup. The top bulbs are used for pickling. Large amounts may be harmful. Livestock eating tops or bulbs of Onions have developed anemia and jaundice. Common. Roadsides, fields, thin woods, most frequent in moist places; n Fla into e Tex, ND, and NB. Apr-July.

Other Onions with flat leaves include: Ramps, *A. tricoccum* Ait., which flowers as or after the broad (2–6 cm) leaves shrivel; n Ga into Minn, NB, Del, and e NC. June-July.

Uvularia perfoliata × 2/5

Uvularia pudica × 2/5

Hemerocallis fulva × 1/6

Allium canadense × 2

Wild Onion   *Allium cuthbertii* Small

Perennial to 65 cm tall. Leaves long, flat, to 6 mm wide, usually withered or withering at flowering time. Bulb covered with a mat of fibers. Inflorescence of flowers only. Perianth segments acuminate. Ovulary and fruit crested. Occasional. Sandhills, scrub oak, open woods, granitic outcrops; ne Fla into e Ala and cn SC; nw and c NC. Apr-June.

A. cernuum Roth also has flat leaves and no bulbs in the inflorescence. Bulb covered with membranes. Inflorescence nodding on a bent peduncle. Perianth segments obtuse or rounded at tips. Occasional. Rocky places, thin woods or in open; n SC into Ariz, BC, and NY. July-Sept.

False-garlic   *Nothoscordum bivalve* (L.) Britt.

Perennial to 45 cm tall from a small bulb which has a faint odor of onions when fresh. Leaves linear, less than 5 mm wide. Flowers 3–10 in terminal umbel. Perianth segments reflexed when fruits are developed. Onions have a strong odor and the perianth is not reflexed. Petals 1 cm or more long. Common. Fields, open woods, pastures, roadsides, thin soil around granitic outcrops; Fla into Tex, se Neb, cw Ind, s O, nw Ga, Pied. of Ga, and se Va. Mar-May; Sept-Nov. *Allium bivalve* (L.) O. Ktze.

N. fragrans (Vent.) Kunth is similar but the plants are taller, to 80 cm, the leaves are more than 5 mm wide, and there are usually more than 15 flowers per umbel. Rare. Sandy soils, roadsides, waste ground, fields; Fla into se La; central coast of SC. *Allium inodorum* Ait.

Carolina Lily   *Lilium michauxii* Poir.

Perennial to 1.5 m tall. Leaves chiefly whorled, the blades with smooth margins and mostly broadest above the middle. Flowers nodding, usually 1–3, or to 15 under favorable conditions, the tepals strongly recurved. Capsules nearly erect. Attractive hardy plants worthy of cultivation and the attention of nurseries. Named for Andre Michaux, French botanist who traveled widely in the southeastern United States. Rare. Dry to rich woods; n Fla into se Tex, e Tenn, s Va, and NC. May-Aug.

Other species with nodding to horizontal flowers are: *L. superbum* L., shown next. *L. canadense* L. with flared, usually lighter-colored tepals. Rare. Wet habitats; nw SC into n Ala, Ky, Minn, and NS. *L. grayi* Wats. with 1–8 horizontal bell-shaped flowers with flared dark-spotted red tepals, and finely roughened leaf margins. Rare. Higher mts; nw NC into ne Tenn and c Va.

Turk's-cap Lily   *Lilium superbum* L.

Perennial to 3 m tall. The leaves chiefly whorled, the blades with smooth margins and usually widest at the middle. Flowers nodding, as many as 65, but more often 25 or less. The tepals are strongly recurved and their inside bases are green. Rare. Moist habitats; nw Fla into Mo, Minn, NB, and n Ga; c C.P. of NC. June-Aug.

Two tall cultivated species with all leaves alternate have become naturalized locally. *L. bulbiferum* L., the Orange Lily, is 0.6–1.2 m tall and has erect lightly spotted flowers. *L. tigrinum* Ker is about as tall and has nodding, heavily spotted flowers.

Allium cuthbertii × 2/5

Nothoscordum bivalve × 4/5

Lilium michauxii × 2/5

Lilium superbum × 1/4

Pine Lily   *Lilium catesbaei* Walt.

Perennial to 60 cm tall, the leaves alternate, narrow, and ascending. The single flower and fruit erect. Petals wider than the similar sepals; the tips of both, and especially the sepals, curved backward; the blades of both orange toward the tip, yellow and purple-spotted toward the base which tapers into a slender claw. Common. Wet pinelands and savannahs, bogs; C.P.—se Va into Fla and s Miss. June-Sept.

Our other species with erect flowers is *L. philadelphicum* L. It has 1–5 similarly colored flowers but whorled leaves. Rare. Thin woods, meadows and balds; nw Ga, mts NC, Pied. Va, Del, and northward into Ky, s Ont, and Me.

Dog-tooth-violet; Trout-lily   *Erythronium americanum* Ker

Perennial from a bulb. The yellow tepals are washed with light to dark reddish-brown. The anthers yellow or sometimes brown to lavender. The tip of the ovulary and capsule may be truncate, rounded, or pointed. Mature capsules are held well off the ground. The leaves are variously reported as emetic or edible as a potherb. Common locally. Rich woods; n Ala into Okla, Minn, and NS; cs NC. Feb-May.

E. rostratum Wolf has a capsule with a prominent beak at the apex. Rare. Moist rich woods; Ala into e Tex, e Kan, and c Tenn. *E. umbilicatum* Parks & Hardin has a distinctly indented apex to the ovary and capsule, and mature capsules are reclining on or just above the ground. Common. Rich woods; n Fla into e Ala, s O, e WVa, and Va. *E. albidum* Nutt. has white tepals. Occasional. Woods and prairies; ne and c Ala into ne Tex, Minn, Ont, Pa, and c Tenn.

Star-of-Bethlehem   *Ornithogalum umbellatum* L.

A bulbous perennial, easily recognized because of the conspicuous broad white filaments below the yellowish anthers. The bulbs are reported to be edible when cooked, but all parts of the plant are also reported to be poisonous to grazing animals. Caution should be taken accordingly. This introduced native of Europe has become naturalized in lawns, fields, pastures, and low places, including woods. Occasional. Ga into La, Neb, and Nfld. Mar-June.

O. nutans L., a native of s Asia and naturalized locally, is similar but the lower flower stalks are about as long as the upper. *O. thyrsoides* Jacq., a native of South Africa, with a dense cluster of flowers, is widely sold by florists. Both species are poisonous when eaten and should be kept from children, especially.

Bear-grass; Yucca   *Yucca flaccida* Haw.

Leaves smooth above, leathery, evergreen, the margins fraying into threads. Rarely with an aboveground stem, then a shrub. Introduced far beyond its natural range. The young flowers are used in salads and cooked. Occasional. Usually dry habitats; fields, rocky and sandy places, and woods; se NC into Fla and Tenn; natzd. into Tex, Ill, and NJ. Mar-July. *Y. filamentosa* L. of most authors.

Y. filamentosa L. is similar but the leaves are scurfy to touch above and not as pointed. Occasional. Dry places in thin woods or open; ce Ga into s Va. *Y. aloifolia* L. (coast of se NC into Fla and cw Ala) and *Y. gloriosa* L. (coastal sands; NC into ne Fla) usually grow into erect shrubs or trees. The former has rigid leaves with minute marginal prickles, and the latter thick leathery leaves with thin tan margins.

Lilium catesbaei × 2/5

Erythronium americanum × 1/2

Ornithogalum umbellatum × 1/3

Yucca flaccida × 1/11

Wood-lily   *Clintonia umbellulata* (Michx.) Morong

Perennial from a knotty rhizome. The 2–6 leaves are basal. Flowers mostly erect in an umbel on a single stem which may be 50 cm tall. Tepals greenish-white. Fruit a berry, usually with 2 seeds and black when mature. The very young leaves have been used as a salad. Common locally only. Rich woods; nw SC into n Ga, e O, NY, and NJ. May-June.

   C. borealis (Ait.) Raf., Corn-lily or Clinton-lily, is similar but the flowers are mostly drooping, the tepals are greenish-yellow and larger, the fruit with more than 2 seeds and blue when mature. Common locally only. Rich moist woods; mts Ga into Pa, ne O, Minn, Man, and Lab.

False Solomon's-seal; Solomon's-plume   *Smilicina racemosa* (L.) Desf.

Herbaceous perennial from a fleshy knotty brown rhizome. Plants finely hairy, to 1 m tall, most often little over half that tall. Leaves in two ranks, usually on the top half to two-thirds of the stem. Flowers small; the tepals 6, white to greenish. Fruit a globose 1–3–seeded berry, reddish when mature, 4–6 mm in diameter. The berries are palatable but are cathartic. Common. Rich woods; Pied. of Ga into Ariz, BC, and NS. Mar-June.

Two-leaved Solomon's-seal; Canada-mayflower   *Maianthemum canadense* Desf.

The small white flowers and fruits are borne in a small raceme above the 2–3 (or rarely 1) leaves, suggestive of a diminutive False Solomon's-seal. The individual flowers are similar to those of False Solomon's-seal, the most noticeable difference being the reflexed perianth segments. Plants are rarely over 20 cm tall, from branched, fine, and extensive rhizomes. The fruits are a favorite food of the ruffed grouse. Common. Woods and thickets; mts of Ga, NC, and e Tenn into Mich, Man, Lab, and Del. May-June.

Solomon's-seal   *Polygonatum biflorum* (Walt.) Ell.

Perennial from an elongated knotted white rhizome. Stems to 1.5 m long, arching. Leaves sessile, glabrous beneath. Flowers, axillary, 1–12 per peduncle. Fruit a bluish black berry 8–13 mm in diameter. The young shoots have been prepared and eaten like asparagus, and the white rhizomes have been eaten as a salad; but as with all wildflowers, neither should be so used except in dire emergency. Common. Rich woods; Fla into e and cn Tex, Minn, s Ont, and Conn. Apr-June. *P. canaliculatum* (Muhl.) Pursh.

   P. pubescens (Willd.) Pursh is similar but the leaves are short and hairy beneath, especially on the veins. Usually not as large. Occasional. n Ga into e Tenn, n Ill, s Man, and NS.

Clintonia umbellulata × 1/4

Smilicina racemosa × 2/5

Maianthemum canadense × 1/3

Polygonatum biflorum × 2/5

Lily-of-the-valley   *Convallaria montana* Raf.

Perennial with 2–3 leaves. The flowering stem sheathed on the lower part of the leaf
bases. Inflorescence to half as high above the ground as the leaves. Plants not in dense
colonies, often scattered. Rare. Wooded slopes and coves; mts. of n Ga into WVa and
Va. Apr-June. *C. majalis* var. *montana* (Raf.) Ahles.

  C. majalis L. is similar but the plants form dense colonies and the inflorescences are
usually over half as high as the leaves. This species is abundantly reported in Europe
as poisonous when eaten. *C. montana* may therefore be poisonous. Rare. Spreading
from cultivation locally NC and Tenn northward into Me.

Sessile Trillium   *Trillium cuneatum* Raf.

This is the most abundant of the 16 species of sessile-flowered Trilliums in the Southeast. Petals 3–4 times as long as wide, purple, brown, green, or rarely yellow. Stamens
less than one-third taller than the pistil, anthers dehiscing toward the ovary or to the
side, prolonged part of connective wider than long. Ovulary not 3-angled, stigmas
divergent to spreading. All species of Trillium are perennial. Common. Rich woods;
Pied. of NC, into cs Miss, cs Ky, and se Tenn. Mar-May.

  There are several similar species. *T. sessile* L. has anther connectives prolonged almost as long as the filament. c Md into ne Okla, e Kan, se Mich, and sw NY; c Ky
into cn Ala. In *T. maculatum* Raf. the ovulary is 3-angled. Rare. cn Fla into cs and ce
Ala, and sw SC. In *T. underwoodii* Small the petals are more than 4 times as long as
wide, the prolonged part of the connective is about as long as the filament, and the
anthers dehisce at the sides. Rare. sw Ala into cw Ga and cn Fla. In *T. decumbens*
Harbison the stems are decumbent leaving the leaves on the surface of the ground
litter. Rare. n Ala into nw Ga. In *T. stamineum* Harbison the stems are erect, the
anthers dehisce on the outer side, and the pollen is brown. Rare. e Miss into w Ala
and c Tenn.

Trillium   *Trillium discolor* Wray

The pale yellow petals are tipped with a small point and have a long narrow base.
Stamens about twice as high as the pistil. Rare but common locally. Rich wooded
slopes; Savannah River system, Pied. and B.R., Ga, SC, and NC. Apr-May.

  T. luteum (Muhl.) Harbison has strongly lemon-scented flowers with yellow or
greenish-yellow petals. Common locally. Mountain woods; nc Ga into e Tenn and w NC.

Narrow-leaved Trillium   *Trillium lancifolium* Raf.

Plants to 30 cm tall, leaves sessile, sepals turned downward, petals at least four times
as long as wide and clawed, stamen tip strongly curved inward. Abundant locally only.
Rich wooded slopes, usually neutral to basic soils; along the Fall Line of SC and Ga;
extreme sw Ga and adj Fla; ne Ga and adj Tenn into c Ala. Mar-May.

  A similar species, *T. recurvatum* Beck, has stalked leaves and petals about twice as
long as wide. Common. Rich woods; cw Ala into nw Miss, nw La, ne Tex, c Mo, e Ia,
s Ill, and w O.

Convallaria montana × 1⅓

Trillium cuneatum × 2/5

Trillium lancifolium × 2/3

Trillium discolor × 2/5

Rose Trillium   *Trillium catesbaei* Ell.

One of our most common Trilliums having peduncled flowers. In this species these are declined or rarely erect. Sides of young leaves turned upward. Petals usually white at first and later turning pink. Sepals, petals, and stamens (when mature) reflexed or curved. Styles fused. Common. Woods; sw Ga, into e Ala, se Tenn, and Pied. of NC. Mar-June.

Two other very rare Trilliums are similar to erect peduncled forms of the above species. In *T. pusillum* Michx. the leaves are obtuse, stamens (when mature) straight or nearly so, and petals merely divergent. Peduncles vary from 5 to 40 mm in length. Rich woods; C.P.—Va into SC; e Tex into Ark and s Mo. *T. persistens* Duncan is much like *T. pusillum* but can be recognized by having acuminate or rarely acute leaves. Deciduous or conifer-deciduous woods, under or near evergreen *Rhododendron* species; Tallulah-Tugaloo River system, ne Ga and nw SC.

Painted Trillium   *Trillium undulatum* Willd.

Leaves acuminate and stalked. Flowers peduncled, with a red to purplish inverted V near the base of the white petals. Ovulary obtusely angled. Locally common. Acid woods, swamps, and bogs (at high elevations southward); mts of n Ga into WVa, NJ, northward into ne O, Ont, e Man, and NS. Apr-June.

T. nivale Ridd., the Snow Trillium, also has stalked leaves and obtusely angled ovulary but the plants are smaller (to 15 cm versus 20–50 cm tall), the leaves are obtuse, and the dark colored V is absent. Occasional. Rich moist woods; sw Va into se Pa, s O, se Minn, and w Pa. Mar-May.

Large-flowered Trillium   *Trillium grandiflorum* (Michx.) Salisb.

Often in spectacular colonies, whose beauty is enhanced by the flowers being held above the leaves by peduncles. The petals are white, up to 8 cm long, usually turning pink with age. Stigmas slender and straight or nearly so, styles little fused, ovulary pale. Common. Rich woods; nw SC into n Ga, e Tenn, e Minn, s Que, and Me. Apr-June.

Nodding Trillium   *Trillium cernuum* L.

The nodding peduncled flowers with white to pale pink petals, separate styles, purple or rarely pink anthers, and pale ovulary identify this Trillium. Occasional. Rich woods; n SC into n Ala, e Tenn, e WVa, ne O, Nfld, and Del. Apr-July.

T. flexipes Raf. is similar but the leaves are sessile instead of very short petioled and the flowers are generally larger. Occasional. Rich woods; cs Ky into se and ce Mo, Minn, s Sask, s Que, NS, c NY, and w Md; ce Tenn.

Trillium catesbaei × 1/4

Trillium undulatum × 1/3

Trillium grandiflorum × 1/3

Trillium cernuum × 2/5

Vasey's Trillium   *Trillium vaseyi* Harbison

This species is often spectacular because of its large size, to 60 cm tall, and maroon or rarely yellow petals which may be 7 cm long and nearly as wide. Much smaller plants are occasional. Flowers are peduncled, nodding, and not ill-scented. Stamens much longer than the purple pistil, the anthers yellow to brownish red, and the styles not fused. Occasional. Rich moist woods; mts of n Ga, e Tenn, sw NC, and nw SC; ce Ala, and sw Ga. Apr-May.

   T. erectum L. is similar but the peduncled flowers are erect and usually ill-scented, the stamens shorter to slightly longer than the pistil; the stigmas short and stout, and the ovulary purple. The petals are spreading from the base, usually maroon, sometimes white, and rarely pink or yellow. Common. Rich moist woods; nw SC into n Ga, e O, s Mich, Me, and Del.

Yellow Star-grass   *Aletris lutea* Small

Plants perennial, to over 1 m tall, with a basal rosette of wide grass-like leaves with very narrow transparent margins. The flowers are cylindrical at time of pollen shedding. A white-flowered form occurs and can be identified by having transparent leaf margins and cylindrical flowers. Common. Wet open places; lower C.P. of Ga into Fla and s La. Apr-May.

   A. aurea Walt. also has yellow flowers but they are obovate at time of pollen shedding and the leaves have no transparent margins. Fla into e Tex, se Okla, C.P. of Ga, and se Md. Apr-July.

White Star-grass   *Aletris farinosa* L.

Similar to *A. lutea* except for white flowers and the leaves without transparent margins. The name *farinosa* means "mealy" and indicates the appearance of the outer parts of the flowers. The rhizome and roots have been dried, powdered, and used for a number of illnesses. Common. Wet and dry habitats, sometimes in thin woods; Fla into se Tex and se Okla; also e Tenn into O, Minn, and sw Me. Apr-July.

   A. obovata Nash also has white flowers but they are obovate and the leaves have narrow transparent margins. Occasional. Moist soils; Fla into s Ga and sw SC. Apr-June.

HAEMODORACEAE: Bloodwort Family

Redroot   *Lachnanthes caroliniana* (Lam.) Dandy

Perennial with a prominent rhizome and fibrous roots, both with red juice. A rhizome exposed by removing the soil over it may be seen in the picture. Flowering plants to 120 cm tall. Leaves mostly basal, resembling those of Iris. Inflorescence yellowish to brownish, very hairy. Perianth segments 3, united at the very base. Stamens 3. Ovulary 3-carpelled, inferior. Reported as poisonous when eaten but doubtfully so. Sandhill cranes are known to consume great quantities of this species. Common. Wet habitats, swamps, thin pinelands, ditches, open places; Fla into s La, lower C.P. of Ga, and se Va; cs Tenn; Del into Mass; NS. May-Aug. *Lachnanthes tinctoria* (Walt.) Ell.; *Gyrotheca tinctoria* (Walt.) Salisb.

Trillium vaseyi × 1/3

Aletris lutea × 1/2

Aletris farinosa × 1/2

Lachnanthes caroliniana × 1/9

Lophiola   *Lophiola americana* (Pursh) Wood.

An almost complete covering of fine white hairs on the upper parts of the plant make it conspicuous, especially when in flower. The small flowers are also striking because the inside of the tepals are maroon and bearded with long yellow hairs. Plants to 70 cm tall. Occasional. Moist savannahs and pine barrens, bogs; Fla into s Miss, c C.P. of Ga and se NC; Del into NJ; w NS. Apr-Jun.

AMARYLLIDACEAE: Amaryllis Family

Atamasco-lily; Rain-lily   *Zephranthes atamasco* (L.) Herb.

Plant with several flat linear sharp-edged leaves from a covered bulb. Flowers like those of true Lilies except with an inferior ovulary, on a leafless stalk. Perianth funnel-shaped. Pistil longer than the stamens, with three stigmas. Leaves and especially the bulbs of this species are known to be poisonous when eaten, less than 1 percent of animal's body weight being fatal. Common. Low areas, usually in woods; Fla into c Miss, Pied. of Ga, nw SC, and se Va. Jan-Apr.

Z. *simpsonii* Chapm. is similar but with the pistil shorter than the stamens. Occasional. Low areas; Fla into s Ga and se SC. Feb-Apr. In Z. *treatiae* (S. Wats.) Greene the leaves are half-round and round-edged. Occasional. Low areas; Fla into se Ga. In Z. *candida* (Lindl.) Herb. the perianth is widely spreading and the stigma 1 with 3 lobes. Rare. Low places; Fla into se Tex; coastal NC. Sept-Oct.

Spider-lily   *Hymenocallis caroliniana* (L.) Herb.

Perennial from a large bulb. Leaves linear, all basal, 2–5 cm wide and to 60 cm long. Flowers 3–9, sessile on a leafless stalk. Sepals and petals alike, long and narrow, white, attached to a long floral tube. Lower half, or more, of stamens united with a white crown which is shaped somewhat like a morning-glory corolla. A sharp line marks differences in colors and tissues between the floral tube (whitish) and the ovulary (greenish). Matured ovulary beaked. Rare. Swamps, river banks and terraces, adjacent wooded slopes, rocky shoals; Fla into cs and e Tex, se Mo, sw Ind, and nw SC. May-Aug. H. *occidentalis* (Le Conte) Kunth.

In H. *crassifolia* Herb. the color and tissue changes between the floral tube and the ovulary are gradual, and the tip of the matured ovulary is cuneate. Swamps, marshes, wet river banks; Fla into se La, Ala, sw SC, and se NC. Apr-June.

Lophiola americana × 1

Lophiola americana × 3/5

Zephranthes atamasco × 3/4

Hymenocallis caroliniana × 1/4

Rattlesnake-master   *Polianthes virginica* (L.) Shinners

Succulent perennial to 2 m tall. Leaves basal, at first erect and then spreading, gradually tapered to a narrow base, abruptly tapered to the weak pointed apex, sometimes
purple-blotched. Flowers scattered in a spike-like raceme. Perianth tubular at base.
Fruit a subglobose 3-carpelled capsule, 1.5–2 cm in diameter. Common. Dry, rocky,
sandy places, thin woods; Fla into e Tex, sw Mo, s Ind, s O, cw WVa, Ga, and c NC;
absent from most of the Blue Ridge. May-Aug. *Agave virginica* L. *Manfreda virginica*
(L.) Salisb.

Plants with purple-blotched leaves have been improperly separated as a species,
Manfreda tigrina (Engelm.) Small.

Yellow Star-grass   *Hypoxis hirsuta* (L.) Cov.

Perennial with hairy grass-like leaves, 2–8 mm wide and up to 30 cm long. They come
from a corm that has a few thin pale to brownish sheaths. Scape to 35 cm tall. Petals
obtuse. Ovulary inferior. Seeds black. Common. Dry to moist thin woods and meadows;
Fla into e Tex, Man, and Me. Mar-Sept.

In *H. micrantha* Pollard the petals are acute and the seeds brown. Occasional. Savannahs, pine flatwoods; Fla into ne Tex, C.P. of Ga, and se Va. In *H. juncea* J. E. Sm. the
leaves are under 1 mm wide. Rare. Savannahs, open pinelands; Fla, se Ala, into s Ga
and se NC. Mar-May, occasionally later. In *H. rigida* Chapm. the scape is very short and
the seeds are iridescent. Rare. Savannahs, moist pinelands; Fla into se Tex, C.P. of Ga,
and se NC. Mar-Apr.

IRIDACEAE: Iris Family

Blue Iris   *Iris virginica* L.

Perennial to 1 m tall. Leaves 1–3 cm wide and, as in all Irises, all flattened into one
plane, at least at their bases. Petal-like structures of the flower are 9. The broadest and
lowest 3 are the sepals, the next 3 are the petals which are less than 2 cm wide, and
the upper 3, which are narrowest, are the stigmas. Under these are hidden the 3 stamens. Occasional. In wet places or shallow water, thin woods or open; Fla into e Tex,
Tenn, Pied. of Ga, and se Va. Apr-May.

I. prismatica Ker has leaves less than 1 cm wide. Rare. Similar places; ne Ga into
c Tenn, NC and along the coast into NS. In *I. tridentata* Pursh the petals are about
half as long as the sepals. Occasional. Depressions and low places in open; n Fla into
C.P. of s NC.

Dwarf Iris   *Iris verna* L.

A perennial from densely scaly rhizomes, the leaves essentially straight, the upright
stems under 15 cm tall, and the yellow or orange band on the sepals smooth. A rare
white-flowered form occurs. When consumed in relatively large amounts any Iris is likely to cause breathing difficulties and intestinal inflammation. Occasional. Sandy or rocky
and thin woods; se Ga into nw Fla, e Miss, s O, s Pa, and DC. Mar-May.

I. cristata Ait. is similar but the leaves are arched toward their tips, the yellow or
light orange band on the sepals with crinkly ridges (the crest), and the rhizomes with
tuberous sections separated by long thin rhizomes that have indistinct widely spaced
scales. Common. Rich woods; Pied. of Ga into e Okla, se Mo, ne O, and DC. Apr-May.

Polianthes virginica × 1/2   Hypoxis hirsuta × 1/2

Iris virginica × 1/3

Iris verna × 2/5

Blackberry-lily   *Belamcanda chinensis* (L.) DC.

Flowers much like those of a lily but with only 3 stamens and an inferior ovulary. When not in flower the entire plant greatly resembles those of Iris except that the roots and rhizomes are orange. Very hardy and drought resistant. The covering on the mature fruits splits and curls downward exposing the many black seeds on the central column, at this stage imitating a Blackberry (whence the popular name). Occasional. Roadsides, rocky areas, thin woods and old homesites; Pied. of Ga into e Tex, Neb, and Conn. June-Aug.

Blue-eyed-grass   *Sisyrinchium albidum* Raf.

Members of this genus have fibrous roots, similar flattened and tufted leaves and stems, linear leaves, 3 united stamens, and inferior ovularies.

This species is a perennial with matted fibers at the base, flowers from between 2 sessile bracts called spathes, perianth white to blue, and ovulary finely glandular-hairy. Occasional. Open places, dry woods, often in sandy soils; Fla into e Tex, s Wisc, s Ont, and w NY. Mar-May.

S. exile Bickn. (*S. brownei* Small) appears somewhat like a miniature *S. albidum* but is an annual, grows only to 15 cm tall, has a yellowish perianth, the stems and leaves are radially spreading, and the fruits are nearly globose. Rare. Wet places, roadsides, fields, swamps; Fla into se Tex. Apr-May. *S. minus* Engelm. & Gray is another annual of a growth form similar to *S. exile*, but to 20 cm tall, the perianth white to purple-rose, and ovary and fruits 1.5 times as long as broad. Rare. Dry sandy or silty soils in open; Miss into s and c Tex. Apr-May.

Blue-eyed-grass   *Sisyrinchium atlanticum* Bickn.

Perennial to 50 cm tall without persistent matted fibers at the base. Scapes narrow winged, 1-3 mm wide, terminating in a spathe from which arise 2-3 peduncled flower-bearing spathes. Fruits 3-4.5 mm long. Plant pale green, mostly retaining color upon drying. Common. Usually low places, edge of marshes, thin pinelands, and deciduous woods; Fla into se Tex, cs Mo, s Mich, and sw NS. Mar-June.

S. angustifolium Mill. is similar but the stems are broadly winged and 3-5 mm wide, the fruits 4-6 mm long, and the plants blacken upon drying. Common. Moist places, fields, meadows, woods, and roadsides; Fla into e Tex, e Kan, s Ont, and se Nfld. Mar-June.

CANNACEAE: Canna Family

Golden Canna   *Canna flaccida* Salisb.

Perennial to 130 cm tall, from coarse rhizomes. Leaves to 55 cm long and 15 cm wide, with sheathing petioles. Upper leaves the smaller. Sepals 3, greenish, 25-30 mm long. Petals 3, yellowish-green, their bases united into a tube 50-65 mm long, the lobes about the same length. The showy part of the flower consists of modified stamens which look like petals. One petaloid stamen bears the only pollen-bearing anther. The style is also petal-like. The inferior ovulary and fruit are covered with small elongated warts. Rare. Freshwater swamps and marshes, ditches, in thin woods or open; Fla into s Miss, cs Ga, and cs SC. May-Aug.

A considerable variety of cultivated plants, which are hybrids of other species, occasionally persist at abandoned sites or more rarely escape into the wild. This variety of individuals in the Southeast is probably best considered as *C. X generalis* Bailey.

Sisyrinchium albidum × 1

Belamcanda chinensis × 3/5

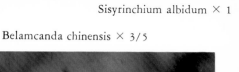

Sisyrinchium atlanticum × 1/6

Canna flaccida × 2/5

Burmannia   *Burmannia capitata* (Gmel.) Mart.

Thin, rarely branched annual 3–20 cm tall. Leaves alternate, merely scales. Flowers up
to 20 in a dense head. Hypanthium 3-angled, but without wings. Perianth greenish to
nearly white. Ovulary inferior. Occasional. Moist places in savannahs, thin pinelands,
ditches. Fla into e Tex, sw SC, and se NC; c Pied. of Ga. July-Nov.

   B. biflora L. is similar, generally smaller, fewer flowers in each head, hypanthium
with three thin wings, perianth blue. Rare, or perhaps overlooked. Fla into e Tex, se
Ga, cs and ne NC, and se Va. July-Nov.

ORCHIDACEAE: Orchid Family

Pink Lady's-slipper; Moccasin-flower   *Cypripedium acaule* Ait.

In Orchids, two petals are similar, the other (the lip) is different, often radically so,
and is an important character in identification. Another peculiarity of Orchids is the
union of the 1–3 stamens and the pistil, forming much of the column, the central
structure of the flower. All have inferior ovularies. None of our Orchid species has been
reported to be poisonous.

   Members of this genus get their common names from the inflated moccasin-like lip.
All are perennials and have 2 fertile stamens.

   Pink Lady's-slipper is distinguished by having only two leaves, both basal. Occasional. In a variety of habitats, wet to dry, thin to dense woods; n Ga into n Ala, ne Ill,
Alba, Nfld, and NC. Apr-June.

Yellow Lady's-slipper   *Cypripedium calceolus* L.

The latin name *calceolus* means "a little shoe." The "shoes," or moccasins, in this species are golden-yellow or rarely almost white and 15–60 mm long. The 1 or 2 flowers
are above the 3–5 leaves. This species is circumboreal, occurring in Europe and Asia.
The North American plants are var. *pubescens* (Willd.) Correll. They are perennials
and may grow to 70 cm tall. Occasional. In a variety of habitats—wet to dry, thin to
dense woods, and 500 to 9000 feet elevation; n Ga into Ariz, BC, Yukon, Que, Nfld,
and c NC. Apr-June. *C. parviflorum* Salisb.

Showy Lady's-slipper   *Cypripedium reginae* Walt.

The moccasins of this species are reddish to pink or less commonly waxy white. Plants
are often larger, to 85 cm tall, than those of the preceding species and have 3–7
leaves. Rare. Moist situations; mts ne Ga, sw NC, se Tenn, R.V. of Va; Pa into nw NJ,
n Ill, s Mo, ne ND, Sask, and Nfld. May-June.

Cypripedium acaule × 1/4

Burmannia capitata × 1½

Cypripedium reginae × 1/2

Cypripedium calceolus × 1/2

Showy Orchid   *Orchis spectabilis* L.

Glabrous perennial to 35 cm tall. Leaves 2, glossy, and basal. Flowers 2–15, very fragrant, the hood pink to mauve or rarely white, and the lip white. This is our only species of the genus. Another occurs in n United States and Canada, and one in Alaska, China, and Japan. Almost 100 species occur in Europe, Asia, and Africa. Occasional. Rich hardwood forests; mts of Ga into n Ala, n Ark, ne Kan, e Neb, ne Minn, s Que, and NB. Apr-June.

Green Woodland Orchid   *Habenaria clavellata* (Michx.) Spreng.

Glabrous perennial to 8–45 cm tall, with 2–4 leaves along the stem and no basal ones, the upper leaves much the smaller. Flowers 3–16 in a terminal raceme, the pedicel plus ovulary about 1 cm long, the spurs some longer, the lip oblong and with 3 short rounded teeth. Common in or at edge of water, usually in woods; Fla into e Tex, Minn, Ont, and Nfld. June-Aug.

   H. integra (Nutt.) Spreng. is in some ways similar but is 30–60 cm tall and has longer and narrower leaves. The flowers may number 70 and are light to dull orange, the spurs shorter (about 5 mm), and the lip obtuse to acute but without the 3 distinct teeth. Swamps, bogs, low pine barrens and flatwoods; chiefly C.P.—n Fla into se Tex, e Tenn, O, and NJ.

Ragged Orchid   *Habenaria lacera* (Michx.) Lodd.

Perennial to 80 cm tall, with fleshy roots and erect leaves, the upper ones smaller. The 2 upper petals oblong, their upper margins entire. The lip is 15–20 mm long and deeply lacerated, hence the name "ragged." Flowers pale yellow to almost white. Occasional, northward common. Moist or rarely dry open places or thin woods; c Pied. of Ga into Ark, ne Tex, Minn, se Man, and Nfld. May-Aug.

   H. leucophaea (Nutt.) Gray is similar. It may be recognized by smaller flowers, lip 7–15 mm long, and the 2 upper petals being wedge-shaped and their upper margins only eroded or finely toothed. Common. Wet places, in prairies and coniferous forests; La into Mo, Kan, ND, e Que, and NS.

Purple-fringed Orchid   *Habenaria psycodes* (L.) Spreng.

Glabrous perennial to 120 cm tall. Roots tuberous. Leaves cauline, up to 5, the upper ones gradually smaller. Lip deeply 3-parted, the 3 divisions both coarsely and finely toothed along their ends. Corolla lilac-lavender to pinkish purple. Spur slender and curved. Occasional. Usually in moist places, thin woods or open, sometimes along small streams; mts of n Ga, Va, NC, and Tenn into e Ky, ne Ill, e Neb, s Ont, and Nfld. May-Aug. *Platanthera grandiflora* (Bigel.) Lindl.

   H. peramoena Gray is similar having purplish flowers but the 3 divisions of the lip are entire or slightly uneven. The middle division is notched. Occasional. Moist places; nw SC into c Miss, c Ark, ce Ind, s O, se Pa, and w NJ.

Orchis spectabilis × 1/3

Habenaria clavellata × 1/2

Habenaria lacera × 4/5

Habenaria psycodes × 1

Yellow-fringed Orchid   *Habenaria ciliaris* (L.) R. Br.

Some plants of this beautiful perennial grow to 1 m tall. The several leaves are largest near the base and gradually become smaller above. Flowers are in dense racemes to 20 cm long. Lips of the flowers are oblong, 8–12 mm long, and prominently fringed. The spurs are 20–33 mm long. Occasional. In almost any type of habitat; Fla into e Tex, Ill, Ont, and Vt. June-Sept.

H. *cristata* (Michx.) R. Br. has orange flowers also but they and the racemes are smaller than in the above species. The spurs are much shorter and the lip is less than 6 mm long. Occasional in s C.P., rare elsewhere; c Fla into e Tex, C.P. of Ga, and se Mass; c Ark; c and e Tenn into nw SC and sw NC. June-Sept.

White-fringed Orchid   *Habenaria blephariglottis* (Willd.) Hook.

This Orchid is almost identical to *H. ciliaris* except the flowers are white. The photograph shows the last flowers of the raceme about to open. The flowers do not all open at once, as indicated by withered flowers below the open ones. It is obvious that fresh flowers occur on each plant for a considerable period. Occasional. Moist habitats usually open; Fla into se Tex, C.P. of Ga, e Va, n Mich, and Nfld; scattered places in Pied. of Ga into mts of Tenn and NC. July-Sept.

Snowy Orchid   *Habenaria nivea* (Nutt.) Spreng.

Perennial to 90 cm tall. Leaves 2 or 3 near the base and nearly erect, grading abruptly into as many as 10 slender erect bracts. Raceme 3–15 cm long and 1.3–3 cm in diameter. Flowers snowy white, rarely pink-tinged. Lip turned upward, linear-oblong to linear-elliptic. Occasional. Pine barrens and flatwoods, bogs, savannahs; Fla into se Tex, C.P. of Ga, ne NC, and se NJ. May-July.

Rose Pogonia   *Pogonia ophioglossoides* (L.) Ker

Perennial 10–70 cm tall with an ascending leaf about midway of the stem, occasionally with 1 or 2 long-petioled leaves arising from base of stem. Flowers 1–3, rose to white, fragrant. The lip 25 mm or less long, lacerate-toothed along its lower margins, and bearded along the middle of the upper side. Occasional in the C.P., rare in the Pied. and mts. Swamps, bogs, thin flatwoods, and other wet habitats; Fla into e Tex, Minn, and Nfld.

Habenaria ciliaris × 2/5

Habenaria blephariglottis × 3/5

Habenaria nivea × 1

Pogonia ophioglossoides × 1¼

Rose Orchid; Spreading-pogonia   *Cleistes divaricata* (L.) Ames

Glabrous perennial to 75 cm tall, with fibrous roots. Leaves 1, or sometimes 2, above the middle of the stem. Flowers usually 1, sometimes 2 or 3. Sepals 3, similar, linear-lanceolate, spreading, brownish to purplish or rarely almost green. Lip and other 2 petals partly united, forming a cylinder. Lip crested and with finely wavy margins near the tip. Rare. Usually moist places, pine barrens, savannahs, thin woods, swamps, bogs; rarely on dry grassy slopes and mountain tops, usually in acid soils; c Fla into se Tex, C.P. of Ga, and NJ; mts of n Ga into e Tenn, e Ky, and w Va. Apr-June.

Autumn-tresses   *Spiranthes cernua* (L.) Rich.

A variable genus, with plants often difficult to name to species. Our 11 species are no exception. The generic name means "coil-flower" in allusion to the spiral arrangement of the flowers of many species.

This species has several spirals forming a dense spike with flowers usually in 3 longitudinal rows. The lip is 6–14 mm long and has 2 small rounded projections at its base. The largest leaves are near the base of the stem and at most are 25 cm long. Common. In a variety of moist habitats; Fla into NM, c Kan, ND, and NS. May to frost.

In the similar *S. ovalis* Lindl. the lip is only 4–5 mm long. Rare. Moist to well-drained woods, palmetto swamplands, hammocks; cn Fla into e Tex, Mo, cw WVa, and e Va. Aug-frost.

Slender Ladies'-tresses   *Spiranthes gracilis* (Bigel.) Beck

Perennial from several thick roots, 20–75 cm tall, sometimes with 2 or 3 stems from the same rootstalk. Leaves basal, usually withered by flowering time, petioled, spreading from base of stem. Flowers small, in a single rank along one side of the spike to strongly spiralled. Lip 4–6 mm long, the central portion green. Occasional. Dry places, less frequent in moist places, thin woods, meadows, pinelands, between dunes; Fla into e and cn Tex, Minn, and NS. Apr-Oct.

S. grayi Ames also has spreading, petioled, and early withering leaves, but the lip is 2.3–4 mm long and is all white. Occasional. Dry places, thin woods, grassy areas, savannahs; Fla into e Tex, c Ark, s Ind, w O, and Mass. June-Sept, rarely as early as Mar.

Spring Ladies'-tresses   *Spiranthes vernalis* Engelm. & Gray

Perennial to 110 cm tall from several thick roots. Upper parts with fine dense pointed hairs. Leaves basal, erect, up to 30 cm long and 1 cm wide, their bases sheathing the stem. Flowers strongly spiraled, rarely as little as in those of the photograph. Stem, ovulary, and bracts densely and finely hairy, the hairs glandless. Lip 4.5–8 mm long, widest near the base. Occasional in C.P., rare farther inland. Moist places, meadows, coastal salt marshes, thin pinelands, savannahs, floodplains; Fla into e Tex, e Kan, sw La, s O, and se NY. Feb-July.

S. longilabris Lindl. has similar leaves and the lip widest near the base, but the upper part of the plant is glabrous or nearly so, the flowers are not spiralled or only slightly so. Rare. Wet places in thin woods or open, swamps, savannahs, pine barrens; Fla into se Tex, C.P. of Ga, and se Va. Oct-Dec.

Cleistes divaricata × 3/4

Spiranthes cernua × 1/3

Spiranthes vernalis × 1

Spiranthes gracilis × 3/5

Kidney-leaf Twayblade   *Listera smallii* Wiegand

Plants 6–35 cm tall with 2 leaves which are somewhat kidney-shaped, thus the common name. Flowers usually 4–10, the lip broadened toward the tip which is split less than halfway to the base. Named for George K. Small, who studied the flora of the Southeast extensively for many years. Rare. Bogs or often under Hemlocks or Rhododendrons; up to 4700 feet in mts of ne SC into Ga, e WVa, se and c Pa, and ce Va. June-July.

    L. australis Lindl. is similar but the leaves are ovate to elliptic and the lip linear and split over halfway to the base. Rare. In rich humus of moist woods, low pine barrens, marshes, and sphagnum bogs; Fla into se Tex, s Ga, and NJ; se Pied. of Ga; scattered localities into Que, Ont, and Vt. Feb-July.

Downy Rattlesnake-plantain   *Goodyera pubescens* (Willd.) R. Br.

Plants of our species of this genus are often in colonies, conspicuous because of basal rosettes of variegated leaves. The resemblance of the leaf patterns to rattlesnake skins is the basis for the common name. The leaves are prominent and attractive throughout the winter.

    This species grows to 45 cm tall and has a dense many-flowered raceme, with flowers on all sides. Common. Dry or moist coniferous or deciduous forests; n SC into sw Ala, cn Tenn, cs Mo, ce Minn, s Que, cw Me, and NC. June-Aug. *Peramium pubescens* (Willd.) MacM.

    G. repens var. *ophiodes* Fern. is smaller, rarely over 30 cm tall. The raceme is 1-sided and only 3–5 cm long. Occasional. Dry cool woods, dense mats of moss, usually beneath conifers; sw NC into se Tenn, s and e WVa, c Pa, n O, ne Minn, BC, Alas, Nfld, and n NJ; also in sw United States and Eurasia. June-Sept.

Grass-pink   *Calopogon barbatus* (Walt.) Ames

Glabrous herbaceous perennial to 45 cm tall. Leaves narrow, 1 or 2 from near the base. Flowers 3–6 in a raceme, rose-pink or rarely white, and inverted, making the bearded lip erect. Petals widest below the middle. Column 7–8 mm long. Common. Low pinelands, grassy swamps, wet savannahs; Fla into se Tex, C.P. of Ga, and ce NC. Feb-May.

    C. multiflorus Lindl. is similar but the petals are widest above the middle. Occasional. Similar places; Fla into s Miss and s Ga. Mar-July. In *C. pulchellus* (Salisb.) R. Br. the flowers are pink to nearly crimson. The column is over 10 mm long and has 2 flanges at its base. Occasional. Low pinelands, bogs, sphagnum swamps, depressions; Fla into e Tex, Minn, and Nfld. Feb-Aug. In *C. pallidus* L. the flowers are usually lighter-colored and the 2 flanges are absent. Similar places; Fla into se La, s Ga, and se Va. Feb-July.

Listera smallii × 3/5

Goodyera pubescens × 1/4

Calopogon barbatus × 1⅔

Coral-root   *Corallorhiza wisteriana* Conrad

These nongreen plants obtain their food from dead plant remains, probably with the aid of fungi. They grow to 40 cm tall but are inconspicuous, varying from tan (usually only at the base) to dark reddish purple. The corolla lip is white, pendant, 5–7 mm long, and conspicuously spotted with magenta-purple. Rare. Light to rich, dry to most soils in various kinds of woods; Fla into e half Tex, SD and several western states, s Ill, and se Pa. Feb-July.

The similar, usually lighter-colored *C. odontorhiza* (Willd.) Nutt. has a lip 3–4.5 mm long. Occasional. Similar places; nw SC into sw Ala, Miss, Mo, Wisc, and Me. June-Oct. *C. maculata* Raf. grows to 75 cm tall, and the lip is 5–8 mm long and unequally 3-lobed. Occasional. Rich decaying humus of upland woods or along stream banks; n Ga into e Tenn, O, BC, Nfld, and c and w NC; other western states. June-Aug.

Adder's-mouth   *Malaxis unifolia* Michx.

Plant glabrous, 6–55 cm tall, from a bulbous corm. Leaf blade solitary, bright green, enlarging during growth of the fruit. Lip hanging down, 2-lobed at the end but with a small tooth between. Occasional. Rich humus soils of dry to moist woods or less frequently in the open; cn Fla into e Tex, Minn, Man, and Nfld. Mostly Mar-Aug.

Our other species, *M. spicata* Sw., has 2 conspicuous bright green leaves. The lip is ascending, and not lobed at end. Rare. Swamps, hammocks, moist woods, rich wooded slopes; pen Fla into se Va. Mostly Aug-frost.

Cranefly Orchid   *Tipularia discolor* (Pursh) Nutt.

Perennial to 65 cm tall, from a corm. The single leaf is green above and purplish beneath. It appears in the fall, remains green during winter, but withers in the late spring. In the summer a leafless flowering stalk develops. It usually bears 20–30 pale-colored flowers which blend so well with the leaf litter that the plant often goes unnoticed. Each flower has a slender spur 15–22 mm long. The fruits mature in the fall. They are ovoid, about 10 mm long and 5 mm wide, and droop parallel to the stem. The dead main stem, occasionally with some frayed fruits, can often be found the following spring. Common. Wet to dry places in hardwood or occasionally pine forests; n Fla into e Tex, sw Ark, se Ind, w NY, and NJ. June-Sept. *T. uniflora* (Muhl.) B.S.P.

Twayblade   *Liparis lilifolia* (L.) Rich.

A perennial from a bulbous corm. The flowers are 5–40. The lip of the corolla is translucent, madder-purple, and over 10 mm long. The 2 upper petals are narrowly linear. Rare. Rich woods; n Ga into n Ala, Mo, se Minn, and Me. May-July.

In *L. loeselii* (L.) Rich. the lip is opaque, yellowish green and long. Rare. Moist places; ce Ala; mts of NC into e WVa, ne O, Minn, se Mo, and NS; e Va, also in Wash and westward in Canada into Sask.

Corallorhiza wisteriana × 2/5

Malaxis unifolia × 1/2

Liparis lilifolia × 3/5

Tipularia discolor × 1/3

Index

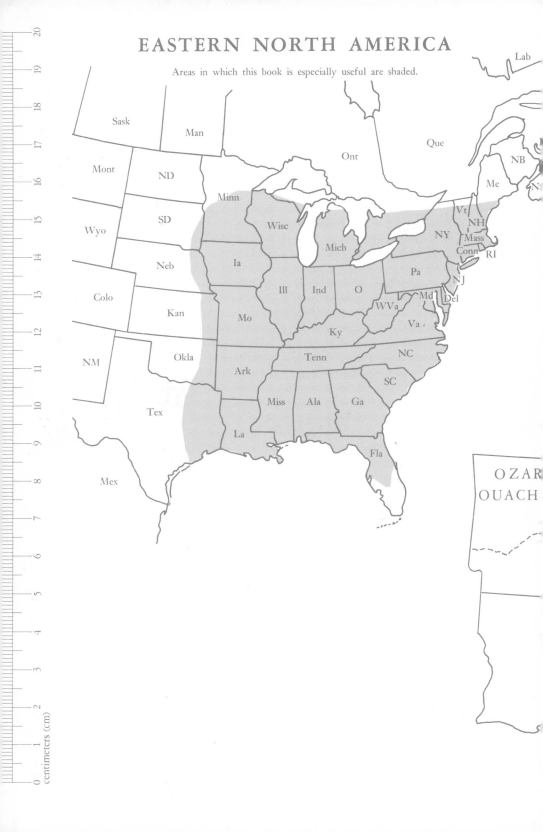

EASTERN NORTH AMERICA

Areas in which this book is especially useful are shaded.